SEBASTIAN COE
BORN TO RUN

SEBASTIAN COE BORN TO RUN

The Authorized Life in Athletics

David Miller

PAVILION

First published in 1992 by
PAVILION BOOKS LIMITED
196 Shaftesbury Avenue, London WC2H 8JL

A CIP record for this book is available from
the British Library.

ISBN 1 85145 7364

10 9 8 7 6 5 4 3 2 1

Printed and bound in Great Britain at
The Bath Press

Contents

Acknowledgements

Sebastian Coe has collaborated extensively in this biography, which, it must be stressed, is exclusively about his sporting career. I am not privy to aspects of his political career and ambitions, and the book therefore has made no attempt to search into Sebastian's life beyond his running and all that has affected it. Many people have given their help and advice in this respect, and to all of them I offer grateful thanks, especially his father and coach, Peter, and his mother, Angela. Others have included Joan Allison, Sir Roger Bannister, Dave Bedford, Mike Boit, Christopher Brasher, Andreas Brügger, Ron Clarke, Steve Cram, Frank Dick, Herb Elliott, Peter Elliott, Brendan Foster, Stan Greenberg, Ian Hague, Robert Hague, Jimmy Hedley, Derek Ibbotson, Svein-Arne Hansen, John O'Keefe, Arthur Lydiard, David Martin, Peter Matthews, Steve Mitchell, Andy Norman, Luiz Oliveira, Roberto Quercetani, Juan Antonio Samananch, Steve Ovett, Wilf Paish, Steve Scott, Wendy Sly, John Walker, Mel Watman, Jane Williams, Malcolm Williams and Harry Wilson.

Those who may have read either *Running Free*, an earlier biography written in collaboration with Sebastian Coe in 1981, or *Coming Back*, the story of his Los Angeles triumph published in 1984, will observe in this book here and there the occasional quotation or short passage that has been adapted from the earlier works. This has been necessary for the comprehensiveness of this volume on the assumption that the reader will not necessarily have seen either of the two previous works.

Steve Dobell has been as always an enthusiastic and sensitive editor, Julie Davis helpful in the production schedule, and I am again grateful to Jane Butterworth and Frances Carman for patient typing of the manuscript. Mel Watman was a proof reader beyond praise. Many comfortable hours were spent talking with Seb in front of the log fire enjoying the hospitality of Nicola Coe, mostly while she herself was busy preparing for Badminton Horse Trials.

D.M.

Foreword by Steve Ovett

Times change, but it doesn't feel that long ago that Seb was chasing me round the tracks of the world. Now my answerphone seems to have taken their place. Whilst away on holiday, Seb and David Miller left several messages asking me if I would write a foreword to this biography.

I suppose Sebastian Coe realises more than anyone that I cannot resist a challenge, and to be offered the chance to write a foreword, and thus to be in front of him, has always been rare and should never be missed.

Let me go on record by saying that Sebastian Coe is without doubt the greatest middle distance runner of the last decade. Now that I've got that off my chest, I can say what I like about the rest of his life!

However, the truth is that I don't know that much about Seb the person or even Seb the athlete, so venomous criticism or lavish praise cannot be accurate. Shame. People's lives are wonderfully complicated, and to try and logically unravel the threads and produce reason is possible. Try doing it with yourself. How on earth can you expect to do it with someone else.

During the time that my life spanned across the track, I was very fortunate indeed to have come into contact with Seb. His mere presence made life more exciting. It would have meant nothing to have dominated without challenge. Nothing to have won everything without defeat. We have, I think, very little in common off the track and yet we are friends. I sometimes think that our saga could not have been scripted or acted out any better than fate dictated. It was wonderful to have tasted some moments of life so vividly. Thank you, Seb.

Seb's life is well documented, and he seems now again to be vigorously chasing goals in numerous avenues much in the same way as before. The Renaissance Man is a phrase that comes to mind in my feelings for Seb: someone whose drive encompasses all aspects of life. A need to excel. I suppose I see this in Seb as I once felt it in myself. I was also aware that excellence has it's price. Not as a total sacrifice from the individuals themselves, as most are willing to pay, but as one of a loss of time for and awareness of others. That is why I suppose that a smile spread across my face when I heard that Seb and his wife Nicky were expecting their first child. Children have an innate ability to punctuate life, not with commas or semi-colons but full stops. They make decisions for you, turn your routine into theirs, or snap you back from loftier pursuits to make you aware of their reality and love.

As people always say, your life is never the same. The fulcrum changes.

The two full stops in my life, Alexandra and Georgie, are and always have been wonderful to their father. That is why I hope that Seb and Nicky have as much fun, love and joy as we do.

Introduction

Fear runs through sport. Fear of the opponent. It is there all the time, whether seen or not. It is there in losers; yet it is as likely to be there in the mind of a winner during some phase of victory. Fear can be both a motivation and an inhibition. Fear exists in the conspicuously physical sports such as boxing or rugby, and every Olympic downhill racer will tell you they encounter fear on the face of the mountain. Yet fear also stalks the competitor in something as unaggressive as golf. So much of sport at its pinnacle is played in the mind. It was fear that was almost the breaking, and thereby the making, of Sebastian Coe in the Olympic Games in Moscow in 1980.

Coe was, in a word, scared. Now, after all the years during which one of the most remarkable careers in sport fluctuated between ecstasy and despair, Coe admits that his defeat in the 800 metres, the distance at which supremely he was world record holder and considered to be unbeatable, was because he was afraid of Steve Ovett. It was not so much the pressure of the Games, which Coe has previously admitted he found overwhelming, an experience that has destroyed many great athletes. It was the fact that he was overawed by the immense talent and reputation of the other man.

SC: The sense of inferiority was on account of what I saw him to be: physically and mentally arrogant. I'd been progressing heat by heat, meal by meal, through the opening days of the competition . . . and Steve, he was coasting through, waving to his girlfriend! I sensed at the time, as I do now looking back, that he was the most talented runner I've ever run against. The talent was prodigious at the age of sixteen. Part of the problem I had in Moscow was that in the infant stage of my own career I'd witnessed the range of his skills. First at Washington, in County Durham, at the English Schools Championships, almost waving on the final bend *then*! And a year later, he was the guy who finished eight places in front of me in the English Schools Cross-Country Championships at Hillingdon in Middlesex, when he was second.

Then you have to remember that, only two years later, the fellow is winning a silver medal at 800 in the seniors' European Championships in Rome, in 1974. The *next* year, he's winning the European Cup Final in Nice. There'd been an argument about his not being sent to Christchurch for the Commonwealth Games the previous year, and I'm sure he would have won a medal there, at eighteen. Although he was only a year older than me, he seemed in another league. A year after his silver in Rome, I was winning a bronze medal in the European *Junior* Championships in Athens! I can't stress it too strongly:

Peter, my father, would never let me dwell on this, but I was making my first tentative steps as a senior in 1976 while Ovett was being heralded as a *favourite* for the Olympic Games in Montreal. In 1977, he destroyed a world-class field in the World Cup, including John Walker, the Olympic champion, who walked off the track shaking his head. I wasn't beginning to develop and become rounded as a senior until 1979. I couldn't go to Moscow and just say to myself, well, 1976 and then 1978 – when Steve had beaten me in the European Championships in Prague – simply didn't matter. I was bound to be in awe of his staggering talent.

In Moscow, I was almost twenty-four, but I'd been doubting whether I could beat him since I was eighteen, such was his stature. The 800 defeat in Moscow was, in part, due to this feeling I had about him: whether I really could beat him, never mind my world record. It wasn't until 1981 that I acquired a comfortable feeling about confronting him in any race at any distance . . . and that was never to happen again when we were both at a peak. When we were having a chat about Moscow together some years later, prior to the Olympic Games in Seoul, Steve said to me laughingly, "I'd have *killed* that day." I said to him, "You did." I'd known immediately afterwards that the problem had been that I was mentally afraid to get into the race. The manifestation of that was that I ran it looking physically weak and frail. I had a feeling of desolation, of total loneliness; and feeling *isolated*. It was a release to go to bed that night, not to have to answer questions. But how long can you hide from yourself? The next day, Sunday, I was just going through the motions. At heart, I still believed the game was up.

That is what most of the rest of the athletics world also thought, bar a handful of competitors, coaches and observers who were aware of Coe's own remarkable depth of talent; of a combination of endurance and finishing speed that had never been seen before and has not been equalled in championship races to this day. That Coe's game was up was certainly the view of the bookmakers in London, who were now giving odds of 11–4 on Ovett to repeat his triumph in the final of the 1,500 metres. If he did that, Coe, as an athlete, would be dead: he would be dismissed as no more than a record-breaker, lacking the mental tenacity, judgement and temperament for the most demanding of arenas into which a competitor ever steps. Coe knew it. And what was more, he knew that his friends and acquaintances knew it. In the Olympic Village people were avoiding catching his eye, were making noises of sympathy and saying "well, now you can do it in the 15", when transparently they believed nothing of the kind. There were a few who remained optimistic, not least Peter Coe, his father and coach; and those such as Chris Brasher, the former Olympic steeplechase champion, who has always sensed the unique quality of this extraordinary runner, and the author, who had seen at close hand during training, never mind four world records, sufficient evidence to be sure that here was no wimp lacking moral fibre.

Indeed, the world of sport was about to see an exhibition of moral fibre, the like of which there has seldom been. Sebastian Coe was to reveal hitherto unobserved elements of character that produced a climax which would literally stop traffic in the streets. The final of the 1,500 metres was watched in Britain by more than twenty million people, many halting to watch the race in the windows of television retail shops. It was the single most captivating *individual* event in the history of British sport. It was the making of Coe as an athlete of legend, possibly the making of him as a person in adult life. It is easy to talk in superlatives, yet a second consecutive defeat could have been so crushing for his morale that he might never fully have recovered, on or off the track: by such margins do our lives sometimes turn. Coe's life now turned on the fact that though he had been afraid, his nature is one that depends, indeed could be said to thrive, on conflict.

SC: Sport at the top is mentally complex. When you need an iron will, when the fires are fiercest, the catalyst can often be your own doubts. There is a side of me that has always doubted what I can do, and that comes from Angela, my mother, though this is not to exaggerate, because there are ways in which she has given me even more than Peter. Yet I *have* felt vulnerable so often, both she and I have been less sure of my ability than Peter. However, the best performances in life, whatever you do, can stem from a conflict inside you, from the combination of a sense of imminent failure and the need to prove, to yourself and other people, that you're not really afraid at all.

The existence of this emotion in her elder son is confirmed by his mother. "I think he was always very nervous," Angela says. "I think it stayed with him, though more and more he was able to control it. I saw it in his respect for other runners, a reflection of his uncertainty, always tending to believe that even modest runners could, on the day, raise their performance above the ordinary. There would be a tension in him, even for the Yorkshire championships: that silent, locked-in look at meetings when even *I* wasn't nervous. I've seen it even as recently as the World Cup in Barcelona in 1989, though very con-trolled. Perhaps it's something you've got to have, just like going on the stage. I can cry for anybody, but get them to laugh . . . ?" Angela Coe was, before she married, a repertory actress, mainly in comedy, at Worcester.

That memorably magnetic race in Moscow was, however, far more than simply the climax to a particular Olympic Games, and to a three-year rivalry between two outstanding runners. It was part of a sequence of historic races, over a period of sixteen years in international athletics, dominated remarkably and predominantly by four British runners: Ovett, Coe, Steve Cram and Peter Elliott. The coincidence of their concurrence in one country is something that has been the astonishment and envy of every rival nation against which Britain competes on otherwise approximately equal terms. The emergence, one after the other, of these four runners, so excellent and yet so different, has been at the heart of the development of athletics in Britain to an extent never previously known.

It has indeed been a golden decade, the most spectacular even for a country with an eminent tradition in middle-distance running. To produce just one such runner would be the delight of most countries: to generate four is something beyond explanation. To have four such runners with not only the talent but the temperament for winning at the highest levels is the more unusual when one considers the climate. Though meteorologically mild, it is predominantly unforgiving to the international runner who must spend the entire five months of winter undergoing the maximum hours of daily endurance preparation, out-doors, that will enable him to withstand all the fires of summer. It has never been sufficiently studied, that I know; but it might well be the climatic factor which contributes to the breeding of great runners. We are, after all, conditioned by environment as well as by genetic inheritance.

Brendan Foster, born and bred on Tyne-side in the north-east of England, a few hundred yards from where Cram would later run his first steps, is firmly of the opinion that the British quartet derive their greatness from their background as distance runners, products of the winter cross-country system at school, county and national level. Foster can claim some knowledge, for it was he, an Olympic 1,500 metres finalist in 1972, a European 5,000 champion in 1974 and Olympic 10,000 bronze medallist in 1976, who helped establish a developing upward trend in British athletics twenty years ago; together with such men as David Bedford, Ian Stewart and Alan Pascoe.

You can say for certain that it will never happen again [Foster says]. You could never expect such a domination of an era by four runners of this quality, all of them with the potential to win any race. Kenya has perhaps come closest in its production of famous runners, but the Kenyans have not sustained it up to the present time, either individually or collectively. By saying that Britain won't have another such era doesn't mean we won't produce more great milers; and indeed Cram and Elliott are not yet finished, for either could still break records or win championships. What has been so specific about the achievements of these four has been that they ran the mile or 1,500 metres. It's an event that every ordinary person can sense and measure and appreciate. The mile in this country is a more significant event than any other.

Svein-Arne Hansen, the meeting director at Bislet stadium in Oslo, scene of countless world records down the years, echoes an appreciation that is to be found world-wide. Oslo's admiration is especially strong for Coe, who in five visits to the city between 1979 and 1983, the last indoors, broke five world records. Ovett and Cram broke one each.

It *has* been an era [Hansen says] we shall never see again. We would not at Bislet be in the position we are today, a Mecca of middle-distance running, without Seb Coe. He made us famous. Maybe we gave him a little of his fame, too, but he unquestionably established our international reputation. The people in Oslo love him because he would go out and do it *alone* from the front. When Ovett waved, when he came here in 1980, the people didn't like that. Nowadays, the public no longer asks who is running: the event is established. We are a sell-out from early in the year. What was so outstanding about the four British runners was that they ran regularly, every year, not like some Finnish runners, who ran a few major championships and didn't appear elsewhere (*such as Lasse Viren*). When Seb began to come here, athletics in Britain and Norway was not a big spectator sport. When he came and broke his first record in 1979, the 800 metres, we knew little about him, other than he'd done some very impressive training. Then two weeks later he came for the Golden Mile, and we had our record crowd of 24,000. We were paying John Walker, the record-holder from New Zealand, $10,000. We were paying Seb $1,000 at that time . . . and he ran away from everyone to lower Walker's record. We would be paying him more after that! There was always a *feeling* that he was going to do something. There was a magic about him. He is much more known in Norway than any football player. The only time Bislet ever appeared in *Newsweek* was after that mile in 1979, which made our meeting a household name in Britain. On my next trip to England, the man at Customs asked me the reason for my visit, and when I said I was the organizer at Bislet, the response was "Oh, welcome, nice to have you here."

Harry Wilson, Steve Ovett's personal coach and at one time the national long-distance events coach, figured prominently in fashioning this scenario of continuous drama.

It was a wonderful time to be around in athletics [Wilson says]. They had a great influence on the sport in general, in that it became a major spectator sport because of them. Dave Bedford had started to bring the crowds, the kind we had originally witnessed in the Fifties at the time of Bannister, Chataway and Pirie, running against Kuts and others at White City. What Seb and Steve did was to bring the television. This new era had a huge influence on British coaches; it convinced the athletics body that you didn't have to go to Finland or America for knowledgeable middle-distance coaching. Now, *our* coaches were being asked to lecture overseas, foreign coaches were following what we did. Administrators in our sport haven't fully appreciated the difference that Steve and Seb made.

Brasher takes this point further.

Coe and Ovett, and then Cram, were successful like no other trio in the world, at the same time and the same distance. *We* had it, and we in Britain didn't appreciate it . . . and didn't do anything about providing facilities for the next generation, born with an enthusiasm created by these three. Where are the stadiums in which they and their successors deserved to be running?

The events of a remarkable decade, indeed of a span of seventeen years if we take the period from the moment of Ovett's international emergence to the present day, have been well documented. The intention here, on the one hand, is to record Sebastian Coe's reflections on momentous days, good and bad, and at the same time to draw together the various threads of emotions and motivations that influenced him and his three rivals and their coaches. The fascination of the period is that it is impossible to consider any one of the four outside the context of their relationship to the other three.

What makes the story especially interesting, I think, is that while the two Steves and Peter Elliott have quite evident and clear-cut personalities, Ovett being overtly the more emotional of the three, Coe's personality has had, and continues to have, at times an inscrutability that not even his family and friends can be sure they can read. The runner who became the only athlete ever to win twice the blue-riband race of the Olympics, and won more individual Olympic medals than any previous British athlete, is an emotional contradiction. At least outwardly. The slim, handsome young man now embarking on a career in politics, who ten years ago became a national sporting idol on account of a combination of aesthetic physical excellence and quiet good manners, has a cold element in his make-up which at times masks the deep-seated emotions. There is a genetic legitimacy to that expressionless face behind which, in public, Coe has so regularly concealed the rages of frustration and disappointment that have been burning inside. He is one quarter Indian.

Coe's maternal grandfather was Indian. Although Angela's father had no sporting pedigree – the genes for this are probably inherited from Peter, a cyclist – there is in the grandson that degree of Oriental, outward equanimity, of *introspection*, never mind that his grandfather was a man of excitable, occasionally excessive emotion. In the grandson, the passions which run deep have been suppressed behind a demeanour of gentleness. The only two occasions in his public life when that expression has been broken by the exploding frenzy within have been the moments of Olympic triumph. They have been the momentary face of anguish, relief, of an abstract kind of revenge; the moment of proof of the way he sees himself, the moment of fulfilment in the manner in which he wishes publicly to be remembered; a seeker of excellence, to the pursuit of which he has devoted 25,000 hours of his thirty-five years.

Those two moments of rage quickly gave way to the customary graciousness. At those times when he has been disgracefully treated – and not he alone – by incompetent British administrators, he has never sought to indulge in verbal pugilism. Dignity has been the watchword of his public life. Although he has never walked away from press conferences – his family and friends would say he has been over-indulgent in his accessiblity to the media – Coe has mostly done his talking, in his sporting career, with his legs. He was not the man to gain revenge with words, even less so when he had emphatically made his point on the track.

SC: There's always been a motivation, an *enjoyment* in proving people wrong as much as consistently winning. Right from the early days, when I was very young and people thought Peter's coaching was all wrong: anything from merely "misguided" to "wicked", in the way he drove me. . . . Proving people wrong from the time I was told at eighteen that I was "too slight" to be a great 800 runner, including by Steve Ovett. I remember a very shaky period at my club, the Hallamshire Harriers in Sheffield, with the whispering behind our backs, and quite a nasty scene at a cross-country race in Graves Park, when I won by a minute and a half. One parent was about to attack Peter physically. In those days, I was half a foot or more shorter than most of the other boys, and this man threw down a tracksuit on to the ground in anger, shouting, "You're just a couple of *professionals.*" At other times, parents and rival coaches would say to Peter, "You're killing him", and Peter would answer, "Yes, all the way to the top." It undoubtedly unnerved my mother, who had no real knowledge of what we were doing but would be standing there loyally at the side of the course.

Peter is sometimes considered, by those who do not know him well, to be a hard man: the truth is that he is disarmingly pragmatic and realistic, and occasionally cantankerous when dealing with people whom he feels do not know what they are talking about. Privately, while objective at times almost to the point of being dogmatic, he can be soft-hearted. For hardness, he is as nothing compared with his son. "Inside," Peter says, "Seb is as single-minded as they come." On his unswerving route, Peter likes to use the term "enlightened self-inter-est". It is one he readily applies to his son.

PC: He enjoyed all the success, though not ostentatiously. It's reasonable to say that, as long as I kept coming up with schedules that advanced this, yes, there was an element of *selfishness* in him. He's egocentric, though in recent years there's been a degree of unselfconscious concern for me, perhaps as I got older! And that's not self-delusion. He's not too worried about other people's opinions, but he'd still like *me* to approve of what he does. I've always told him to be a *pro*, don't dabble, *go* for it. I don't think he was ever in any doubt that what I was doing was for his benefit, not mine.

Peter, tall and slim, had in his youth been a competent racing club cyclist. There is an element of the authoritarian in him, and when peering over or through his dark-rimmed glasses he bears more than a passing resemblance to Old Chalky, the schoolmaster in the Giles cartoons. It might have been asked whether Peter was disposed to push his son more than he might have done for the very reason that the pushing was accepted, yet behind the austere exterior beats a tender heart. He knew unerringly how sensitively his young son would need handling. He admits to having driven both of them hard, of being at times impatient. "He knew better how to live with me than anyone in the family," Peter says, having had three other children: Miranda, a former dancer with the Royal Ballet and then in cabaret in America, who is now modelling; Nicholas, a successful businessman in San Francisco; and Emma, who works in interior design in London.

As mentioned, Seb's mother, Angela, had been a repertory actress before her marriage. Her mother, half Irish, half Welsh, was the daughter of an artist who was an RA, and herself had to give up dancing when she broke an ankle, having danced with the legendary Pavlova. If Seb's equanimity comes from his mother's side of the family, none who know her would doubt that his resolve comes from his paternal grandmother, Violet, who is the personification of Londoners who endured the Blitz, of the Flanagan and Allen line, "Who do you think you are kidding, Mr. Hitler?". Granny Violet has that kind but determined demeanour which would have seen off Rommel with an umbrella. The unbending attitude was evident in Peter, who insisted upon an academic diligence from his elder son as severe as that applied to his running. Athletics itself became an almost academic exercise for Peter, who, starting from a position of ignorance, educated himself in the esoteric field of training, biomechanics and athletics physiology, to the point where he knew almost as much as anybody in Britain, and he set about applying his knowledge to the particular, idiosyncratic qualities of his own son. When people accused him of allowing athletics to become an intellectual exercise, his answer was, "You're dead right!" It was an extraordinary partnership that developed between father and son. Being an engineer, Peter was sound on mathematics, but knew little of statistics. When Seb was taking an "A" Level in statistics, Peter enrolled two nights a week as a mature student at an open college in order to be able to help. His devotion to his son's cause has been extreme, yet instead of the stresses that can so often arise in such an intense relationship between father and son, they have to this day remained the best of friends.

It has been a relationship which few outside the family have been able to comprehend. Others often sense, understandably, that Peter is dogmatic, unsympathetic and dictatorial. This, to a degree, is true; but one needs to know the other side of the man, and one of my lasting memories, seen only in the darkness through the driving mirror of a Moscow taxi, is of Peter with his arm round Seb following the 800 metres defeat, as consoling, in silence, as with a child who has woken from a nightmare in the middle of the night and come to its parent's bed for reassurance.

It would be difficult to overestimate the contribution, the emotional balance, given to her two men by Angela. She has been strong without being too demonstrative, supporting without being fussy, influential without interfering, bringing to the intensity of their situation the soothing ministrations of a mother and wife. Throughout the arduous years in which they were driving towards distant objectives, she was able to hold the emotional tiller as they negotiated rapids which at various times could have capsized one or both of them.

I was amazed that Seb never complained about the routine, at the sheer pain in his hands from the cold when he came back from training sometimes in winter, up on the hills, with ice on his hair, when he was told how many hours' sleep he had to have . . . at his "O" Level stage I felt it was very much in the balance whether he continued. Even Christmas Day had a timetable, including training and, say, two hours' geography revision. I can remember Peter saying, "You can do it, one helps the other." Somehow Seb managed it, the same with "A" Levels, his self-discipline was astonishing. There were times in the early days when I wished, I suppose, that he wasn't so good at running. Sports days were embarrassing. I'd find myself thinking, "*please* lose something." You could hear other mothers muttering, "It's only going to be Coe again, I don't know why we bother to come." . . . For years I accepted Peter's saying, "He's going to be world class," while I was tending to think to myself that I hoped it didn't blow up in his face. I didn't want either of them to be disappointed. Because I saw less of what was happening up there on the hills, I suppose I probably had less faith in the ultimate success.

Angela's collaboration was in every way as important as Peter's: every extra training session, every race, meant a whole day reorganized in terms of meals, laundry, co-ordination of the younger children.

Besides the hill runs, where much of the long-distance endurance work was done, there were many sessions of critical repetitions that took place along almost the only flat stretch of road around Sheffield that runs through the Rivelin Valley, between precipitous farmland on one side and wooded hills and allotments on the other. It was along this road, a fraction over three miles before it reaches the city near the Sheffield Wednesday football ground, that some of the most remarkable runs of all time were made, observed only by mothers with prams and a few disinterested motorists. Along this stretch, it is possible to fit in six consecutive half-miles, and it is these sequences that built in Seb the exceptional stamina that was to produce so many exceptional times. So impressive were the figures in the early days that Peter refused all requests to come and film Seb in private action. Here, Peter would drive the car ahead of his athlete, drawing him out to performances that most other athletes or coaches would not have believed possible.

PC: Managing an engineering business successfully demands co-ordination on a whole range of aspects. To get something done, you call upon the best resources. When I came into athletics I didn't know much about physiology but I knew of people who did. There was any amount of advice, much of it conflicting. I read a lot, went to conferences, discarded much of what I read and heard. I realized that nobody actually *knew* for sure. There is nothing revolutionary in what I did with Seb, but it was tailor-made for his physique. An athlete to a great extent determines his own training by his responses to the tasks you set for him, and by his racing results. The coach must adjust to the athlete. I never told him a false time to encourage him. Seb is not a mindless automaton, but I had to be certain that he would adhere to the programme when I was not there, yet that he would vary it when necessary because of the weather. He was exceptional because his trust in me was total. The coach can only work with the athlete's consent. The measure of the athlete is the extent of his consenting to do things within his capacity. The danger for the coach is that if the athlete's trust is total, he may consent to anything. In conversation with other coaches, I never heard of one athlete who was as dedicated as Seb.

It was at an early age, from the first days of competitive running at twelve, that Coe was learning to live with public comment provoked by his performance. If there were the subjective, frustrated parents accusing this wisp of a child of being a professional, merely because he was so superior to their own progeny, there was also the quiet satisfaction of hearing the murmur that would run through a crowd, even in boyhood days: "*Coe is here.*" He liked winning; even more, he liked winning *by a mile*. Angela remarks on the inconsistency in a child of outward equanimity: that the two areas he has chosen to pursue, sport and politics, are a contradiction of the quiet life, "when you have to eye-ball people", as she says. Part of the genetic inheritance of equanimity, Angela thinks, may have come from her mother's father, a painter who was a friend of Sickert, and a man of unfailing composure. Coe, observing his mother's unusual mixture of nervousness and calm, senses that his element of restraint comes from her; though he differs with his father on one main point: "*He* doesn't care what anyone thinks, I *do*. But he shows his feelings more."

If Coe has had the image of the clean-cut professional, then that comes from conforming as a child to parental background, rather than from education. He had the fortune to inherit from middle-class parents the old-fashioned ethic known as hard work.

SC: From childhood, we were disciplined from Monday to Saturday if we stepped out of line. That's one of the reasons why I never see any cause to antagonize the press, who mostly wanted to ask sensible questions. If there has been an element of *emotional selectiveness*, it's because early on I calculated that this was the best thing. All energy is consuming: emotional energy is as draining as physical effort. By my mid-teens, I'd realized the necessity of conserving my energy for running fast.

This degree of calculation in Coe's conduct has resulted, after the initial national euphoria at the glamour of his racing, in the younger generation considering he had none of the sex appeal of the more spontaneous Ovett and Daley Thompson. He took himself too seriously, they said: the young and even the not so young. Coe thinks it is important that people are allowed to be themselves, that they should not be subject to sports psychologists smoothing off their differences.

SC: That way, you're left with ordinariness. Daley without his informality, Steve without his brash to-hell-with-them attitude, would not have been the same athletes. My best performances have come from peaks of internal conflict. Would the victory in the Olympics in Los Angeles have come without the set-back of illness during the two previous years? Would the victory in Moscow have come if I had *won* the 800? Would the 800 victory in the European Championships in 1986 have come had I not believed my career would be a failure without it?

Coe hated failure, and he hated criticism – and it is the latter trait, incidentally, which makes some wonder whether he can survive in the political arena, where criticism is so often unpredictable, unfair, and unanswerable. "Seb took criticism very personally," says Jane Williams, with whom he shared much of his private life for five years from the winter of 1983. "The element of public disbelief at another virus attack hugely upset him after he had come out of hospital. 'But I *did* have it,' he would say repeatedly. I knew well enough, because I was making the soup, and trying to help him endure the painful drugs he was taking to correct his glandular condition."

The mocking of the Gateshead public in 1983, which followed the announcement that he was having treatment for an injury when he missed the presentation ceremony after losing to Cram, the local hero, may not have reached his ears beneath the grandstand. But scepticism by public and press, that surrounded his elimination through illness from the World Championships that year, provided much of the fuel that would drive him to athletic immortality a year later. Coe is fond of a comment by Alec Stock, the venerable manager of Fulham, when they reached the FA Cup final in 1975. On the morning of the match, Stock had said: "There are some players who will have woken up this morning hoping that they are going to play brilliantly but thinking that perhaps it's not going to be the greatest of days. And there are others who will have woken and felt that this is a day that they can die with blood in their boots."

Angela says that even as a small boy, her son had not fought other people so much as he fought himself; that the pressures on him were predominantly self-created, and that this was the same even with his school-work, in which he failed his 11-plus exams. She thinks if there was stoicism, it came from Peter, not from her. "If I had been there in Moscow, I'd have said to Seb, 'It doesn't *matter*, you've got the silver, never *mind*.' Winners don't need people like me around."

Personally, I feel the Moscow victory was attributable as much to perversity as stoicism. Foster, who was one of those who expected the reversal of fortune in the final of the 1,500, had noted the steely mentality from the time of Coe's first international races.

Immediately after the Olympic Games in 1976, Seb had run against Walker, the Olympic champion, and *led* all the way. Walker caught him at the finish. In the next race, Seb did the same, and this time Dixon (the 5,000 metres bronze medallist) caught him. I thought to myself, here's a little fellow from Sheffield with the mental maturity to challenge the best current runners in the world, to explore his own limits. Yet I think that one of his faults, later in his career, was that he felt he was carrying everyone's expectations; that he couldn't afford to run when physically at less than his peak. The common experience of *all* athletes is that of losing. In any big race, there'll be someone who's under the weather on the day, so I don't think anyone should get too intense.

Foster's view is legitimate; and Coe, his long-time friend, will accept it, though he and Peter would both say that Foster has not understood the degree to which they have lived their athletic co-existence in the permanent pursuit of excellence. Brasher says, comparing Coe with Ovett: "Coe has always been regarded as far more calculating, as putting himself first. Ovett was outwardly more the ideal club man, the runners' runner. Seb would never be that. Roger [Bannister] was the same, never one of the heart of the athletics family." This perception of Coe as being exclusive, being apart from the rest, is commonplace, yet partly a misconception borne of the deliberate conditions imposed by Peter Coe on his athlete, as he liked to refer to him, in competitive events. The perception is echoed by Steve Scott, six times the breaker of the US record for 1,500 metres and a mile, and a frequent opponent.

Seb was the complete opposite to Ovett [Scott says]. In his approach to athletics, and now to his political career, Seb has been very exact. He's planned everything meticulously: his training, racing, his schedule for the Olympics. He wasn't one to socialize, he didn't come and have a drink after a race too often. Not that he was unfriendly, but difficult to get close to. If he was going to have a drink, it would be with the promoter, the sponsor, the press; something that would further his career. At least that's how it seemed to some of us.

Coe, unsurprisingly, justifies his attitude:

SC: I know that tends to be the view of other athletes. At major championships, at Grand Prix events, my narrow focus was easy for me, that was what I was there for. I didn't over-race, and I was brought up to recognize that because there were few of them I should make each race serious, especially championships. There are probably only half a dozen, even less, potential great races in your career, so make them count. Yet in terms of the range of where and how I would race, I don't think anybody ran at as many different levels as I did in any season. In 1980, I ran in the county championships, the area championships, the inter-counties, and then went on to win the Olympic title. If you talk to those I ran against at lower levels, they will tell you I had a very different attitude to what I had at international meetings. If you're racing like Scott, or Ovett in 1980, or Cram, and racing mainly at *one* level, then you can't keep that focus all the time. I could keep it at all the big events without a problem. When I went in at international level, yes, I suppose I *was* the outsider. I didn't arrive at international races with a group of friends. I don't race the US winter season on the boards, for money. I must have looked stand-offish. It wasn't, however, a considered thing, it was the way it tended to work out. If I wanted a lighter side, that came with racing in my university or club colours. I had a clear accessibility to the (different) social side of competition.

It was not a deprivation at a major meeting not to be chatting at midnight. Moreover, it would be difficult for some senior athletes to make themselves accessible, because I never saw them in Games villages – Ovett, Cram or Elliott – because they were usually in hotels. If I went to Oslo, Zurich, Viareggio, it was usual that I had come straight from London for the race, and not from Nice or Koblenz or some other European meeting. I was never around on the circuit as much as Dave Moorcroft and Brendan were, I didn't have their appeal.

The irony of the confrontation between Coe and Ovett in their initial years on the track – emphasized by differences of opinion that were evident in a previous book in which I collaborated with Coe, entitled *Running Free* – was that subsequently they have become good friends. "I thank my lucky stars that Seb came along and hugely increased my enjoyment," Ovett says. "Three world-record miles in a week between us (in 1981) – we could have gone on and on. Jeffrey Archer could not have invented the story. We did a lot together, against each other, and came out of it friends, which is nice. Different backgrounds? Not that much. We're close in some ways. We've expressed so many common things in the sport, we care about individuals, we are bound to be close."

The alleged personal conflict was highlighted, Coe reflects, because of the publicly exaggerated contrast in personalities between the two runners: nice and nasty, brash and cool.

SC: I was no more coherent than Gary Lineker, David Hemery or Bobby Moore. The differences (in personality) with Steve were such that everything was exaggerated by the press, by the public perception. The important thing is that there were no more than half a dozen quotes by either of us about the other. At the level of conflict there was for a while, it could have become unpleasant.

It was little short of unpleasant in the summer of 1980, during the count-down to the final of the Moscow 1,500 metres. Not only did Coe know that his reputation would be in tatters should he again come second – imagine it, being viewed as a flop by the public if you have taken two silver medals in the Olympic Games! – but he was aware of an impending plan by Ovett and his advisers to embark on a series of races around the world, for the highest, though then athletically illegal, stakes; and from which Coe would be excluded. The amount riding on this one race was immeasurable, in every sense. The day following the calamity, for Coe, of the 800, Peter – who had quietly told him the day before that he had "run like an idiot" and had been rash enough to talk to the press in terms of "humiliation" – had backed off. Coe went for a long, mentally cleansing run through the suburban countryside of Moscow, pursued by a bevy of photographers. Not that he would know, but the headline over one of the photographs the following day would read: "Trail of Shame". Such had been the level of expectation.

By the second day, Peter was starting to put the knife in again, metaphorically; to drive his athlete back into action. Coe did a series of severe repetitions, 6 x 800 metres, with only two-minute intervals.

SC: He worked me very hard. It was getting close to the heats of the 1,500, but Peter probably thought that the preparation had become too cosy. The need was more mental than physical, and for a couple of days he was fairly brutal in stirring me up. By the Tuesday, three days after the 800, I myself was starting to become angry. I'd pulled back the curtains that I'd used mentally to shut out the memory of the first event, to eliminate the details: though to this day I have *no* recollection in the usual way, almost stride by stride, of how the race was run. If I watch a video of the Moscow 800 today, I have no sensation or recall of what it was like at the time. I have no relation to the race, which reveals the degree to which I had frozen on the day.

It was during those three so-called rest days that Coe began to generate the willpower that divides winners from runners-up. Frank Dick, Britain's chief national coach, likes to quote Lady Macbeth on the mental quality that separates the great achievers from the merely successful: "[Thou] art not without ambition; but without the illness that should attend it." Coe, he considers, has that "illness" that demands the ultimate victory. "The champion needs that additional edge," Dick says. "There has to be the ruthless element, and I think Ovett may have had it to a degree; but when a year later or so he totally changed his public manner, when he launched his clothing company, suddenly being nice to the press, I said to Daley that I thought he would never win another championship." Ovett was to win once more, the Commonwealth 5,000 metres in 1986. The other point that Dick makes is the extent to which world records are irrelevant in major championships. You can pick your own day, so to speak, for an attempt on a world record, in company with sympathetic colleagues, "but for gold medals the date is picked for you". This was something that Mike Murphy, in 1980 a BBC television producer, well understood. "Get your effing head up, Coe," he said laconically as they passed each other in the Village the day before the 1,500 heats. The way in which Coe got his head up is recollected in a subsequent chapter.

If the victory in Moscow was to make Coe a renowned figure from Singapore to San Francisco, his reputation was given lustre less by what he won, which was extensive, than by the way he ran, which was beautiful. There was an aesthetic cadence about his stride, a production of speed without visible acceleration, of extremes of endurance without grimace. Stan Greenberg, a long-standing expert in that esoteric field of track statisticians, and one who has watched every runner worth seeing for over forty years, is among a small number who not only appreciated the visual elegance which gained Coe acclaim wherever he went, but understood what lay behind the way the Coes planned their racing. He knew, more than most, the refinement that went into every race, in a ceaseless search for perfection.

I remember one early race in 1989, when Seb was making a return to form [Greenberg recalls]. Seb went flat out for 700 yards, then died in the straight and was nearly caught. There were people busy saying "It's all gone", when it was clear he was just trying to find out how he was. It was an incredible run at the time of year. I went up to him and said, "Great", and Seb said, "Thank Heavens there's someone who understands." The year before, in May, he'd run an 800 in world-class speed in the Middlesex Championships at Enfield, winning by seven seconds, and he'd floated round. I'd said to him beforehand, "Nice day", and he'd winked and replied, "Pity to waste it." He had this ability, when he was fit, to run amazingly on any day, irrespective of the opposition. Peter and he were always looking for the opportunity to test himself. There are very few athletes really prepared to do this. Back in the Sixties at the White City, Keino ran a very fast first lap in a mile, and I said to a colleague that Alan Simpson (a prominent British middle-distance runner) would have a *fit* when he heard the lap time. A few yards later Simpson ran off the track; and said to the press afterwards he just couldn't understand what had happened. The fact was the pace had scared him: his problem as a miler was that he never found out what he could do, which was something Seb was doing from the time he was a boy.

In the training diary that Peter kept from the time his son was twelve, there was a page of projections on progress year by year. It estimated, in 1970 when Seb was fourteen, that by the time of the Olympics in 1980, Seb should be able to run the 1,500 metres in 3 mins 30 secs. The world record in 1970 was 3:33.10. Seb was to win a slow tactical race in Moscow . . . but by 1986 he had fulfilled the prediction with 3:29.77.

Andreas Brügger of Zurich is another of the leading promoters who has reason to be grateful for the emergence of Coe's record-breaking runs. Two were achieved in Zurich: including, in 1979, the 1,500 metres, Coe's third in forty-one days, which was a sensational prelude to the Games the following year.

I consider him one of the finest athletes we have ever seen [Brügger says]. He set not just new records but new standards, in the way he ran. He turned the

800 metres into a sprint. Fiasconaro of Italy and then Juantorena of Cuba had started this, but Seb took it even further. Seb, when he was in top shape, gave the impression that he was not touching the track. With other runners, you could always see when they were working hard. With him, there was a quite different sensation.

This appearance of effortlessness stemmed from innovative, exploratory training schedules. As Brasher has said, a coach has to take an athlete beyond a point at which he thinks he is going to die. Such preparation enabled Coe, for instance, to break the indoor 1,000 metres world record in Oslo in 1983 without even looking out of breath, turning round at the end of the race with a shrug of ignorance, wanting to know what the time had been. Peter considers that his outdoor 1,000 metres record of 2:12.18, set in 1981 also in Oslo and still standing, is possibly his best. The more remarkable, in that the distance is being run far more often, is his 800 metres record: first lowering Juantorena's record by more than a second in Oslo in 1979, with 1:42.33, and then improving this two years later in Florence to 1:41.73. The twelve years (up to the time of writing, June 1991) for which Coe has held the record, an exceptional duration, approaches the longevity of the record when it was held by Harbig of Germany, including war years, from 1939 to 1955. Not the least of Coe's unique qualities was that in the autumn of 1989, the season of his retirement at the age of thirty-three, he was running a first lap in Berne in 50.4 seconds: almost the same as when he was first setting the record ten years previously.

SC: You don't appreciate fully what you've done till later. Only now can I look at my career in the round. The records may appear as though they were run to order. In reality, they were achieved against a background of clinical appreciation of my potential by my father. *I* knew in '81 that I couldn't be beaten. I never felt that in '79. That was still an experimental year. It was the first time I'd started training in the morning! Peter's attitude to the training of some other athletes was "an excuse for not thinking". I only ever made six deliberate record attempts: the 1,500 metres in Zurich in 1979 and 1980 and Stockholm in 1981, the 1,000 in Oslo in 1980 and 1981, and the mile in Zurich in 1981. Four of them were successful: but in *none* of them did I know for sure who was going to be making the pace. When I set the 1,500 record in 1979, I had to run the last two laps on my own, and for the 800 and mile records, in Oslo, Florence and Brussels, there was no pacing specifically organized for me.

In my time on the track I have seen three generations of athletes. I came in at the end of Juantorena, while Mike Boit, Andy Carter, Moorcroft and Foster were there. I coped with Ovett in his second and third phase; then Cruz, Steve

Scott, Johnny Gray, Gonzalez and Abascal; and then almost a fourth generation in the late 80s, with Bilé, Kiprotich, McKean and Ereng. Throughout the last two generations there have also been, of course, Cram and Elliott, and they remain leading forces. You have to adapt all the time. Where were the young lions to which Tony Ward (the British Board press officer) referred when I was not selected for the Olympics in 1988? I beat them in the Commonwealth trials the following year, and none of them have done anything much.

Steve Scott has said: "Some of the rest of us were racing here, there and everywhere. For Seb, the Olympics were everything." Elliott ruefully asks why there is no "Sebastian Coe Stadium" in Sheffield. "After all he has done for the city, that would be better than the 'Woodburn Road Stadium' we now have."

Coe's list of career achievements reads as follows:

World Records (9)

800 metres:	1:42.33, *Oslo 5.7.79*; 1:41.73, *Florence 10.6.81*
1,000 metres:	2:13.40, *Oslo 1.7.80*; 2:12.18, *Oslo 11.7.81*
1,500 metres:	3:32.03, *Zurich 15.8.79*
Mile:	3:48.95, *Oslo 17.7.79*; 3:48.53, *Zurich 19.8.81*;
	3:47.33, *Brussels 28.8.81*
4 x 800 metres:	7:03.89 (4th leg, 1:44.01), *Crystal Palace 30.8.82*

Olympic Record
1,500 metres:	3:32:53, *Los Angeles 11.8.84*

European Record
1,500 metres:	3:32.80, *Oslo 17.7.79*

UK Records (3)
800 metres:	1:44.95, *Crystal Palace 9.9.77*;
	1:44.25, *Brussels 18.8.78*;
	1:43.97, *Crystal Palace 15.9.78*

World Indoor (3)
800 metres:	1:46.00, *Cosford 11.2.81*;
	1:44.91, *Cosford 12.3.83*;
1,000 metres:	2:18.58, *Oslo 19.3.83*

UK and Commonwealth Indoor (3)
800 metres:	1:47.6, *Dortmund 19.2.77*;
	1:47.5, *Cosford 26.2.77*;
	1:46.54, *San Sebastian 13.3.77*

Major Honours

1973	English Schools 3,000 metres gold, AAA Youth 1,500 metres gold
1975	AAA Junior 1,500 metres gold, European Junior 1,500 metres bronze
1977	National Indoor 800 metres champion, European indoor 800 metres gold, Emsley Carr Mile winner, European Cup 800 metres 4th
1978	UK 800 metres champion, European Championships 800 metres bronze
1979	National indoor 3,000 metres champion, European Cup 800 metres gold
1980	Olympic Games 1,500 metres gold, 800 metres silver
1981	National Indoor 3,000 metres champion, AAA 800 metres champion, European Cup 800 metres gold, World Cup 800 metres gold
1982	European Championships 800 metres silver
1984	Olympic Games 1,500 metres gold, 800 metres silver
1986	European Championships 800 metres gold, 1,500 metres silver
1989	AAA 1,500 metres champion, World Cup 1,500 metres silver

If athletics has been the mainstream of Coe's adult activity, his life has been much broader than that of the average professional sportsman; which is what he has been legally entitled to call himself since the regulations were changed by the International Amateur Athletic Federation in 1982. He gained a degree in economics at Loughborough University; worked on a post-graduate thesis for a doctorate; was a member of the Sports Council for six years and its vice-chairman for two-and-a-half years, rejecting the offer from Colin Moynihan, the Sports Minister, to become chairman; is a board member of the Health Education Authority; is a member of the Athletes Commission and Medical Commission of the International Olympic Committee; is chief executive of the UK distributors of Diadora, the Italian sports shoe and clothing manufacturers; and is partner in a marketing company, Comodale. Now he is heading for a career in politics. Why?

SC: It's been the only thing I ever wanted to do outside sport. It's something I've thought about, had at the back of my mind, since I was taking my 11-plus exams. The conviction that this was what I wanted to do sharpened during my time with the Sports Council, when I had to work at close quarters with civil servants, Ministers for Sport and even Secretaries of State. That kind of involvement enabled me to see how the political process worked: how if you pressed the right buttons, things happened. That was fascinating. I was interested in politics during my time at university, and was treasurer of the Young Conservatives. I think I am a natural Conservative, but with reason to find some differences on some issues of strategy. I have made a number of speeches about the melody of my type of Conservatism. This is the management of *change*, but it is also about the essence of our national tradition that the Conservative Party considers to be timeless: the tradition of freedom, the value of competition, the freedom of the individual to develop talents within the framework of the law, with as little State hindrance as possible.

He might be a wettish, liberal Tory, but his main interest is in health and the NHS, with views that make him anything but a right winger. Peter is very much from the old school of self-made working-class Tory. It is Angela from whom her elder son inherits his liberal tendencies. Peter's views are trenchantly work-ethic orientated. "Peter thinks I am too liberal," Angela says, "a supporter of the underdog, the other point of view. It almost killed Peter that I enjoyed reading John Updike. Peter is very black-and-white: grey is a sign of weakness. I have all the greys. Of our four children, Seb is the more self-aware, which is often true of the eldest, a sense of responsibility. When we travel, it's Seb who has usually telephoned to see if we've arrived."

Coe's political aspirations are the bafflement of some of his closer friends, worried about the political jargon in which they have observed him becoming trapped, in radio and television debates. The *Observer* referred to his "terrible ungainliness" when he tries to talk like a politician, as during his appearance in *Any Questions?* on Radio 4. He was pulled up sharply by Jonathan Dimbleby, and invited to "deal with the question that was asked". Yet in his campaigning as a prospective parliamentary candidate for Falmouth and Camborne he showed himself to be commendably clean and classless; and with a reputation among the electorate that encouragingly stretches beyond being a famous sportsman and a "decent chap". He has shown that he cares, has a willingness to learn the local problems, and familiarize himself with the needs of the electorate in a constituency far from London, where he and his wife, Nicola McIrvine, the Badminton three-day event champion of 1990, have bought themselves a cottage.

It remains to be seen whether, at thirty-four, Coe entered the political arena in time to make serious impact. Christopher Chataway, another famous runner who reached junior ministerial level before being forced, for financial reasons, to seek another career at the time of the fall of the Heath Government in 1974, has said: "Today, it seems to me that if you have been very well known as a sportsman, it is hard for people to see you in a different way. In terms of political ambition, it may help you to be interviewed and selected, but not necessarily to be taken seriously."

Coe's athletics career has been distinguished by careful planning and achievement of measurable objectives. Such predictability is impossible in politics, which has been described as "initially a lot of hanging around". Even if with a seat in parliament, it must be wondered whether Coe will have the patience and the tolerance for something so imprecise. No-one who knows him doubts that he will have the energy.

I · Devastated

The controversy aroused by the British Amateur Athletic Board's denial of a place for Coe in the Olympic team for 1988 tugged at emotions and prejudices almost stronger than did the Coe–Ovett saga eight years before. Now the *dramatis personae*, in an issue that took place primarily off the track, involved different rivals for Coe: Steve Cram and Peter Elliott. There were other runners, too, featuring in the competition for places in the two middle-distance events in Seoul, South Korea; they, with the subjective self-justification that is an essential part of any competitor's psyche, saw no reason why the veteran Coe, approaching his thirty-second birthday, should be the recipient of privileges from the selection committee. In truth, neither did Coe himself; but in the emotional and often distorted way in which the circumstances were presented to a bemused public, rationality was seldom evident.

Chris Brasher wrote in *The Observer* that not to allow Coe to defend the Olympic title he uniquely held in the 1,500 metres from the past two Games "is a crime which makes me angrier than it does him". The only inaccuracy of that heart-felt statement was that Coe, behind his habitual restraint and public moderation of manner, was so angry that, when the time arrived, he could not bear to watch the unfolding of the races in Seoul. He believed passionately, yet rationally, that he still held as good a chance as any British runner of bringing back a medal from Seoul, indeed better than most. The argument justifying the decision of the Board, loudly proclaimed by them and supported by a sizeable minority within the sport, was that Coe's exclusion was wholly a consequence of his own lack of form at the critical time of selection. The argument of Coe and his father, and many others including members of a selection committee that was over-ruled, was that the selection system, and its timing, was counter to the interests of any runner with genuine expectation of winning a medal, as opposed merely to gaining selection.

The record of the British Board when it comes to selection is not a happy one. As far back as 1964, there had almost been a strike by the athletes over the handling of the team for Tokyo; at almost every subsequent major Championships there would be some allegation of incompetence in selection. Athletes, as we know, are subjective, and those omitted from teams on narrowly decided issues are often unhappy. What makes the situation more uncomfortable is when it is known that those having the final say, not necessarily the selection committee, are unfamiliar with the needs, schedules and planning of potential medal-winners. Some British Board members would have difficulty identifying individual athletes if they met them in the club-house, never mind judging their merits; and there was the instance of Brendan Foster being wished good luck on the massage table by a team official half-an-hour after he had finished his race. The Board still operated in the style of the much-maligned international selection committee of the Football Association, prior to the appointment of a team manager in sole charge of selection in 1963. In what is now a professional sport, it is imperative that the Board should listen to, or give more authority to, the professionals within their own ranks. In 1988, the greatest runner in British history was denied an Olympic place, by one vote, among a British Board council of twenty-one, among whom barely half a dozen would genuinely understand the physical cycle of an Olympic medallist's season. But this is running ahead of the story.

The ambitions of Steve Cram for 1988 were always going to be intensely challenging to Coe's presence, following Coe's defeat of Cram in the 1,500 metres final in Los Angeles. This had denied Cram the one supreme goal which remained for him after he had won the Commonwealth, European and World titles during the previous two years. Much as Cram would, understandably, wish to play down this blank in his credentials, he recognized as well as anyone that Olympic performance is the ultimate measure of any athlete: however arbitrary that judgement can at times be. Immediately following the disappoint-ment of the event in Los Angeles, and being about to attempt a world record in Budapest, Cram had said: "With Seb now expected to move up to 5,000 metres, there's only the slightest possibility of our meeting again. I've got to accept that. I don't want to get preoccupied with chasing Seb. And if I did beat him, it would never make up for *not* being Olympic champion . . . I'd like something to add to my silver before the season is out. The public becomes blasé. If you don't win gold, you are just 'another' medallist." Cram was speaking from the heart. He would be twenty-seven by the time the Games in Seoul arrived, and he would know this was his last chance to gain the most prized title. He would not want anything to stand in his way as the time approached; though before then, at the European Championships of 1986 at Stuttgart, he would split the gold medals with Coe for the two events, and be reminded that the older man was still a force to be respected.

SC: What I started to think about, that winter following Stuttgart, was that I woud step up the mileage in training, run a few extra road races in the new year, and that at some stage in '87 I would, for the first time, get involved with the 5,000. This had originally been the intention after 1983, but the plan had been shelved because of my prolonged illnesses. The plan now was that I would probably run the 1,500 in the World Championships in Rome, but that I would incorporate in the season one or two races at the longer distance; and then might be able to consider 5,000 for Seoul, after two winters of longer-distance work. After the first couple of road races, I was moving well; having finally won the 800 title the year before that had been so elusive, the cards were increasingly right for considering the 5,000. I ran a fast indoor 3,000 at Cosford to win the UK finals.

Next came a 400 relay leg in the National League, confirming that my basic speed was OK. From there I dashed off with friends to Wimbledon to watch a greyhound called Bandit. I had become a half-owner, courtesy of Jarvis Astaire, following a dinner of the National Sporting Club at which I was speaker, and where the greyhound was auctioned. Bandit won his race, and we all went off to spend the winnings on a meal in Wimbledon. The dog went on to have a better season than I did. A few days later, out training at Estoril in Portugal, where I'd gone for a weekend on a seminar sponsored by Barclay's Bank, I discovered I had a sore heel. A day off training, and ice packs, did nothing to alleviate it.

The trouble didn't respond to physiotherapy, and no diagnosis in Britain could initially give an answer. Then an X-ray picked up a small piece of detached, floating bone, and there was talk of an operation. I spoke by telephone to David Martin, an expert in sports physiology at Georgia State University in Atlanta, whom I had been consulting for some years, and he said that an operation would necessitate cutting tendons. I did not want that, and spent another six weeks or more trying to find a natural cure. Training was at a standstill. I went as a spectator to the AAA Championships, which were being used as a guide to selection for the World Championships, in order to watch a couple of colleagues from my Haringey club in the 10,000. Afterwards Les Jones, the British team manager, and Tony Ward, the Board's press officer, asked me how I was: I'd been preselected for Rome for the 800. I said I thought I just might make it to Rome, but they would be advised to scratch me. I could hang on to see if I improved, but that way I would screw-up other runners trying for selection, and with a good chance, such as Steve Crabb and John Gladwin. I wouldn't want them to embark on a series of races that would be unhelpful if they were going to be involved in Rome. Jones and Ward pressed me to postpone my decision, but I told them I didn't feel I would be able to do myself justice, wouldn't come back with any medals, and that they would be better off alerting other runners so that they could be given time: those such as Horsfield, Morrell, Crabb who were beginning to emerge.

Coe was not to find the same charitable, rational attitude extended to him the following year, by athletes or officials. In August, he went to Chicago for consultation with John Durkin, a specialist in what Americans term "pediatry", who for several years had been designing the orthotic inserts for Coe's running shoes which helped give a correct foot placement.

SC: I'd been seeing him since 1982. The mistake I made was not going to consult him earlier in the year. I flew to Chicago in the morning, had an X-ray in the afternoon; half-an-hour later, the loose piece of bone had been identified, and Durkin injected a special dissolving solution. The heel was a bit sore, but I went sailing with him on Lake Michigan. Two days later an X-ray revealed that the floating piece had gone. A whole season had been unnecessarily wasted.

Back home, I was invited by a long-time friend at the BBC to join the commentary team in Rome, for analysis of the 1987 world championships. I would deal with the middle-distances, Brendan long-distances; Dave Moorcroft would be the link in the studio. It seemed like a nice week-and-a-half in prospect, but proved to be a major error. Suddenly I became aware of the monumental egos within television. I sensed a resentment of outside involvement. One of the senior editors announced that if I worked he would resign. Part of the problem was that this editor previously had a friendship with a girlfriend of mine, though their relationship had been over several years beforehand. The upshot was that, after the first round of the 800, I was told unless McKean fell over I was no longer needed. It was an odd decision, given the sophistication of the home audience. I found myself standing beside the track, in temperatures over 80, feeling I'd be better off up in the stand watching events properly. I joined a couple of journalists who correctly read the situation . . . and the next day I received an offer from ITV! Yet Steve Ovett was already working with ITV, so what did they need me for? The whole thing was so unprincipled on both sides, though no fault of Rowlinson's. He managed to sort it out: I previewed and summarized the semi-final and final of the 1,500, Elliott having taken the silver behind Konchellah of Kenya in the 800, and Bilé of Somalia emerging as champion in the 1,500 rather than the frustrated Cram. And that was my season.

The two races had been respective disasters for McKean and Cram. McKean stumbled down the back straight of the second lap, seemed to make no effort to recover, and came in last. As Jimmy Hedley, Cram's coach, observed: "I've always got my heart in my mouth watching Tom. I think he tends to panic a bit, it's in his nature. I'm delighted when he wins, he's so talented, but you can never be sure of what will happen." Konchellah was never seriously challenged in a fast 1:43.06, while Elliott drove past Barbosa of Brazil to take the silver. Elliott gives his due to Eddie Kulukundis, a Greek shipping millionaire and self-effacing philanthropist, who has done much to support British athletics, individually and through his work with the Sports Aid Foundation. Kulukundis had paid for Elliott to spend ten days training at Formia, the Italian national training-centre north of Rome, immediately beforehand, as a break from his shifts as a joiner at the Tinsley steel mills between Sheffield and his home in Rotherham. "I'd been tired, and that break turned it for me," Elliott says.

Cram had started to experience persistent injury problems, existing since 1984 but now even more frequent. "His training had been interrupted, and he'd been trying to train with injury", Hedley says. "It gets to the stage he doesn't really know whether he's injured or not. He's *expecting* injury, he tries to compensate, and then other things go wrong in consequence. I'm in agony watching. The failure in Rome was simply lack of condition." Andy Norman and Mel Watman are less sure, expressing a view that Cram has never been the same since his unexpected defeat when finishing second to José Luis Gonzalez of Spain, in the European Cup final, in June the same year, in Prague. "It was something you could never have expected," says Watman, for many years the editor of *Athletics Weekly* and now consultant editor of *Athletics Today*. "Subsequently, Cram has been patchy, and I don't understand why he did not see the right specialists to get his calf muscle right. You sometimes wonder about his lifestyle, and whether he spends too much time playing snooker with his young Jarrow colleague, David Sharpe." In Rome, Cram took the lead before the bell, but in spite of a surge round the penultimate bend, he could not sustain his drive, Bilé strode to victory ahead of Gonzalez, and Cram limped home eighth.

SC: I was back into training in the autumn, and after Christmas I went to Florida for some sun with Wendy Sly and Peter Wirz, the Swiss runner, both of whom are coached by Peter. My father and I rented a small apartment; I used the golf course at the university of South Florida for endurance training, and the track at the University of Tampa for speed work. I was regularly going for physiology testing with Dave Martin at Atlanta. A detailed analysis showed there was no deterioration in the biochemistry of my blood, in the aerobic capacity to absorb oxygen. As Dave says, age is merely a number, not an index of fitness. If I was considering seven races in nine days in Seoul, as in Los Angeles, it would need a really hard winter's preparation, a commando's fitness. Such a series of races is as much a matter of strength as of speed, and in Florida I was also able to have the use of a first-class gymnasium.

For a break, I went to an indoor 3,000 at Meadowlands, New Jersey, though I had a cold and shouldn't have run. It was a nightmare twenty-four hours. The plane was delayed twelve hours, arriving at 11 pm; the taxi from the airport, with Peter Elliott and his new coach, Kim McDonald, had a flat on the Jersey Turnpike; and the driver couldn't change the wheel because the nuts were rusted. We took a second taxi: there was no one at the hotel reception desk, and when I eventually found a room, there was a child crying next door and I had about three hours' sleep. The surface of the wooden track was horrendous, I had to scribble my own race numbers by hand, and unwisely chose to run without spikes. I was slipping on the curves, was troubled by my cold, and found Brian Abshire running the second fastest time ever. Three laps from the finish, unable to breathe properly and not holding the floor, I pulled out mid-race, the only time in my career. Returning home a bit jet-lagged, I ran second to Adrian Passey over 3,000 at Cosford in the match against America, the first major race since running my best ever 1,500 in Rieti in Italy, just after the European Championships in 1986.

At the beginning of the '88 outdoor season, I wasn't in a hurry to force things. There was no point in being in good shape for the Olympics too soon. In '84, I wasn't right even four weeks before the Olympics. The problem this year was that the Games were at the end of September, and the trials, in which I was obliged to run, were at the beginning of August. This presented an eight-week interval between two peaks that would be required: the first, in the opinion of Peter and me, and also Cram, being too early and a disadvantage for the second. Therefore, my condition in July, in preparation for the trials, had to be on training background, only picking up on the quality track work in August. I planned to run the trials, and then two Grand Prix races in Europe; then an early departure for Seoul for time acclimatization, via Australia, which is an eight-hour flight from Seoul but on the same time-zone latitude.

Following uneventful, stepping-stone 800 metres races at Enfield, Portsmouth and Lausanne – beating Paul Ereng of Kenya in the latter, the man who was to win in Seoul, and finishing half a stride behind Bilé – Coe confirmed his steady progress with a fluent victory at Crystal Palace in early July, still almost three months away from the Games. He ran away from young Sharpe, for whom Hedley, his coach, had forecast a "mould-breaking" win on his twenty-first birthday. Also in the field were Ereng, again, and Steve Crabb, who was to play an increasingly prominent role in developments. Coe, who early in the season had been publicly voicing his disapproval of the selection system, with its new policy of mandatory qualification for the first two and only the third place discretionary, was partially satisfied with the race.

SC: I beat everyone I was *allowed* to beat. Anyone who was at risk of being eliminated by my beating them was not allowed in the race. Hedley had said beforehand that I didn't deserve to go to the Olympics, that I hadn't done enough, that Sharpe would show me the way home. This race was the best indication yet, by anyone in Olympic contention, of their fitness.

The first misfortune of the season then overtook Coe in Dublin. Looking for the necessary qualifying time for Seoul, in his first 1,500 race for almost two years, Coe was spiked, slightly pulled a hamstring, and had to drop out. Within a few days, the wolf pack of critics gathering at his heels – he was in his thirty-second year and had not competed seriously since 1986 – were starting to come into the open.

By now the plot had taken shape. It was not going to be possible to run both 800 and 1,500 metres trials and Coe, with no exceptional performance at either for two seasons, could not expect with confidence to be given the discretionary place in either; even less so now that antagonisms towards him within the Board, as well as among younger rivals, were becoming evident. An interview given by Crabb revealed the mood of things, following a stipulation by the Board that Coe had to run the trials in one event or other.

I agree with the decision [Crabb said]. If I had my way, the first *three* past the post would be chosen for the Games. You can't pick a man who hasn't run the distance for two years, no matter who he is. Either Coe or Cram run the trials or one of them misses the Olympics. It's only the big earners who are against the new system. They're the ones with everything to lose. Non-selection for the Games would be quite a blow to their sponsorship deals. Ninety per cent of athletes feel the new system is fair. Everyone has his chance on the day. I don't think Seb can win in Seoul, even if he qualifies. It was great to hear a British Board official saying Seb still has to prove himself . . . Coe and Ovett were my boyhood heroes. If the selectors thought that way, they'd still be picking them when they're forty-five.

The expressed view of Ward, on behalf of the Board, was that Britain currently had seven of the world's top twenty at 1,500 metres, on the year's times so far, and that Coe had yet to run the qualifying standard. "We may be nearing the end of an era", intoned Ward. "It seems to me that Seb's the guy with the weakest hand at the moment. We cannot go on sentiment forever." The reasoning of both Crabb and Ward was fragile. Those against the selection system were those who in the past had proved an ability to produce a peak at the right time, that they had the temperament for major championships. Britain figured so prominently in the rankings precisely because leading athletes around the world were *preserving* their efforts for nearer to the Games. Coe set off for altitude training at St. Moritz increasingly conscious that there were officials wishing, as they say, to put the boot in.

SC: St. Moritz in the summer is wonderful for training, with its woodland paths around a lake. Peter and I went not so much because it is at high altitude, but because Peter Wirz regularly goes there, to an "athletes" hotel run by friends of his. By the end of the week, however, I was feeling a bit dodgy with a cold. I went down to race at the town of Rapperswill because I needed a qualifying time. Ward's statement, after I had left for Switzerland, that, if I didn't run the 1,500 in the trials, I could not expect to get a selection at either distance, was forcing my hand. I couldn't expect the discretionary place at 1,500, nor was there any guarantee of the 800. I was the only athlete being told that I had to run. This was clear indication to Cram, in my opinion, that he as good as had the discretionary 1,500 place, and to Elliott the same for the 800. He was not being told that he had to run *anything*. That was when I began to feel the cards were stacked against me. If the AAA Championships were open, why was I being given directives? I was doubly handicapped because I needed a qualifying time by selection date, and therefore had to run at Rapperswill. I could have easily have run a qualifying time later.

I was aware that the return to sea level, and to Birmingham, from altitude could be difficult, and discussed with Dave Martin the right timing. He thought the optimum interval before the heats in Birmingham was four or five days. It's all to do with pressure on the arterial system. The cold from St. Moritz was only a head cold, but I was feeling a bit lethargic, and now I was in a cleft stick for the trials. If I said I had a cold, and didn't run, the Board would have said I was ducking the issue.

Andreas Brugger was present for the qualifying race at Rapperswill, and sensed the fine line that Coe was riding. "It was like the old days, he was floating, not sprinting, *schweben* as we say, suspended like a gazelle, not in touch with the ground. I was convinced he could have done the same again in the Olympics, it was clear that he was coming into shape to run 1:43 or 3:32. The mistake he made in St. Moritz was to cool down after training without wearing a sweater."

At home, Elliott was tightening the screw. Sensing that the discretionary 800 place was his, in the light of his World Championship silver medal the year before, he was now increasing pressure on Coe by entering the 1,500 in the trials, with the intention of doubling up. That had been his wish for LA four years before; the selectors had then preferred Coe, wisely in the event, while Elliott had fallen foul of injury during the 800. Now he was gunning for Coe in every sense, as he showed in an interview shortly before the trials.

If necessary, I'm ready to run Seb Coe out of the Olympics [Elliott stated]. If it came to a straight choice between Coe and me, and the selectors couldn't decide, I'd be prepared to meet him in a head-to-head . . . you can take sentiment only so far. Seb has been great for British athletics. He has everybody's respect, including mine. But he has to run in the trials. If he wants to be picked, he's got to record a decent time. It was four years ago that he retained his Olympic title. Who says he's going to win another gold? He's thirty-one now. I'm twenty-five. I have a feeling that I can even run close to the world record. This is my big year . . . I believe in the old bulldog attitude.

Steve Ovett, whose performances in Los Angeles had been agonizingly undermined by respiratory problems, would also be attempting to qualify in the 1,500. A shade older than Coe, he too disagreed with the selection system and was sympathetic with his old adversary.

The policy of guaranteeing a place to the first two past the post is wrong [Ovett said]. You have to *think* your way through the Olympics, it's as simple as that. There are guys who can run a single race well, but facing heats semis and finals in the Olympic Games is something altogether different. You need experience to deal with that situation. That's why the selectors are so wrong to pick people on the strength of one particular day and one result. You challenge them, and they say but so and so has run over a second faster, so he must be better. They pitch inexperienced people into a pressure cauldron.

Although the allegation of expediency was strongly denied at the time by John Bromley, the Head of Sport for ITV, there was little question that the integration of trials for the Games into the AAA Championships hugely elevated the television interest, and therefore the viewing figures, irrespective of who took the decision. In all probability it was rampant opportunism by the AAA, the more frustrating for Coe and others who were similarly trapped by the system. For instance, there was competition for a discretionary place in the 5,000 metres, with Jack Buckner, the European champion and World bronze medallist, and Tim Hutchings, fourth in Los Angeles and European bronze medallist, both hampered by injury at the time of the trials.

SC: I didn't complain about Cram deciding not to run in the 1,500 and to go for the 800 place by running in the trials. My complaint was that I was given an ultimatum. I might have preferred to run for a place in the 800 and continue training for the possibility of a 1,500 inclusion later. After all, Cram had done nothing consistent at 1,500 since 1986, and came eighth in Rome the year before. When I had been putting myself on the line against Bilé and Ereng in Lausanne, Cram was being beaten domestically by Sharpe and Morrell at 1,000 metres in Birmingham. I was *criticized* for being in Lausanne and running a reasonable 1:45.50. When it came to discretionary cards, my hand was not that bad.

Yet it became known that prior to the trials, Elliott and Wilf Paish, his coach, had written letters to the selectors stating he was "the man in form", and should be selected. Cram had a sketchy season, ran well in the trials at 800, but came fifth in the Grand Prix in Nice. He was clearly inconsistent. Warming up for the heats at the trials, I passed Elliott, who called out, "Don't believe what I've been quoted as saying, it's just paper talk". Yet close friends of mine had heard him saying the same thing on radio. I had a last warning in the warm-up from Ovett: "Don't cock it up".

Coe knew he had a problem as soon as the heat of the 1,500 metres began. The first lap was just over 60 seconds, but in his current condition it felt more like 56 seconds. The 800 went by in two minutes, and when the pace started to intensify at the bell, he was struggling to react to what was only an average change in pace.

SC: I was having difficulty sucking in enough oxygen. I tried to challenge at 200, held the leaders but could not gain on them; tried to sprint 80 metres out, raised my pace for six or seven strides, but then slumped and trailed home fifth. Immediately I'd finished, Mel Batty [the former world 10-mile record-holder, who is now an equipment distributor and also assists the media at major meetings] was beside me in a flash. He must have once been an ambulanceman in the States, first on the scene, on commission. "Anything to say to the boys?" he asked expectantly. I could only mutter "No".

With the first four through to the final, Coe was eliminated. As he walked to the changing tent, the stadium was hushed, the crowd numbed. People do not like intruding on private grief, and a path between milling people opened, to give Coe a corridor of silence away from the track, whereas so often in the past they would have been thumping him with congratulations. As he reached the changing area, Helen Thorpe said, in a matronly tone: "How many times have you been told you shouldn't run with a cold!". Such advice was irrelevant now. As Coe put on his tracksuit to leave the stadium with Steve Mitchell to drive back to his house in Loughborough, he observed to a press colleague: "This is a hell of a place to end an Olympic career. But . . . it's a bit like Noël Coward dying in Slough".

The result of the trials, with Cram and McKean taking the first two places at 800 and Elliott and Crabb at 1,500 meant the selectors had the following choices for the discretionary places: Elliott or Coe for the 800, Cram or Coe for the 1,500. The six-strong selection committee, chaired by Ewan Murray, also the chairman of the Board, were due to meet on the Sunday evening, immediately following the final of the 1,500. The committee consisted of Frank Dick, the chief national coach; Andy Norman, the Board's promotions officer and cland-estinely the most influential man in the sport for fifteen years; and four team managers of different periods, Mike Turner, Les Jones, Joan Allison and Pam Piercy.

Allison was one who disagreed with the selection policies imposed on the committee, and had sympathy for Coe's situation. Not only that, she was on good ground for supporting his inclusion in the team, at any rate for 800 metres, because of his current status of four victories in five races and a relatively fast time this year of 1:45.50 – never mind his proof of temperament in the Olympics. After the opening discussion, Turner, Dick, Piercy and Allison were in favour of Coe, Norman and Jones of Elliott. With further discussion, Norman and Jones came on board, for a unanimous decision that Coe should be given the vacancy at 800. Allison and Dick were of the view that Coe could cope with both races, and believed he should be allowed time to prove his fitness for 1,500.

Before the committee met the full council of the Board the following morning, Turner privately spoke with Coe and his coach, attempting to discover when Coe would be fit. He wanted to be armed with sound information. The first hour-and-a-half of the Board's meeting, however, concerned itself with a debate on its own future; following a deficit of £300,000 in the previous financial year, a resolution was made by the AAA at its own AGM that the British Board should cease to exist at the end of the current year. The council then turned its attention to item four on the agenda: "to receive *recommendations* from the selection committee and to *select* the team to represent Great Britain and Northern Ireland in the 1988 Olympic Games". The fact that the council was usurping, and not confirming, the decision of its appointed selection committee was a further twist in the tale. When proceeding through the competition events one by one, the council skipped the 800 and determined first the 1,500, approving the selectors' choice of Elliott, Crabb and Cram. They then reverted to the 800 decision. The discussion seemed clearly again in favour of the selectors' choice: Cram, McKean and Coe.

In the opinion of the selection committee, it was Murray who muddied the water. For a start, although chairman of the selectors, he did not make it clear that they had been unanimous about Coe, and did his best to direct the council towards questioning whether the decision was right. Eventually Murray called for a vote, and did so prematurely before the issue had been fully debated. In the matter of the vote, he also influenced the outcome by not asking the AAA representatives whether they wished to use their new "weighted" votes. Since bailing out the Board's deficit the previous year, there were now some AAA members carrying three votes rather than one. Instead of taking a ballot, Murray asked for a show of hands: not in favour of the selectors' recommendation, but "those in favour of Elliott". The count was 11–10 for Elliott.

Those in public office carry serious responsibility for what they do. The breakdown of the voting was reported as follows:

In favour of Coe:
3 AAA representatives: Bill Ferguson, chairman; John Lister, treasurer; David Bedford, Southern Counties.
4 Scottish AAA representatives: Jim McInness, president; John Brown, treasurer; Bob Greenoak, secretary; Ruth Booth, women's rep.
3 Northern Ireland AAA representatives: Les Jones, chairman; Tom Welsh, treasurer; Claire Brook, acting women's hon-secretary.

Against Coe:
3 Women's AAA representatives: Margaret Oakley, chairman; Susan Deaves, assistant secretary; Patricia Green, Midlands.
3 AAA representatives: Mike Farrell, general secretary; Roy Mitchell, Midlands Counties; Charles Rice, Northern Counties.
3 Welsh AAA representatives: Bill Evans, secretary; Margaret Elgie, women's secretary; Heddyd Davies, treasurer.
2 International Athletes representatives: Mike Winch, Judy Simpson.

Two points should be made: firstly, if the weighted votes of the AAA representatives, split 50–50 on a show of hands, had been included in a ballot vote, then the decision would have been 15–15, and the debate should have been re-opened for a new count. David Bedford tried to achieve this, but was refused, while the members of the selection committee, other than Les Jones wearing his Irish hat, were not permitted to address the meeting. Secondly, as Chris Brasher points out, Ewan Murray, as chairman of the selectors, should have voted, to make the show of hands 11–11, and then given his casting vote, as chairman of the Board, in favour of Coe. "Some of us were stunned," Bedford says. "We were never prepared for this to happen. We should have lobbied beforehand, and could have got a couple of votes to go the other way. It was like a bad dream."

Joan Allison felt impotent in the face of a selection system with which she disagreed. She and her selection colleagues were embarrassed by the tone of the debate, in which Margaret Oakley, the first to support Elliott from the floor, hinted at class factors between north and south. It mattered not that Coe's athletic upbringing had been almost exclusively in Sheffield, a few miles from Elliott in Rotherham. The turning-point on the show of hands came with Farrell and Evans turning against Coe, together with the two international athletes: both of the latter, in the opinion of one of the selectors, being "the epitome of second-grade international competitors".

The minutes of the meeting merely recorded, on this traumatic day: "The recommendations of the selection committee were then received and discussed. The team was then selected as recorded in the minute book".

"It was one of the saddest days in athletics", Allison says. "I still feel . . . not ashamed, but so sad that it happened".

SC: On the Sunday, I'd been for a jog with Mitchell back in Loughborough. After lunch, there was a phone call from Mike Turner, who'd been a good team manager at the European Championships a few years before. It was a two-way conversation with Les Jones, wanting to know what had gone wrong. They asked what I thought had been the effects of the altitude training, and I said that perhaps I hadn't calculated the possible side-effects of going down to run at Rapperswill. They asked if I'd be prepared to demonstrate my fitness in a subsequent race, and I said of course, whatever distance they wished. They indicated that they thought I had little chance for the 1,500, but reckoned I would get the discretionary place for 800, because of my fitness before the trials. Jones promised they'd do what they could! When I told Peter about the conversation, and that the 1,500 was out of the question, he rang Frank Dick to say that if they would give me a fitness test for the 800, for heaven's sake why not for the 1,500? The next day, the day of the Board meeting, I went to see Dr. Malcolm Read, the Board's doctor, together with Dave Martin. I had a blood test, which was clear, but Read advised me not to rush back into racing because I was obviously under the weather.

Leaving Read, I was driving round the M25 when I heard the 3 p.m. radio bulletin, with the announcer saying bluntly: "Sebastian Coe's international career is over, he's not been selected at either distance". I felt devastated, but at eighty in the fast lane of the M25 you tend to concentrate on the road ahead. Dave was speechless. When I got back to my house at Twickenham, the press and photographers were three-deep around the front door, so we slipped in by a side-entrance. I wasn't going to speak, merely put out a statement. On the basis that I would say nothing, I felt the Board behaved badly: they were goading me under pressure from the press – particularly with Tony Ward saying that our planning hadn't worked, starting with the Lausanne "fiasco", and returning too late from altitude, and that these things "had been influential in the pros and cons of the Coe v. Elliott debate".

The Board's comments would lead to demands by Peter Coe for a retraction, on the grounds that Coe's illness could not be blamed upon inadequate training and preparation. Amid the speculation before the announcement of the Board's decision, Elliott had been particularly confident of his double selection, guaranteed as he was of the place for the 1,500. "I can't see how they can pick Coe ahead of me", he said in an interview. "I've proved I'm the man on form and should be allowed to double up. I've heard suggestions that I might be asked to take part in a run-off for the third 800 place. No chance. I would refuse. Coe knew what he had to do and failed to produce, so he can have no complaint".

The entire episode had been deeply unedifying. ITV had wrung the last ounce of hyperbole from their promotion of the trials during the preceding days. When word on the grapevine had suggested that Frank Dick and some of the selectors were opposed to the selection policy, Ewan Murray found fit to say that Dick was an employee of the Board and would have to abide by policy. Throughout the television coverage of the meeting, ITV commentators had presumed the selectorial role. The vacillation of Jones, initially supporting Elliott at the selection meeting even after talking to Coe and promising he would "do his best", was disappointing. Worst of all was the emergence of prejudices existent among the Board members. There was undoubtedly lingering resentment over the role of Coe as chairman of the Sports Council's *Olympic Review* committee, which in 1985 had recommended that athletics should receive *no* additional grant towards preparation for the Olympic Games, because it was already better funded than any other Olympic sport and was considered to make inadequate use of its resources.

Coe's statement, released to the Press Association at 5.30 on Monday afternoon was simple:

I have only two comments to make. Firstly, this represents, of course, a great personal disappointment. But, secondly, I want to wish the very best of luck, fitness and form to all those selected. They have before them the highest honour in sport – to represent their country at an Olympic Games.

Unfortunately, Peter Coe had been caught by a situation which he might have read better. Following the Board's announcement of the team, Peter had received a telephone call from a reporter of the *Sun*. Peter was rash enough to say that the Board had stabbed his son in the back. Not only did the *Sun* run the story, beneath mega-headlines – news v. nicety is no contest with the *Sun* – but Peter's comments had been shared with every other journalist in attendance at the hotel in Birmingham, where the Board's meeting took place. Every breakfast table had "Coe stabbed in the back".

In the aftermath of the furore, two fresh developments began. On the Wednesday morning, two days after the selection announcement, the *Daily Mirror* started a "Coe Must Go" campaign, which the newspaper was to run right up to the time of the Games. Some 70,000 people responded, over two-thirds of whom thought Coe should go, irrespective of the system into which the Board had locked itself. It was the biggest response ever recorded in a newspaper phone-in of this kind. Simultaneously, I had telephoned Juan Antonio Samaranch, the president of the International Olympic Committee, with whom I was on good terms, in order to discover his reaction to the exclusion of one of the most famous of all Olympians. I found Samaranch surprised, even when apprised of the circumstances. Without solicitation on my part, Samaranch said that he had in mind writing to the British Board, requesting their re-consideration. This seemed to me ill-advised. Apart from knowing the reasons underpinning the Board's decision, it was out of the question to de-select competitors already nominated, and therefore would be seeking an undemocratic process.

It might be more to the point, I ventured to suggest to Samaranch, that Coe should receive an *ex gratia* invitation directly from the IOC. This would be an unprecedented move, but we were talking of a competitor without precedent. I was well aware of the horror that such a step would provoke among the bureaucratic and the average: those who become instantaneously resistant to anything not done before, and anything which seeks to elevate an individual. We tend to be governed by conformity: the motto of the Olympic Games is about excellence.

Predictably Samaranch's appeal to the Board was swiftly rebuffed, with expressions of surprise, not to say "astonishment", at such a request from such a source. The Board did, however, find itself obliged, after initial reluctance, to issue a statement of apology for impugning Peter's preparation of his athlete for the trials. The key passage in the statement read:

We accept totally that the reason for Seb's bad performance last weekend was the respiratory infection he had picked up just beforehand, and that in no way was his preparation to blame.

The *Daily Mirror* continued to hound Elliott, unfairly portraying him as a donkey. This was absurd denigration of a runner who had won a World Championship silver medal; and inappropriate because Elliott was not even the runner whose selection should be questioned. The two whose performance in Seoul was unlikely to carry them to the final, let alone a medal, were Steve Crabb and Tom McKean. The Board was committed to them, by the policy of first-two-past-the-post.

Yet the pressure was beginning to weigh on Elliott's nerve. At one stage Peter Coe received a call from Elliott's manager/agent Kim McDonald; it was uncommon for either to call the other. McDonald came quickly to the point. Elliott was distressed with the criticism of his selection for the 800, was beginning to doubt whether he should double up, and was concerned to learn that he had not been the recommendation of the selectors: perhaps the thing to do was to run against Coe to settle the argument. McDonald suggested the Grand Prix in Zurich the following Wednesday. Peter knew the possibility was slim, because his son's infection had yet to clear; he said he would talk to him.

It was a one-sided deal. Coe was less than fit, and short of races, so the gamble for Elliott was worthwhile; it could remove the pressure. Conversely, the offer was unattractive for Coe; even though it had become apparent, with the failure of Konchellah, the world champion, to gain a selection for Kenya, that the 800 was an even softer race now than Coe and his father already believed it likely to be. A decision by the Coes became unnecessary, however, when McDonald called back and said that Elliott had changed his mind, and felt he could now take on two events.

During the campaign to get Coe to the Games, there were those who were scornful; they considered that the concern for a former champion was misplaced. Apart from athletes, with their own vested interests in participation, and those such as Winch and Simpson on the British Board who would always champion a chance for mediocrity, included were some experienced commentators: Peter Hildreth of the *Sunday Telegraph*, a former international hurdler, and Cliff Temple of the *Sunday Times*, also the coach of some aspiring athletes. Temple took the view that Coe had been failed by no one but himself, that he did not deliver on the day, under a system in which he had months of fore-warning. Temple spoiled his argument by being drawn into tacky sniping about Coe's university degree, as though suspicious of all excellence. Hildreth had for years exhibited an ambivalence about Coe, obsessed with the frequency with which he was unwell.

The situation returned to the melting-pot with the revelation that Samaranch had indeed extended an independent invitation to Coe, provided that both the national and international federations, and the British Olympic Association, approved. The BOA, through Charles Palmer, its president, was quick to give his blessing; while the British Board, with no rule behind which to take cover, pompously gave its agreement. Palmer had said that, while pleased for Coe, he questioned the principle behind it. Murray announced on behalf of the Board: "I have now told Charles Palmer that if Coe is invited in this way, we would regard him as a member of the British team, wearing our colours, *and benefiting from the coaching and training advantages of our other athletes*, and with his fare to Seoul paid by the BOA. After all, *he has always been a good judge of his form* and I would expect him to tell us straightaway if he did not feel he should go to his third Olympics as a competitor". This was an extraordinary statement by the chairman of the organization which so recently had paid no heed to Coe's assurances, to the selectors, that he would be fit if given the chance to show it in the way he had previously done. Coe knew from repetitions in St. Moritz that he was close to the condition he had been in for Los Angeles.

However, while the BOA were waiting for the International Amateur Athletic Federation to rubber-stamp Samaranch's initiative – something that Primo Nebiolo, the IAAF's president, was unlikely to refuse, for all his sometimes tense relationship with Samaranch – the initiative was torpedoed elsewhere. Prominent athletes in Britain and abroad voiced opposition; although there were those who approved, it was the voice of dissent, needless to say, that found newspaper space. The most vociferous of all was Steve Cram.

What I object to is the rules being changed for one person [Cram said]. I live in a part of the world where people have to work for what they get, and it's not appreciated when people have things handed to them on a plate. If they want to change the rules to invite all Olympic champions to defend their crowns, then that's something to be considered. But to do it for one person three weeks before the Games is ridiculous. At this stage, for the IOC to play the old pals act is totally unfair.

Others to express indignation were Said Aouita and Ed Moses, while there were said to be private objections to Samaranch from his IOC members in the United States, Robert Helmick and Anita DeFrantz. Although Kevan Gosper, a 1956 Olympic 4×400 metres relay silver medallist for Australia, who is on the IOC executive board and is a potential future president, was in full support, Samaranch was unable to sustain his initiative in the face of public opposition. A leader in *The Independent* for example, had welcomed the right of defending Olympic champions, as a non-nationalist development. Samaranch disappointingly shrank away from his unilateral stance: the wild-card offer was withdrawn. "I'm sorry at the opposition to what would have been a fitting honour for a great athlete and sports personality," Samaranch said, having spoken to Coe to inform him of the withdrawal. The final loop-hole having closed, Coe issued the following statement:

Through various issues and controversies of the last two-and-a-half weeks, I have kept my own counsel. I refused constant requests for interviews. I released only two brief statements. At no time have I been in discussion with the British Amateur Athletic Board, the British Olympic Association, the International Olympic Committee or the International Amateur Athletic Federation. Like everyone else, I have followed developments through the media.

Mr. Samaranch did phone me personally this morning to say that he did not feel able, after all, to extend to me his personal invitation to compete in the Seoul Olympics. That was my first direct communication of even the prospect of such an invitation. These weeks have been something of a switchback ride.

During them, I have simply concentrated on getting well again with the help of the BAAB doctor, Malcolm Read, and I have carried on training. As an athlete, I must aspire to compete in the Olympic Games. In my particular case, there has been the additional, understandable ambition to defend a proud Olympic title that I have won twice in succession. I am very grateful to those who made efforts to get me to the Games. I shall look forward to competing in the coming weeks.

Samaranch would have persued his intention of offering Coe a wild-card entry had it not been for voluble objection from Coe's British contemporaries. The British Athletics Board, the British Olympic Association and the I.A.A.F. were all stepping into line, and the IOC executive board was in approval. "I thought, for many reasons, that Coe ought to have the opportunity, after his two Olympic victories" Samaranch says. "He was a very special athlete in the history of the Olympic Games, but once other British athletics came out against him, how could I defend him?" Why had Cram reacted so outspokenly? There must be suspicion that, even if subconsciously, he was motivated by a wish to keep Coe out of the Games. Cram, of all people, would be aware of Coe's potential if fully fit, and the spectre of Coe once more being there to deny him his expectation would understandably have given him the shivers. If that were so, then Cram was to be dealt the harshest poetic justice. Cram's response to events, indeed to misfortune, is normally so relaxed that the sting of his comments on this occasion had been out of character. Yet he remains unrepentant about the views expressed in 1988. "The blame really has to be laid with the British Board", Cram says. "It was a ridiculous policy. It was unfortunate it was Seb [that suffered], but I would have said the same whoever had been offered a wild-card entry. It did me no good – from the hate-mail I had, you'd think it had been my fault."

Jimmy Hedley is at variance with his own athlete. In his opinion, the selectors should select.

There is usually a situation in which one or two should be pre-selected [Hedley says]. The selectors know where they stand, how good the athletes are. Your 2 hours 16 minutes marathon man will never do 2:08. It's the same for the javelin, for the 1,500. There are a lot who are just going for the British track-suit, and therefore it's the lesser people who want head-to-head trials. If the selectors are honest, they *know* who should go. The good people won't go if they're not fit, because it will push their market value down. Of *course* Coe should have been selected. Look at what he'd done. He wouldn't go if he wasn't ready. Why not pick reserves? There are too many who are fighting and tripping just to be there. *That's* their gold medal. The champions are never going for the ride.

Paish, Elliott's coach, likewise felt that Coe should have been selected. "First-past-the-post and *two* discretionary places would be the better solution," Paish says. "If selection had been totally unbiased, Seb should have gone. I wouldn't have selected Cram: all the indications were that he was not running well. But I totally disagreed with Samaranch's proposal, *and* with Elliott being reinstated for the final in Split in 1990. There are stacks who have been tripped, and didn't get in".

The pattern was clear: knowledgeable coaches and athletes who had nothing personally to fear from Coe's presence are almost unanimous that he should have been selected, while Bilé and Cruz, both potential medallists, had no objection even to a wild card. "I think he would have gone close in Seoul," John Walker, the former champion runner says. "He knew enough to get himself right. If he hadn't run the 800 too hard, he'd have won the 1,500. Cram was over-trained and over-raced and lost confidence". Steve Scott is in favour of Olympic champions being allowed to defend their title, provided they have the qualifying time. Luiz Oliveira, Cruz's coach, is the most emphatic: "If Coe had been there in '88, he would have won. In a slow race, he would have out-kicked them". Mel Watman goes further than Paish; he is not against the winner of a trial qualifying, to give some incentive to outsiders, but would be happier with all three places being discretionary, putting the onus upon the selectors. "Seoul remains a disappointment. I thought it might have been the race of the century: Bilé, Aouita, Cram, Elliott and Coe. Yet it turned out to be one of the poorest. I would give more powers to the selectors provided they know what they are doing. In '88, my gut feeling would have been for Coe to have been there: though maybe that's subjective". Foster and Brasher, self confessed Coe advocates, are in no doubt.

You really can't select Morrell or Crabb instead of Cram or Coe [Foster says]. In my heart I know the 1,500 should have been Elliott, Cram and Coe. Given the chance, of course Morrell or Crabb would say, . . . to hell with the others, I'm going. They also get up at 7 am! The selectors should know that someone like Coe will never go when not fit, they don't go for the bus ride. Coe, when he looks back, can come to terms with Moscow, or Barcelona in 1989, where disappointment was on the track, but not with what bureaucracy denied him in '88. That was sad.

Brasher's view is that the Coes' *timing* (in training) was one of the great feats of athletics. "It annoys me so much, because I believe he could have won again in '88. And I believe the reigning champion has earned the right to be there. Selectors have got to select, instead of applying some formula". Yet Norman, the old owl, was not a policeman for nothing. He knows his fellow men. "Seb had said too much beforehand," Norman reflects. "He should have talked about himself only, but he'd alienated people by criticizing the whole set-up. And when it got to '88, the Board couldn't justify him by talking about a champion. He wasn't the same person".

The sporting letters column of *The Times* produced some interesting contributions. Edward Grayson, a barrister and specialist in sport and the law, wrote:

Is the most illuminating test, by which to judge the bizarre behaviour of the British Board's decision, to consider the comparable circumstance for the no less demanding standards for four-legged thoroughbreds? On Saturday week the world's oldest classic horse race, the Doncaster St. Leger, will be run, followed a few weeks later by the Arc de Triomphe at Longchamps. No one would ever suggest that the Jockey Club, Weatherbys, or the Doncaster Race Committee should require that trainers responsible for bringing their charges to a peak condition at either occasion should suffer the arbitrary hoops operated by the BAAB . . . anyone with the faintest awareness of the true human endeavour within sport at all levels knows how different individuals peak at different times . . . by abdicating selectorial responsibilities the BAAB has manifested its intellectual as well as moral unfitness to administer its great inheritance . . .

From Jonah Barrington, former squash champion:

Sebastian Coe is a special case and he should have been chosen. His unique and proven quality, unwavering commitment, and his continuing search for perfection, should have won more respect and understanding from those who sat in judgement on his moderate recent form. He has been shamefully stood down, indeed insulted by, in the main, mean-spirited, mini-minded officials who have no concept of true excellence.

From Mrs Sylvia Disley, a former athlete:

The projected offer of a wild-card for Sebastian Coe opened up the prospect of a return to the true original concept of excellence in competition of the ancient Olympic Games. At present, the Olympics are nothing more than a glorified international match, with their rigid limit of three competitors per nation per event. The inevitable result is that in some events, while some countries can send the full quota of three mediocre athletes who just make the grade, other countries have to leave at home potential finalists and medal winners simply because they have a surfeit of excellence in a given event . . . surely the aim of the Olympic movement should be to allow those athletes who are faster, higher and stronger than the rest of the world, to compete. To this end, the

IOC might consider allowing one athlete per nation and then select the remaining competitors for each event from performances at certain recognized meetings . . .

Perhaps the most consoling letter of all for Coe was a personal one received from the Master of Pembroke College, Oxford – Sir Roger Bannister:

Dear Seb, You have been thoroughly philosophic in public about last weekend's disappointment, but I feel I must write to say how sorry I felt that the doubtless temporary effect of altitude and infection did not give you the chance to come through the trials successfully. Your own career is indisputably the best of any middle-distance British runner this century – and the longest by far. I know that some future opportunities for your inclusion might occur, but if not, we face sadness that you may not get your chance in Seoul to win your third Olympic gold medal at 1,500 metres, which would be a record I cannot conceive any other runner ever equalling. May I just end by sending you my very best wishes for your races yet to come, the Sports Council, and whatever further careers you choose. Yours sincerely, Roger.

My own feelings were almost as much for Peter as for his son, having known them an equal length of time. I know how I would have felt in a similar situation, after having done so much together: mortified. More than any other athlete or coach, Peter would have known what genuinely was possible, and I have never met anyone so starkly objective if he knew there to be *no* case.

PC: The cost of illness and injury is the penalty you have to pay because the level of sports medicine (in Britain) is not that great. We wasted a season in '87, with calf and heel problems, but for which there might have been more visible continuing proof of Seb's status. John Durkin in Chicago designed and supplied all the orthotic felt inserts for Seb's shoes, and cured the calcification of his heel with syringes. The price doesn't have to be that high if you can find the right people.

The future for athletes operating at Seb's level has to be monitoring in the fashion of the Eastern Bloc (that was). At this stage of Seb's career 30–34, it wasn't that he couldn't take hard sessions. He could. But recovery after hard sessions, and during illness, took longer. After his 1,500 peak in 1986 (3:29.77) I would have been happy to pack up and go home. Yet I couldn't see anyone around at that time who had better qualifications for representing Great Britain. Without any bragging, I *knew* he could come away with medals in each event in Seoul. A banker. So: let's go. It was his wish to do so, however, not mine, and everything was going well in '88 till the middle of July. Seb made all his protests about the system, a bad one, early on. Afterwards he didn't join in the debate. It's demeaning having athletes writing to the Board: Dear Sir, please pick me!

He should never have run in the trials, because the cold hung around longer than usual. By the end of the month he was getting better, and the wretched thing is, Elliott apart, we did so badly in Seoul. Would I have thrown my son to the wolves, just to get the ride? Would he, with his honesty, have wished to be there? If I didn't think he was right, he wouldn't run. Recovery in those situations is so fine a line that you can decide not to run one day and be OK the next. Of course he could have coped with the seven races in Seoul, the series would have set him up the way it did in LA. We had the proof that his quality was still there in the World Cup the next year. Never mind me, Seb's pride is such he would never have chanced it himself.

Coe's first race after recovering was when coming second to McKean at the Berlin Grand Prix. It was there, preposterously, that he was advised by Andy Norman that there was a £25,000 subvention available if he would return to run at Crystal Palace in the Peugeot Games; and that if he went instead to race in Koblenz, the Board would block his entry. Coe quietly asked Norman if the Board was ready to spend two months in court on restraint of trade. It was an unbelievable affront that the Board, having conspired to prevent Coe representing Britain in the Olympic Games, should now demand his presence, backed by colossal financial incentive, to help boost the attendance and television viewing figures in a domestic meeting.

He ran in Koblenz, finishing second by a couple of strides to José Luiz Barbosa. The Brazilian, who was to finish sixth in Seoul, recorded the fourth fastest time of the year, 1:43.34: Coe the eleventh fastest time of the year, and the second best by a Briton, with 1:43.93. It made Coe the seventh fastest individual in the world, for the year; and the same time in Seoul would have given him the bronze medal behind Ereng and Cruz. In 1988, Elliott failed to beat 1:44 and McKean to beat 1:45.

The selectors, the British Board, the doubters and the critics had received their answer, in slightly under four weeks from that wretched Saturday afternoon in Birmingham . . . and there was still almost a *month* to go before the Games. From Koblenz, Coe went to Rieti where, still with traces of respiratory problems, he ran a 1,500 metres in 3:35.72

SC: Steve Ovett was there in Koblenz and told me to have a holiday and forget about everything. If I could run that time four weeks before the Games, still marginally less than fit, what might I have done in Seoul, given the time and the chance? After my 1,500, I stood watching Cram attempt the record for 1,000, but he pulled up after 2 laps with a calf problem. Elliott had run the 800.

I remember thinking: I'm here because my season's *over*, whereas I'd planned to go to Australia at this time to prepare for Seoul, and here are these two running in races they don't *need*, Elliott running with a hip and groin problem, Cram going for a record four weeks before a double bid in the Olympics. Three days later, the Board rang Cram to find out if he was OK for the double attempt, and were told everything was fine. Yet I'd been ruled out four weeks earlier, with a cold!

I find it remarkable that Coe was able to talk to me, over a year later, for the purposes of this book, without a trace of resentment over something which, at the time, had been the end of his world. The discipline and the control never desert him, rain or shine, whatever the fires that burn within.

However, not only were the Games in Seoul to prove the moral rightness of Coe's case, but were to bring some honour to Elliott: even though it remains questionable whether Elliott should have wished to double up, or indeed should have been allowed to do so.

Crabb and I only did what we were required to do [Elliott maintains]. I was the one in all this who earned his ticket. People somehow thought because I'd been given the discretionary place for the 800, I'd kept Coe out of the defending of his title at 1,500. The *Mirror* campaign was depressing, people gossiping all the time, and it was getting at me. I was glad to get out to the training camp in Japan. I was receiving hate mail, and sections of the press were waiting with knives. I remember warming up for the first heat of the 800 and thinking determinedly, "I'm going to do this journey seven times". Maybe I didn't achieve what Seb had done, but I *was* in two finals. Maybe it would have been better if I'd run only one event in Seoul, but I'd planned all year for both, and it could have worked. The pelvic strain came when warming up for the final of the 800. I seized. Malcolm Read, the doctor, gave me an injection. I don't know what happened. In '84, I'd pulled out of the semis of the 800 with a stress fracture, and I wasn't going to let that happen again. I'd take the risk for the 1,500, because I didn't want to sit and watch two finals I thought I could win.

I felt I had a chance in the 800, and didn't see the point in giving up a final I was already in, and maybe have to pull out anyway in the heats of the 1,500. They don't think I did any damage. At the time I was worried about what I was doing, lying on the bed between races, hardly able to walk. I had five injections in all, and for each race was able to do little more than a few strides warming up, then the race, and a warm-down.

To have finished with fourth place, and a silver medal behind Peter Rono in the 1,500, was indeed the mark of a man with courage. Cram and McKean both went out in the second round of the 800, and Crabb in the 1,500 semis, while Cram could only finish a slowish fourth in the 1,500, behind bronze medallist Herold of East Germany. Coe's "unfit" 3:35.72 in Rieti was faster than Rono's winning time.

The arrival of the Games, via television, was an agonizing time for Coe. He watched Cram fail to qualify, and McKean disqualified, and thought, "I can't take any more". It was worse the next morning, when he woke up to hear Mike Channon, the former England footballer, doing a middle-distance commentary! He rang a travel agent to say, "Take me anywhere, I'll be at the airport in three hours!". He departed with Jane Williams for Sicily.

When someone's as dispirited as Seb was [Jane reflects], there's not a lot you can say. "Oh, never mind" is not much help. His entire circle of family and friends were so shocked when he was left out. We were all thinking, "well, it's happened before, he'll still go." I think he was half confident that somehow things might change, that Samaranch might swing it. The day of the final of the 1,500 we took off on a boat to another small island, just to get away from television. Back at the hotel in the late evening no one seemed to know what had happened, and Seb would refuse to ask, so I called my mother to find out. When I told Seb, he whispered, "nothing to cheer about there". There were some Brits about in the corner. He cared so intensely that Britain had performed poorly. It mattered so much to him: the belief that he could do it in Seoul where no one else could. For him, at that moment, it proved what he'd always thought . . . that he could have won the gold medal for Britain a third time.

Objectives

I used to say to Steve in any race [Harry Wilson, Steve Ovett's coach, says], don't give yourself a problem, give your opponents the problem, sit in tight, don't get boxed. He had the kick to run it *his* way. Nobody but Aouita has had the same, and not even Aouita at 800 metres. Mind you, the best kick I've ever seen was that of Susanj of Yugoslavia, in winning the European Championship in 1974. He suddenly went with 250 metres to go, and within 30 metres he's gone eight or ten metres up. Steve was a bit trapped at the time, but he said afterwards that he was astonished that anyone could win a race within such a short distance.

Wilson, a short, amiable man, had originally been an amateur football player, and had come into athletics casually. As he had been a winger, it was thought he should be a sprinter, but his legs were never long enough for that, and by the time he was approaching thirty he had switched to long-distance road racing. The turning point in his athletics career had been a summer school at Loughborough, where he met the celebrated Geoff Dyson, the chief national coach. It was the influence of that week that convinced Wilson his true vocation would be coaching. In his biography, *Running Dialogue*, Wilson wrote:

More important than my long-distance efforts, I was meeting all the great authorities on running: Gerschler, the German coach who developed Barthel, the 1952 Olympic 1,500 metres champion; Igloi, the Hungarian whose athletes at one time held every world record from 800 metres to 10,000 metres; Franz Stampfl, who had coached the Oxbridge trio of Bannister, Chataway and Brasher; Lydiard, the New Zealand coach to Olympic champions Snell and Halberg; and Cerutty, the eccentric Australian, mentor to the great Herb Elliott. I was struck by the contrast between Lydiard and Cerutty. Lydiard seemed to have little time for discussing running with someone not well established, whereas Percy Cerutty was willing to talk, he made an indelible impression on me. He was a man of great charisma, capable of investing even batty ideas with the strength of his personality. Of course, I wasn't even a proper coach in those days. And even when I was and I visited Percy at his famous camp in Portsea, Victoria, he insisted I sit on the ground like a small boy while he delivered an oration.

Ovett and Wilson came together by chance at a coaching week at Crystal Palace in 1972 when Ovett was sixteen. In their different roles as coach and athlete they were going to have a profound influence on each other. Ovett, tall and strong, was already a man while still a boy.

In 1974, aged eighteen, he equalled Bannister's historic time of 3:59.4, to become Britain's youngest-ever sub-4-minute miler. The previous year, he had won the European Junior Championships at Duisburg in West Germany., worrying Wilson by leaving his finishing kick until dangerously late, but assuring Wilson afterwards that "it never entered my head that I wouldn't win". Six weeks after equalling Bannister's time, Ovett astonished an international audience by taking the 800 metres silver medal at the senior European Championships in Rome, behind Susanj, with a time of 1:45.77. "He was fully developed at eighteen, a grown man," Mel Watman says. "I was mesmerized by him that time in Rome, it was an amazing achievement. Yet talking to him that evening, he was so disappointed he didn't win, so self-critical after what was the race of his life at that stage. I considered him a possible gold medallist for the Olympic Games in Montreal."

Controversially, Ovett was ignored in 1974 for the Commonwealth Games in Christchurch, New Zealand. It was the familiar story of lack of understanding by the selectors. The Games had come early in the year. Ovett's 1973 race form should have been enough to convince the selectors, but in the trials he faded to finish third, and Andy Carter, Peter Browne and Colin Campbell got the vote. Ovett's reaction was that never again would he leave the selectors in any doubt about his right to selection.

When it came to Montreal, the favourites for the Olympic 800 metres were Wohlhuter (US), Susanj (Yugoslavia) and Juantorena (Cuba) . . . and Ovett. One of the problems in Montreal was the lane-break after the first bend. It had been decided two years before that the first 300 metres would be run in lanes, though during the interim the regulation varied from one meeting to another; it was only sub-sequently that a lane-break after 100 metres became standard. In the final, Ovett had the extreme disadvantage of drawing lane eight, thereby being out of touch with the other runners for much of the first lap, and he finished a disappointing fifth behind Juantorena, Van Damme (Belgium), Wohlhuter and Wüldeck (West Germany). It was, nonetheless, invaluable experience for a twenty-year-old. In the 1,500 metres, he qualified comfortably in the heats, and was drawn in Walker's semi-final. Coming into the final straight well positioned, Hill of Canada fell just in front of him, throwing Ovett badly off stride, and he was eliminated in sixth place. It was the opinion of many that by 1976 Ovett was concentrating on the wrong event. "Maybe I was," he admits. "I think I probably always was a 1,500 runner, and I should have concentrated on that sooner. I reached the target a year later, but in Montreal fate obstructed me in the semi. You just have to bite the bullet – like Peter Elliott in 1990 in Split." Whatever the Montreal frustrations, Ovett was already a figure on the world stage. The runner who was about to become his closest rival had not yet broken cover.

Robert Hague is a neurologist at Barnsley Hospital in Yorkshire, and has known the Coe family for many years, taking an interest in Sebastian from his earliest days as a runner; in later years occasionally giving advice during periods of Sebastian's glandular illness.

We all know that people tend to speculate about their future and their ambitions, but much of it is no more than dressing-room chat, people get lost in fantasy [Hague says]. One particular occasion, I remember talking at the side of the track when Seb was about fourteen, and he was discussing, blandly and dispassionately, his plans together with Peter. He was referring, in a matter-of-fact way, to development over previous years: and said that if progress continued at the same rate, then he would win the Olympic Games in 1980. That was some *ten* years distant and he was still a boy! There was not an element of boastfulness. He was simply saying: "This is the incremental improvement, Dad and I reckon if we do this next year, then that and that, we'll be in a position to win in the Olympics in 1980." That was remarkable, and even more so that they learned enough to nurture Seb's talent with such confidence. They had their training-record book, in which there was an extrapolation that contained the figure of 3:30 for the 1,500 metres by the Eighties. This would have been in the early to mid-70s. I made some comment, and Peter just became grumpy and took the book away. Theirs was an extraordinary perception at that time, and it was remarkable that Peter developed his skill and knowledge to bring Seb to a particular point on a particular day: to balance between *no* work at one stage and an *intense* amount at another, and to be certain that the balance was right a week or a month before a race.

There was something about him that struck me the first time I met him, when he was a lad. I had a registrar's post at Manchester, and came over to Sheffield at weekends to run with Hallamshire Harriers. My brother Ian, who was a PE teacher at Abbeydale School, kept saying he had this skinny child who he thought would be a fine runner. What impressed Ian was his *guts*. He'd sometimes turn up not feeling well, and usually still win. My brother is fairly reserved in expressing admiration of potential in an athlete, so that's why I was interested to have a look. One day I met Seb at the track. He was doing mile interval running. I tried joining him on alternate laps. He was very small and frail, with the trunk of a child and the legs of a man. I was determined he was not going to go past me, but he kept streaming by, and there was nothing I could do (*Hague, then in his thirties, was a 2:02 800 metres runner*).

All along, they both had an uncanny confidence of where they were going. There was never any doubt. Yet Seb was so scrawny. I would never, as an athlete myself, have believed he could do it. Peter, with *no* previous experience as a coach, decided Seb could do it. I remember one race in which older runners swept past Seb, and seeing him with Peter afterwards in the warm-up area, Seb was looking like a beaten whippet. As soon as I could talk to him, separately from Peter, I said, "That was marvellous, those were *men*." But Seb was very non-committal, and Peter was hovering, with that grimace of his. Seb was unresponsive to my enthusiasm. I felt Peter had been getting at him and that it was a bit unjust. They would listen intently to each other. The body language was different from others'. They would stand face to face, looking directly at each other, talking earnestly, and Seb had this capacity to act upon it. As the years went by, you began to see glimpses of what was going to happen. For a time I never saw him race, but then went to a meeting at Cosford, where he was running 3,000 metres. Seb led for much of the way, and remembering what I had seen before, it gave me a real cold shiver. He looked smaller than the other men, but he had this elegance, this lightness. There was the realization that here was someone you personally knew, who was going to be up there joining the likes of Herb Elliott.

Seb never became steamed up. They invited me once to Gateshead stadium, he was racing against Henry Rono. I was on edge travelling up there, and Seb was calming me down, saying "relax, don't worry". Yet once, in the match between Loughborough University and their great rivals, Borough Road College in London [*the college of Alan Pascoe*] Seb was running the last leg of the 4 x 400 relay. As he walked on to the track, the Borough Road crowd began to hiss, in that mocking undergraduate way. His race number had started to come off, and he ran to the edge of the track to ask me to pin it back. The hissing had got to him. He was quite white, and sweating profusely, almost shaking. I'm sure it was anger. It surprised me, because it was so contrary to the cool, controlled image I knew. Borough Road had a substantial lead when Seb took the baton, but he caught them, running a personal-best 400.

He could have this strange effect on people. On one occasion, after 1980, we walked into the Broom Hill Tavern in Sheffield. There was quite a crowd, but he was spotted. An Asian man came across, and shook his hand repeatedly, saying "Great, great", unable to say anything else. Some people would be embarrassed, but Seb could carry it off without the bat of an eyelid.

Robert's brother, Ian Hague, had a responsibility within the city for Sheffield Schools cross-country organization. He is a former 400 metres hurdler, and as a PE teacher he had first encountered Coe, then aged thirteen, at Tapton School. Coe subsequently went to Abbeydale Grange and came under Ian's direction.

I dealt with many pupils who did well [Ian Hague says], and they were all precocious, *physically*. They were youngsters who were shaving twice a day. Seb was very small. At sixteen he was looking like fourteen. Yet at cross-country, after 400 metres he'd be in front, with the others trailing, yet most of those went on to be good county runners. Seb came to my school firstly to get good "A" Levels, secondly to get good races, because we travelled all over the country, and thirdly to make use in his free time of the gymnasium. Peter saw

Abbeydale as particularly relevant to the racing, and would say, "Give me a list of races that you'd like him to run, and I'll have him fit on schedule." Already, Peter was synchronizing training with races. When Seb joined us at sixteen, I was playing for the local rugby club. One night after training, during bar-room chat, I said there was this boy who was going to be a world champion. They all laughed.

Yet it was apparent so early, with the combination of Peter's vision and Seb's competitiveness. People may have said Peter was *killing* him, but he wasn't. I was aware of the training that anyone had to do to be successful, and what Peter was doing wasn't cruel. I had an impression of Peter, before I got to know him, that he was difficult. If you casually picked up what he was saying, you could misinterpret it. Some thought he was being too hard, but Seb could handle it because they had such a fine relationship. They were friends! If people didn't see the love that was there, they would think Peter an old rogue. Well, in a way he was! But what he did was so well-judged. With most training, say 8 x 200, if it's in the diary, you *do* it. There's a psychological hang-up, bad for character not to complete the day's work. Yet I've seen Peter pull Seb out after five or six repetitions, often because it was going well rather than badly. Peter was very clever at recognizing signs in Seb that nobody else could see, which he knew because he was his son. Within that slight frame was an exceptional aggression. Once, running for the school against King Henry VIII at Coventry over 6 x 2 miles, Seb ran the last leg and fastest of the day, running for the team and not for himself, pulling us up from sixth to fourth. He worked desperately for the third place bronze, and was absolutely shattered at the finish. You were aware he was running for the others.

He always came across at school as being confident. His geography teacher thought he was arrogant: mainly because, asked what Bakersfield in California was famous for, Seb answered that it was where Jim Ryun ran the mile world record. (Bakersfield has the world's largest inland oil refinery.) I'd like to think I did have some influence in his progress. Peter used to use a group of us to talk through ideas, because there are many different ideas that go to producing good athletes. I saw Ovett at training when he was seventeen with David Hemery, doing 300 repetitions with incredibly short recovery-intervals. Athletes vary.

It is said that coaches know a lot about athletes; whereas, as Harry Wilson has stressed, they know a lot about *individual* athletes. In his opinion, the relationship between Peter and his son was critical to their achievements. "No-one would have been able to do the job Peter did," Wilson says. "The British Board has a Master's coaching award with seventeen recipients, and the fact that Peter never received it sticks in my throat. People say that father/son relationships in coaching cannot work in the majority of instances. It did for Seb, and I don't think anyone else could have got out of him what Peter did – just the fact that they knew each other so well. Seb's record is better than Steve's. Part of Steve's asset was his range (of distances); maybe that diluted him. Seb, although he said he was going to move up to 5,000 metres, never did, and his continued specialization maybe helped him." Angela Coe admits that sometimes Peter's demands on his son made her shudder, but that his honesty as coach was something which enabled Seb to keep going, because Peter never misled him with optimistic or exaggerated figures or expectations.

Wendy Sly, Silver medalist at 3,000 metres in Los Angeles, testifies to the special abilities of Peter as a coach, having worked with him for the past five years, through a series of set backs. "I would probably have given up running but for Peter and my husband," Wendy says. "He is so positive, and his belief in me has been so strong. I needed a change, and his approach has been so refreshing. So much coaching is hit and miss, coaches giving you sessions without knowing why. Everything Peter does has a reason, it all has a scientific base. Every time I went out of the door, the run had a purpose, a means to an end. That was why he was so good at getting Seb ready on the day. That's where so many get it wrong."

SC: You're always under test with Peter, there's no half-way house. If he hears an idea he likes, he will want good evidence before he opens the door to it. Those who have had the most difficulty with him are those closest to him. He has a gut instinct, and is not often wrong, though there are hidden levels of compassion that are not widely apparent. He's taken some pretty serious decisions about my career, but has always said you can only coach by consent. Without our having an employer/employee sense, there's never been for Peter a "that's what I think, like it or lump it" attitude. There have been times when I've not thought a training session was relevant, and we'd discuss it. I would have rebelled had I not shared a similar streak of individuality. There was probably an element in me that wanted to be different, to have team officials tearing their hair out at my personal routine that had the endorsement of someone who was my coach. He was the hand-on-arm, cooling influence on me in the early years. It was in later years that he was much more demonstrative. I've always said that *I* was in charge, right from the start, but especially between eighteen and twenty.

In some of the early school races I was terribly nervous, and threw it away. But one of the things Peter realized was the existence of a variable during racing periods, that things went badly when he was not around. Therefore he was vital as a *valet*, physical and mental, which could not have happened if he'd delegated control to schoolteachers. Typically, for schools championships, I would travel on the team bus, share rooms with competitors in an alien environment, and be expected to produce my best in a major field. These were not the circumstances for good performances. At some expense to his own career, Peter found the time to take me out of this. It made me hugely unpopular. In the under-18 championships at Wolverhampton, I arrived on the day of the race and went home the same afternoon. It was the right solution: not a matter of being sociable or unsociable, but when we were both committing so much, we couldn't leave any stone unturned.

I don't think it necessitated mental compromise on other areas too much: if there *was* a time, it would have been from about the age of sixteen to twenty, and then again after the world records in 1979 up to the time of the Olympics in LA when I was twenty-seven. Athletics does impose a restraint on your life. When I reached the level of county teams at fifteen, the whole thing started to change quite dramatically. It wasn't an imposition by Peter, but a realization that I was willingly being pulled into something that would take inordinate mental and physical effort. There were times when I was around with other children, and was conscious they had so much more time to themselves than I did, even though my decision was voluntary. It was particularly true of the holidays, after "O" Levels, when others were off and free. My holidays were harder than term-time. Everyone else was slowing down, I was deeper than ever into training.

When it came to emotional control, Peter could be too excitable. He wasn't just working with me, but was working *for* me. He was mature enough to accept this, and although everything was felt to be shared, I was the one who carried the can for any inconsistency when I became prominent. What Peter could get away with at the Yorkshire Championships, emotionally, he couldn't in an Olympic Village. The worst aspect was that he could be very dogmatic, and sometimes would argue for the sake of it, which could be wearing if you didn't know how to take it. Yet I never felt I was being dragged into anything.

After telling me I ran like an idiot in Moscow, there was a much more cautious attitude even when he felt there'd been an injustice. Peter could be as sensitive as anyone. I remember the national junior championships at Liverpool, when beforehand we sat on the Mersey Ferry, crossing the river backwards and forwards a dozen times, just relaxing. At the more subtle end of psychology, you've got to find the focus for a race, but not start too early, or you mentally exhaust yourself before the race has begun. I recall Bobby Gould, the manager of Wimbledon when they beat Liverpool in the Cup Final, relating how he and Don Howe had the team training for three hours the day before, and saying "When you've got Vinny Jones and Wise in your team, you don't give them too much time for thinking." We had to have a strict racing discipline, meal times, bed times, three or four days beforehand, and there were schedules even during non-racing periods.

From the age of fifteen, to achieve mental equilibrium, Peter instilled the necessity for lying down if possible before a race. Being a large family, we always had an estate car, and could keep cushions in the back. Peter was splendid at not allowing low-points to dog one's consciousness, and keeping me hungry for new achievements, so that I would arrive mentally fresh. So that when I look back now to major races, I tend to think how lucky I was, even with gold medals, considering what might have gone wrong. It means that now that I've stopped racing, I don't actually *miss* it, I'm not longing to be in Brussels or Zurich.

From 1979 onwards, I realized that I was under the public microscope, though for a while didn't appreciate the full extent of it, the steady drip, drip, of comments on the most irrelevant things you do and finding them there in the tabloid press or the post bag. Nothing would ever be the same again. We both admit the relationship couldn't have continued to work if I hadn't left home at eighteen and gone to university, physically separating us. Peter thought that to remain in Sheffield, in the same town, would not be good. The benefit I received from my mother was in giving me a more balanced attitude inside the extremes of what I was doing with Peter. She would be *pleased* in my school days if I came home late after being out with friends. Of the three of us, she is the one who has been obliged to change the most. In the early days she worried, she didn't like what she saw, and would sometimes be flippant, which would annoy Dad because she was not understanding us. With the development of my racing success, she became happier. It was apparent that I was not being forced. By degrees she became more ambitious for me.

After Peter Snell broke the 800 metres and mile records in 1962, primarily on the platform of his immense strength, there developed the principle, attributed to his coach, Arthur Lydiard, that an athlete must run a hundred miles a week to reach the top. The obsession with mileage, and with the need to be big, continued through to the 1970s, given impetus by champions such as Juantorena and Walker. The Coes arrived on the scene to challenge this principle, of the necessity for size and strength as the basis for middle-distance success. Peter has always looked for the mental iron in a runner; and in his son's early days as a senior runner, he would often send him out with tactical instructions "to see what the bastards are made of". The two of them were constantly into exploration. Long ago Peter set out the five-point principle on which he and his son worked; something that was no secret, as was often alleged, but the simple adaptation of existing formulae to the needs and specialities of his own athlete:

- The way I use 300 metres sessions was influenced by Wilf Paish.
- My little knowledge of physiology is enhanced by Dr. John Humphreys and others. These people's works are freely available.
- When I attended coaching conferences, so did many others. We all drew from the same pool.
- I build Seb's programme year by year with the bricks of my training Frank Dick would call this periodizing using micro and macro cycles.

- The energy systems I seek to develop and use are those explained in the publications of work-physiologists. The duration and intensity of the stimulae is known to many others.

PC: What is special is only that Seb's training is tailored specifically for him and his requirements, by a coach who is in a unique position of being able to have detailed knowledge of his charge. My point is that there are not any magic formulae. A logical and intelligent application of widely known acts, damned hard work by an athlete and coach alike, no neglected details, meticulous care, dedication . . . these are the requirements. If I bring anything new to coaching, it is what I said at a seminar in America: think like a good modern industrial manager, identify your short-term and long-term objectives, marshall your resources and co-ordinate your help. Above all, think first, and then act with conviction. In the UK, all that you require are better facilities and nationally-organized sports medicine as a back-up for our coaches.

An example of this attention to detail was the discussion, before Coe attended Loughborough University, between Peter and George Gandy, a biomechanical specialist and a coach at the university. Gandy would supervise the intense and essential weights programme in the gymnasium through the long winter months.

PC: One of the joys of training Seb was that he understood what I was after, what I was working towards. Of our four children, he was the one who listened. I could get behind him and push. When he was short-listing his "A" Level choices, or his university options, I always tried to bring in my produc-tion-engineer's attitude: the pre-planning, what would *fit*. I only once gave him a major choice, "this or that". He looked at me surprised, and said, "That's your decision, *your job*." And, with a smile, "That's what I keep you around for". Seb is shrewd. He has an instinct for getting people to do things for him, a natural delegation. I told him early on not to feel he was stuck with me, that if he felt he was not going far enough or fast enough, to say so. If you look at the programme we set out to achieve, perhaps there wasn't perfection, but what I said would happen *did* happen. It was a relief when he became an adult, that I had less worries, that my involvement tapered off, and I could concentrate exclusively on the training schedules and races. He always allowed me to pick the races. It was teamwork. It would be difficult to convey the extent to which he listened, and how much he did on his own.

In the trials for the Olympic Games in 1976, aged nineteen, Coe ran poorly, in spite of a personal best of 3:43.2, finishing seventh in his heat. There had been another hassle with the authorities, because he was in the middle of exams and had difficulty arriving at Crystal Palace on time. In the subsequent AAA final, after only three weeks of serious training, he improved his time marginally, finishing fourth behind Dixon (NZ), Moorcroft and Clement of Scotland, beating off the challenge of Quax (NZ). The next week at Gateshead, running in gale conditions and setting the pace from the front, he finished third in a mile behind Walker and Moorcroft. Back at Crystal Palace, still experimenting, he led for three laps in the Emsley Carr Mile, was brushed aside on the final lap and faded on the run-in to finish seventh, though beating four minutes for the first time, with 3:58.35. Moorcroft won a fine race from Bayi of Tanzania, the former world-record holder. Coe had learned more about himself.

It was a small British team, spearheaded by Coe, which went to the European Indoor Championships in San Sebastian the following spring. Coe and I chatted on the way out, and shortly afterwards, on arrival at the hotel, he was surprised to be given a stern warning by Marea Hartman, *mater familias* of the Women's AAA, that he would be well advised, for reasons about which she was unspecific, to stay well clear of both me and the late Ron Pickering. Some of those with administrative power, who, in their honorary positions, in many instances enjoy status which far exceeds that in their daily working or social life, do not take kindly to the inquiring eye and ear of the media.

It was a memorable occasion for Seb and young Jane Colebrook, coached by their father and mother respectively, each winning the 800 metres. Colebrook slaughtered the combined might of Eastern Europe to equal the world best of 2:01.1; while Coe, leading from gun to tape, was a tenth of a second outside the world record of Carlo Grippo of Italy, with 1:46.5. "As a coach, I started to say to Steve that we would have to take this fellow into the reckoning," Wilson recalls. "You don't consider this until someone becomes dangerous, and that was happening now. I'm not saying Steve was complacent, but we both recognized the threat was there. *And* 'on our own doorstep'."

Although, proportionally by age, he developed two or even three years behind Ovett – partly owing to Peter's restraint – Coe was emerging as a force. He was beginning to gain the benefit of the speed and weight training with Gandy. In the Europa Cup final in Helsinki that August, still a lightweight physically, Coe was violently obstructed when about to make his finishing kick in the final straight, being handed off by Wülbeck of West Germany, and faded to fourth in an 800 race he might have won. Two days later, in Brussels for the Ivo Van Damme memorial – the precocious young Belgian silver medallist in the Montreal 800 and 1,500 metres had died in an accident – Coe ran a personal best of 1:46.31 behind Mike Boit of Kenya and Mark Enyeart (US). He won the Emsley Carr mile this year with a new personal best of 3:57.67, to become the youngest winner of the event; though this time, run at the age of almost twenty-one, would be substantially improved by teenagers Graham Williamson and Steven Cram within the next few years. It was the first time that Coe had earned a back page headline, with the *Mirror*'s "Bold King Coe" on the Monday morning. And although he now gained the UK record for the 800 metres with 1:44.95 in his final race of the 1977 season, Ovett held both the 1,500 metres and the mile, with Coe not even ranked in the UK all-time top ten.

In the warm-up area following the 800 metres record, which he had taken from Ovett, he was mildly surprised when Ovett studiously ignored him. It was easy to understand why. Now Ovett had a rival for his status as the golden boy of British athletics: never mind that six days previously Ovett had won what is regarded as the most perfect race of his entire career, when defeating Walker and others in the World Cup 1,500 metres in Düsseldorf. There have been instances in the past of such rivalries as Ovett and Coe: Ryun v. Keino, Pirie v. Kuts, Bannister v. Landy, though they were not from the same country. The real intensity occurs when you set compatriots against each other, such as Hägg and Andersson of Sweden, who broke the 1,500 metres and mile records ten times between 1941 and 1945. The projected Bayi v. Walker confrontation of the Olympics in Montreal had been baulked by the African boycott.

One of those whom Ovett had thrashed in Düsseldorf was the American Steve Scott, a brilliant runner over a period of more than twelve years, who failed to achieve the highest honours only because of mental frailties on the big occasion.

I'd beaten Ovett the previous year in Jamaica at 1,500, his last loss before he began that remarkable winning streak that ran through to Moscow [Scott recalls]. As an American, I'd never heard of him, not yet having been involved on the European circuit. It was my first year as a senior, and I didn't look beyond America. It wasn't until after I raced him that I heard of what he'd done before. In the build-up to Düsseldorf, John [Walker] had been everywhere, running great times, but this was the big one. I expected Walker to win because he had the basic speed, though I don't know quite how much John was bothered; he was obliged to run as the Oceania representative, and it was the end of a hard season. I'd "rabbited" for him in Brussels a fortnight before, when he was going for the 1,500 record. I remember being in pain in Düsseldorf at the pace of the thing. Discovering what money there was to be made in Europe, I'd raced myself out of form by then, here, there and everywhere, so that I was on my knees. But I was still surprised by the unbelievable sprint from Ovett, with 200 metres to go, that left everyone looking so silly. The one thing that really irritated me about Steve, throughout his career, was his showmanship down the final straight. That's not my nature.

Geoff Dyson considered a video of the race should be kept in athletics archives as a work of art and an object lesson in middle-distance running. The modern new German stadium had been packed, which undoubtedly brought the best out of Thomas Wessinghage, the national hero. He led from the gun for the first lap but was then overtaken by Walker, with Scott lying third at the 800 mark. Three laps were passed in 2:54.9, faster than Ovett had ever run before: yet he looked composed and was breathing easily. Walker held his lead until Ovett put in his ferocious kick down the final back-straight. By the time he was into the finishing straight the race was over, and a disillusioned Walker was seen running off the track after he had been passed. Ovett's new UK record was 3:34.45, three seconds inside his previous best, in what was his first season as a serious four-lap runner. Watman was another of those to describe it as the perfect race, in *Athletics Weekly*, and recently said: "Steve had never before really exerted himself. It was the first time he had to go through a fast race, but he still had enough for that spectacular finish."

Walker, who at the time of writing was beginning his preparations in New Zealand to become the first runner to beat four minutes at the age of forty, said: "That race in '77 was my downfall, and then two years later Coe took my mile record. The emerging British runners were all younger than me, and they all had that English cross-country club background, the grassroots of middle-distance running." For Ovett it remains a moment of nostalgia. "Yes, I guess it was perfect," he says. "That night I could have been at least a second faster. There are nights when you don't put a foot wrong, your body can do anything you demand. When you try and reproduce it, it seldom works. Such days don't happen that often."

In 1978 it was not athletics which compromised the path of Coe's life, but the reverse. He was studying for his finals at Loughborough, was on a training basis of under fifty miles a week, and early in the season had suffered a serious injury when putting his foot down a gate-post hole while out training. Though recovering, the injury had further retarded his preparation for the racing season; and he and Peter had decided to forego the Commonwealth Games in Edmonton and to preserve their efforts for the European Championships in Prague at the end of August. For that event, he won the selection race in Edinburgh in July, and a month later lowered his own 800 metres UK record to 1:44.25 in Brussels. A first lap of 50.5 showed that he'd recovered much of the lost ground, and was now coming within range of Juantorena's world record of 1:43.4. As he set off for Prague, it was with the knowledge that he was now the fastest in Europe and over a second inside Ovett's best time. Ovett had also opted to by-pass Edmonton.

SC: Prague was cold, wet and wretched. The accommodation was gloomy, the food poor, and many of the team went down with a stomach bug. I was one of them and, with my weight already down to eight stone, it further drained my strength. I was already annoyed that I had been obliged to run in the trials where others were excused, in spite of the fact that I was ranked first in Europe; and in Prague I was further annoyed to find that Steve was being allowed to postpone, right up to the last minute, his decision on whether he would run the 800 metres as well as the 1,500 metres. Within what was supposed to be a team, this was clearly unhelpful to the runner who needed help in his first championships. The Board allowed Steve to play a psychological game with me. Irrespective of that, it had always been my intention to run from the front. Peter and I wanted to test the concept that no-one could kick when running at sub-1:44 pace, or even sub-1:45. And we proved it. What happened was that I slowed most, then Steve, with Olaf Beyer of East Germany managing to sustain his speed a little bit longer. Approaching world-record pace, it comes down to who fades the least. Kicking is not a last 200 metres in 26, it's in 23. A 26 is just maintaining your form. Most people thought I was nuts, though Adrian Metcalfe of ITV was one of the few who had anything good to say. Steve said afterwards that he should have made his effort earlier, though I feel that at the pace of that race he would have simply faded earlier.

The mind at work behind the surprise East German victory was that of Bernd Diessner, a coach from Potsdam just to the west of West Berlin, a quarter of an hour on the "wrong" side of the Wall, that was. Diessner was himself a European 5,000 metres bronze medallist in the 1960s: his runners would tend to be firmly based on endurance. He had always thought Beyer should win a medal, as he told me recently, in the middle of attempting the transfer of his current charge, Jens-Peter Herold, the European Champion of 1990, to a West German Club.

Beyer had run a 47-flat 400 [said Diessner]. He combined speed with endurance, for he had a background of being able to run anything from 800 metres to a half-marathon. His focus for the Olympics in Montreal had been for the 800 more than 1,500, and it was the same for Prague through to Moscow in 1980: a four-year plan. Unfortunately, he badly sprained an ankle in a fall after Prague, which was the turning-point, because he was never afterwards able to train totally free of pain and eventually had to have an operation. In Prague he was wanting it to be a hard, fast race. Coe was not to know, but his spectacular first lap of 49.32, never run previously, played right into our hands. I was confident after I saw the time at the bell. Beyer never ran so fast himself before, but he had the endurance background, and I thought it would pay off.

Coe had held his lead into the second back straight, with Ovett tucked in behind, and then the 21-year-old maths student from Potsdam. As they came off the final bend, Ovett moved past the fading Coe, only for Beyer to overhaul him fifty yards from the line. Beyer's time of 1:43.84 made him the fifth fastest ever, while Ovett's 1:44.09 lowered Coe's two-week-old record. In his manner of that time, Ovett refused to attend the official press conference, saying he had no need of "useless publicity".

Wilson and Ovett had banked on Coe setting the pace, but in the event had followed the wrong man. It would be fair to say that Ovett's priority was the longer race; and *that* he duly won imperiously, in a championship record of 3:35.59, ahead of Coghlan of Ireland and the new Commonwealth champion, Moorcroft. "I certainly didn't expect to win both, though I'd thought I might," Ovett says. "I knew Seb was in great shape, from his run in Brussels, but didn't realize I could be so fast over two laps. Seb ran a brave, exceptional first lap, and I was stretched to follow him. He started to tire down the back straight towards the 600 mark. I closed and eased fractionally, sensing the race was between the two of us. If I'd gone earlier, I think I'd have run half a second faster, and made it more difficult for Beyer. It was exciting that an unknown beat us, that's the sport. Lucky for me I had another race."

The tale of the 800 is revealed by the splits: 12.2 by Coe for the first 100, then 13.1 for the fifth 100 round the third bend, and 13.8 for the sixth down the second back straight.

SC: After Prague I reckoned it would do me good to run two miles in the Coca-Cola at Crystal Palace to end off the season, but before we left Prague, Alan Pascoe told me I was down for the 800; and I subsequently learned through Andy Norman that I had been kept out of the two miles because Steve didn't want me in the race. I felt flattered. In the event, I managed to regain the UK record from Steve, becoming the first Briton under 1:44, with 1:43.97. Steve set a world two-mile best of 8:13.51, beating Foster's record and in the process defeated the remarkable Henry Rono, who that year had established a unique quartet of world records at 3,000, 5,000, and 10,000 metres and the 3,000 metres steeplechase. Steve stared at him as he came level in the finishing straight, and then waved as if to say "goodbye" as he sprinted for the tape.

Steve Mitchell, a schoolteacher and close friend of Coe's from their time at Loughborough together, admits that during his own running career he didn't know what hard work was until he encountered George Gandy. He was to get even more of an idea during his countless runs with Coe.

I was so disappointed when he failed in Prague [Mitchell says]. He'd been running 400s for the university, turning out 46 and 47 on relay legs, and I was sure he would have won if he had held off a little, but of course he was experimenting with Peter. For Seb, although athletics has been central to his life so far, it's been in perspective, and that must have helped. He never talked athletics socially, mostly quite the reverse. The day I met him was at a cross-country club dinner that I organized in a local pub; when I put on some jazz tapes in the ballroom, Seb came up enquiring whose music it was. That's much more his interest off the track. I'd heard about Seb before I met him, with George going on about him during a summer school coaching course that I organized while the Olympics were on in 1976. During the Loughborough years we'd go twice a week, the athletic squad, in a couple of mini-buses to the Harvey Hadden Stadium in Nottingham, an all-weather track. Ours was then still cinders. Seb didn't stick to his own sessions religiously, and would often be doing what the rest of the group was doing. Just as when he joined Haringey in London, he'd be an *ordinary* club athlete, and run club events. International athletes would never see all that. He went abroad to *win*, not to be part of the bread-and-butter circuit. Yet in 1979, we'd been living so much in the shadow of Juantorena from Montreal, that when Seb broke the world record, which I watched on the news, and saw the margin by which he did it, I momentarily couldn't believe it, even knowing him as I did.

You would expect that the tough, hard element inside him would be apparent to his friends, but it's not. You won't see it. Yet nothing limited him, the existing standards. He could see beyond them. His grasp of what was possible, his sight *beyond* the apparently possible, was without anything remotely brash. You couldn't look at him casually and see a champion. I personally feel he never realized or fulfilled all that he might have done on the track. He liked to have people around him he knew, with whom he felt comfortable, that's why Malcolm Williams and I would sometimes drive with him to foreign meetings. He's so casual: he forgets to cash cheques, there's still a video in my house that belongs to him, he'll lend you his car. He's the reverse of ostentatious. Some people don't know how to handle money when they get it. If you didn't know him, you saw him in the street, you would never realize he had money.

David Martin, the Atlanta physiologist in sports research, was gaining his first experience of a European track event in Prague in 1978, and was impressed by the general level of performance. America, in spite of its size and affluence, has not the quality and depth of the European arena. Martin was particularly surprised at the pace of the 800, and that it was possible for two runners still to have a sprint to the finish. Most American races, at least prior to 1978, tended to be slow before a burst to the finish. A central theme to Martin's research has been the preservation of energy in races with an aerobic content.

What is needed, if you are to have spent everything by the time you get to the line, is a well-developed yet innate sense of what you can manage [Martin says]. I first met Seb having lunch in the press room. The East Germans had come in with him, no doubt to compare his background with Beyer's, several days before the race. They spoke no English and he no German, and were getting nowhere. Looking forward to meeting him, I offered to help, only to be asked, "What the hell's an American doing in Prague at the European Championships?" The day after the race, I congratulated Seb, who thanked me for helping out at the interview. We did not meet again until 1980. I was head coach for our team at the World Cross-Country Championships in Paris, which Craig Virgin of America won; and then went on to a ten-kilometre road race in Italy, taking a small number of our runners. Seb was there with Nick Rose, who had been at college in the USA and was good friends with Tom Byers, one of our middle-distance men. They'd been to my lab. Peter was bitching and moaning about the Italian course, which he'd been told was flat, but was the antithesis of safety, with mud holes, rocks and stones. It was a good opportunity for another discussion, and from that point Peter and I started corresponding; the file is now three inches deep.

What interested me was Peter's knowledge of biochemistry, in which he had no formal training. In a muscle cell there are mitochondria, the power house of the cells, filled with enzymes that break down fuel and which provide the energy for performance. The more enzymes you have, the more fuel you can break down. So the aim is to try to increase the size and number of mitochondria through training. Peter had read just enough to know the basics: training an athlete who goes into oxygen debt requires the proper sessions that will both increase fuel storage and oxygen diffusion. Anaerobic metabolism provides only one-nineteenth of the energy of aerobic metabolism, yet anaerobics are the name of the game in middle-distance running. Peter was thus left with the burning question of how to raise Seb's VO2 max high enough so that, when coupled with anaerobic explosiveness, Seb could cruise at any speed necessary to win.

Was it altitude training, Peter asked? What you need, I said, is enough aerobic training as a base before you emphasize anaerobic training. In other words, you can't do Prague-style first lap on low mileage. The secret of the training is that each athlete is an experiment of one. The more élite the athlete, the more unique the experiment. So figure out for Seb the right mix of aerobic and anaerobic work.

I started the lab in '75, about the time the Peachtree road-race was starting to get an entry of seven thousand. A lot of athletes were coming to run; there were regular clinics that I would take. We were trying to put into layman terms the scientific evidence so that they could do more intelligent aerobic training: the base mileage for endurance. But how much is enough? VO2 max, as it's termed, the capacity to raise oxygen absorption, is variable. If it can be reached with sixty miles a week for ten weeks, why train at eighty miles for twenty weeks? Excessive training will only increase the risk of injury. The vogue with coaches at that time was mega volume. We used treadmill stress testing to help any athlete identify the right kind and type of training to use. If, say, Seb takes five weeks off and now trains for eight weeks at 60 miles per week, what will be his VO2 max? Then, will more or harder training raise it?

You learn by doing physiological analysis. Trial and error observation had never been done before with élite level athletes tested repeatedly over months or years. There had only been cross-section testing: fifty athletes tested once to get average values. But athletes don't relate to anyone else. I was probably the first outside the Eastern block doing this work, though they were probably more interested in technique. We were into longitudinal testing, of the same individuals over a period – using each athlete as his/her own control, fine-tuning their training so as to give the optimum gain from the best strategy.

It isn't as important to compare Byers with Coe as it is to make Byers a better Byers and Coe a better Coe. Then, fire the gun and watch the fun of them both operating at a higher level. The lab was assisted by the availability of shoe company funding, because athletes could now travel for testing and analysis. I had research grants for testing expenses. We were improving not only equipment but data. The object of my research had been to discover what is the least amount of the most specific training that will work. Then you move on from not just how many miles, but how to compete. Many athletes don't have personal coaches, and many coaches have little physiological knowledge. I couldn't believe that so many athletes were working without a written training plan, and simply by instinct, which typically was to do too much. The performance of great athletes in competition goes way beyond merely running high mileage for aerobic training. You have to be able to think under extreme stress. When you are swimming in a sea of lactic acid in an 800 metres final, you still have to think and not make a mistake. That's the mark of a champion. Peter was in the potential situation where a little knowledge could be dangerous. However, he'd read so much, and I didn't see anywhere he was off-base physiologically. He had a sixth sense coupled with his technical knowledge. As Seb's father he knew when he had to back off. What he wasn't aware of were the precise mechanisms by which certain kinds of training translate into improved performance. He was also intrigued by whether physiological changes were reflecting psychological changes: the interaction of mind and body.

Martin's analysis runs slightly ahead of events. In 1979, Coe's prime aim was to get a degree, and everything was subordinate to that, though the training programme had remained similar to previous years: a reduction from March onwards, exams in June, then a build-up of training afterwards. His father and Gandy and he had calculated that, towards the end of the racing season, he should be able to get somewhere near Juantorena's world record. He was therefore only in mid-phase, just after completing his finals, when he ran in the European Cup in Malmö, winning in a relatively moderate time of 1:46.63. The main value of the race was the opportunity to switch from expending mental energy to physical energy. From Malmö, Coe was due to travel to Oslo, but first had to overcome resistance from the British Board. Doug Goodman, the Board's official in Malmö, was attempting to saddle the promoter of the Bislet Games with half a dozen British make-weights; and Coe was told he would not be cleared to run unless the Norwegians would pay expenses for the additional competitors. It was two in the morning before Coe was informed he was cleared to travel only hours later.

"I'd been for a jog with Seb in Malmö, along the sea front," Chris Brasher recalls. "We'd talked about his exams, and the fact that he was still only eighty per cent fit. Yet what he now did broke the accepted truth: that the 800 was for big strong men who could sprint. Here was a lightweight, down to two days' training a week, breaking one of the best records in the book." The moment about to arrive in Oslo was no surprise to Foster, who had observed Coe switching from 3,000 metres down to 800, and getting faster all the time. Frank Clement, who had watched Coe beat Rono at Gateshead the previous year, had said to Foster, "He'll be the next British record miler." Foster had replied, "Big deal – the next world record holder."

Bislet, nestling near the centre of the city and surrounded by high buildings which protect it from the wind, has been an historic setting for countless world records. It was here in 1955 that Moens of Belgium broke Harbig's sixteen-year-old record for 800 metres. Ten years later, in the faint aroma of the nearby Frydenlund brewery, Ron Clarke of Australia removed no less than 36 seconds from the 10,000 metres record. These and many other records had established a tradition which made Oslo the hunting ground of the great, urged on by a knowledgeable crowd who pressed close upon the six-lane track with its tight turns. The youthful Coe was peacefully unaware of most of this, as he quietly checked in at the Panorama Somerhotell, high up on the fringe of the city beside the Sognsvatn lake.

SC: I went out training on the Tuesday afternoon, after a loosening run on the sandy paths around the lake when I first woke, and a series of warm-up 150 metres at midday. I sensed I was in good shape. Grete Waitz – the Norwegian holder of the then women's marathon world record and the former world 3,000 metres record – and her husband Jack were watching, and without my knowing it, Jack had been timing me. He said with a smile that I was going well. I felt that I should report the session, and back home Peter said, "Go out and have a go. Run the first lap in 50/50.5, then hang on and see what happens." My own feeling was that if the wind died when the sun went down the next day, I might get somewhere near the European record of 1:43.7.

The next evening, Lennie Smith of Jamaica set a fast early pace, closely followed after the first bend by Coe and Mike Boit, but before they reached the 200 metres mark in under 25, it was obvious that something special was happening: Boit and Evans White of America were already 20 metres adrift behind Coe. Smith took Coe through the bell in 50.6, and now Coe was on his own, maintaining his rhythm all the way to the tape. Adrian Metcalfe, commentating for ITV, yelled, "I don't believe it". As Coe crossed the line, he turned and saw Alan Pascoe, who looked shaken. "What was it?" Coe asked, barely out of breath. "Well, I've got 1:42-something," the astonished ex-hurdles champion answered.

Walker had watched the race. "The way he ran was just unbelievable. He looked like he could run under 1:40, he never tied up at all." When Juantorena set a world record of 1:43.5 in Montreal, it was supposed that he would dominate the event for several years, but he only succeeded in removing another tenth from that time. In seventeen years, the 1962 record set by Snell had advanced less than a full second. Now, Coe sent a ripple throughout athletics by lopping a complete second off Juantorena's time, with an incredible 1:42.33: more than one and a half seconds faster than he himself had run before. Mel Watman recalls: "Seb was a revelation. The record was a knockout, the margin by which he improved it was extraordinary." And this was only the beginning.

SC: I had no particular sensation of speed, and I think I could have run even faster. I wasn't exhausted at all at the end.

The first IAAF "Golden Mile", in Tokyo the previous year, had found the world's best milers reluctant to travel to the Far East at the end of a hard season. Ovett had been persuaded to go, and won a slow race in 3:55.5. In 1979, his attitude seemed to be that the best mile race of the season ought to come to him in London; and by the time it was scheduled instead for Oslo, he had effectively talked himself out of participation. The race, he said, would anyway be hollow without him. The field on the day was to be formidable. Walker would be defending his record; Scott would be looking for the American record; Wessinghage, the European record-holder, had agreed to help make it fast. Coghlan was there; so was Williamson, who had geared his season to this race; and two other leading Americans, Masback and Lacy. For Coe, this would be only his fourth race over four laps in four seasons. Only Bjorge Ruud, a Norwegian who would set the early pace, and Ishii of Japan, had not recorded a faster mile than Coe.

Father and son had no thought of a record, merely the hope to win the race. They reckoned it would be fast, and Peter's instruction was to get close to the front, stay there . . . and see how it worked out. At the gun, Coe jumped the twelve other runners to avoid the mêlée, but Lacy led the runners into the back straight. He had agreed to set the early sacrificial pace because he was weakened by a cold. Entering the second lap Coe lay fourth. At the end of two laps, there were still seven or eight in contention.

Now Scott, pursued by Coe, burst clear, opening a gap into the fifth bend, with Wessinghage and Coghlan ten yards adrift. With no sign of help from Wessinghage, as had been promised, Scott was obliged to drive harder and earlier than he would have wished. It was his effort over the next 300 yards, in the relentless pace of the third lap, which now set up the record, killing off all but Coe. Approaching the bell, Coe was relaxed, without sign of stress. He moved smoothly past Scott, who initially thought it was Wessinghage belatedly making his contribution to the last lap. Coe had covered the feared third lap in 58, and now needed fractionally under 56 to break Walker's record. Struggling past Coghlan in third place, Walker heard the lap time and knew his record was gone. Around the last lap Coe, never straining, stretched his lead to fifteen yards, with the 20,000 crowd agog with expectation. Continually Coe glanced back, expecting a challenge, but none was there, and he marginally slowed without need as he crossed the line for a new record of 3:48.95. Scott, making the same error, missed Ryun's twelve-year-old American record by one-hundredth of a second.

This had been my opportunity to make amends for the mess I made of the previous year [Scott says]. All the talk beforehand, about who to watch, was around Seb, because of his 800 performance. We all knew what we could do, but what about him? He obviously had the speed, and the distance background. My thinking was that I'd go for the pace I needed for the record, and anyone who wants to come with me can. When Seb went by on the last lap, I couldn't believe the ease of it. I felt Ovett made a big mistake by not being there. Seb had set up something very substantial for himself for the future. That night was the beginning of the new era between him and Ovett. At the time, I was rooting for Seb, on account of Steve's actions towards other athletes on the track. I felt that Seb's ability at the shorter distance would make him superior between the two, in the long run. The only question was his frailty: could he withstand the training, compared to the muscular Ovett?

The awe with which Coe was now regarded by the rest of the athletic world would be hard to exaggerate. His own contemporaries were standing to applaud him when he went to dinner that night, and almost shyly collected his self-service tray in the communal restaurant. As Brasher says, it was as though he had been defying gravity; and, frankly, I think it was something that he himself took some time to comprehend. There was opportunity enough to consider it when he returned home for a fortnight, to be besieged night and day by press, radio and television, with incessant phone calls from all parts of the globe. Howard Cosell, America's most egotistical commentator, telephoned at 2 a.m., Peter putting the 'phone down saying, "Never heard of him!"

Yet there was more to come. In Turin, at the final of the European Cup, Coe avenged the foul on him two years before by Wülbeck, winning a tactical race with ease, with Wülbeck finishing third and Beyer fifth. There was one appointment remaining. Coe was due to run for the first time at the prestigious Weltklasse meeting at Zurich; and discovered that complications were being created by Ovett, who was attempting to talk himself into the 1,500 metres event for which Coe was scheduled. There was now the tantalizing prospect of Coe breaking his third world record in 41 days; but he knew that this was unlikely if Ovett were included in the field. Ovett had suddenly been motivated by the publicity surrounding Coe's latest feats; and the man who for several years had repeatedly said, privately and in public, that world records did not interest him, was now becoming eager to get in on the act.

We had invited Seb many times to Zurich [says Andreas Brügger], but all I'd ever received were messages that Peter said "No". When I finally managed to contact Peter in 1979, he said he'd never received an invitation. They'd all been sent to the British Board. Our event began in 1973, and it had been clear to me how important it was to have television: and to do that, we needed the best athletes. In 1976, we had broken the South African boycott, having the New Zealanders *and* the Kenyans after the Olympics: Dixon, Quax and Walker plus Boit and Waigwa. Boit, when he appeared, received a five-minute ovation, which delayed the start of his race. When we had the Cubans, we had to reward their Federation by sending half a ton of spare parts for American cars.

Ovett had been invited as well as Seb, but we'd had no reply. Seb had said he was willing to attempt the world record. It was my decision, when Ovett called from England the day before the race to ask if he could run, to say the only event available was the 800. Seb was happy for Ovett to race against him, but said that this would mean it was most unlikely the record would go, in what would become a tactical event. One of the promises that I'd made to Andy Norman was that if Coe and Ovett both came, I would take the Cubans. That's the way these meetings are set up, and Andy is a central figure. I'd already announced to the press that both British runners would be there. We were already a well-established meeting by 1979, but Seb's appearance lifted things. If, subsequently, I could say he was running, it would put several thousand on the gate, and not just youngsters. Sponsors, bankers and insurance companies responded, they could identify with him.

SC: I was fully aware of the crowd's expectation at the start. Waigwa of Kenya set off at what I knew instantly was too fast a pace, and at the end of the first lap Peter was bellowing for me to slow down. He didn't need to tell me; and though we covered the next 400 metres in only 59, I was now nearly twenty metres up on Boit. We'd thought beforehand the field might get me through two and a half laps, but with 750 metres to go I realized I was no longer getting any help from Waigwa, so I had to move in front. Suddenly the track ahead was empty. With an 800 time of 1:53, I knew the record was there if I wanted it badly enough. Years afterwards, I can still hear the roar that night of the Swiss crowd as I went in front, and it was that which spurred me.

The third lap was 57.6. Coe needed 56.9 over the last lap, and made it with a tenth of a second to spare, clocking 3:32.03 to clip by a fraction Bayi's glorious run in Christchurch five years before. In 41 days, he had run himself indelibly into history. No man had ever held all three records simultaneously; 800, mile and now the metric mile. Great runners of the past, such as Glenn Cunningham, Sydney Wooderson, Ryun, Hägg and Snell, had held two of them, but never all three; though Ryun had held the 880 yards in 1:44.9 at the same time as the mile and 1,500 in 1967.

"Seb's records in '79 didn't change my view, that winning races was the most important thing, but the public pressure did," Steve Ovett said as I discussed it with him in 1990, when he came south from his home in the Borders to attend Coe's wedding together with Rachel, his wife. "When you've got two guys running like mad, winning big races and breaking records, of course you get intense comparison. It was fuel on the fire. The promoters wanted the records. I didn't feel there was anything wrong about it, I just tried to avoid it for a year or so, and then got caught up. Seb and I would both have been good without each other, but wouldn't have been so good without the incentive provoked by the other. It added a great deal of excitement, of competitiveness, a unique feature in the environment of the athletics of a single nation. Seb's presence added to the enjoyment immensely. It's no good being on your own.

Frank Dick pays tribute to what the emergence of the two runners meant to him:

I realized I'd come into the sport at the very best moment. As a coach, you need time. Ovett, Coe and Thompson gave me results up front, providing a shield. There's a wrong attitude that sometimes exists in coaching – "Do your best, that's all that matters." The essence must be to go out to *win*. These athletes were a buffer for me, and an example to every other athlete. Ovett and Coe changed the image of middle-distance running. Soviet Union textbooks quoted Britain as an endurance/cross-country based nation. These two were bound to take middle-distance records forward because of their basic speed, at a time when a lot of coaches were still arguing for endurance as the fall-back. These two highlighted the fundamental importance of having speed. I knew Seb's 400 potential, which is why I wanted access to him for the World Cup relay in Rome two years later.

III · Summit

"Steve Ovett knew that he had ability, but he needed self-belief and confidence", Andy Norman says. "He didn't have it". This may come as a revelation to those who, over the years, watched the amiably arrogant Ovett come waving his way down the finishing straight, as often as not with a smile from ear to ear, seemingly without a care in the world. This was due to the fact that in most races, for a period of some three to four years from 1977 to 1981, he was capable of winning as he pleased, whatever the opposition. Sebastian Coe was the first to cloud his horizon; there are others besides Norman who will testify to Ovett's insecurity away from the public eye. As Norman says with irony, one of the problems for Ovett in the Olympic Games in Moscow was that he had, for once, a shade too much confidence.

Norman became increasingly involved as an advisor to Ovett following the European Championships in Prague. Prior to that, Ovett's racing-manager had effectively been his mother, Gaye, a dominating woman whose sharp handling of the press could at times make her son seem positively benign. Mrs. Ovett had produced her son in her teens; as he grew up, the age difference between them was less than for many children, and there developed an intensely close relationship that veered towards jealousy on her side, in the degree of her protectiveness. For all his athletic precociousness, his physical maturity and his appealing indifference to etiquette – for those who admire rebels – Ovett was in some ways very much his mother's boy. None could have been more caring than his parents, market traders, who devoted hours of time and effort to enhancing the rapid climb of their talented son towards achievement and fame.

By the time Ovett became European champion in 1978, there was a need for the advice and attention of someone closer to the corridors of power. Who better than the Bromley police sergeant, who was developing a string of contacts at every level that were to make him one of the most powerful figures in athletics throughout Europe, and a key figure in the development of the sport in Britain?

I went to talk to his family, to his mother, though it was a year or so before I was exerting a real influence [Norman says]. I had nothing to do with his training, but was advising him when to run, where and against whom. I was discussing with him how to win two gold medals in Moscow. We'd agree, and agree to disagree. One of the things that I did in 1979, for instance, was to get him to run, within the space of three days, a mile in Berlin, an 800 metres relay leg in the Southern Counties meeting at Crystal Palace, and an 800 metres in

Cologne, where he was beaten by Robinson of America . . . in order to simulate the conditions that he would encounter in the Olympic Games. Then in May the next year, two and a half months before the Games, he did the same, with races in Houston, Texas, then Eugene, Oregon and then Kingston, Jamaica within the space of five days. We were reproducing the Olympic pattern. When it came to the races in Moscow, I would use my knowledge of the other runners, from my involvement in helping to arrange meetings around Europe, to advise him on their strengths and the likely tactics they would use, and what was therefore the best course for him to adopt. Another aspect that was important was the close involvement of Bob Benn, a close friend who had run with him at junior level and wasn't going to make it as an international, but could be a loyal and dedicated companion and would regularly do some of the pacemaking at one-off meetings.

For Coe, the winter of 1979–80 was passed in the soothing, gentle sunshine of southern Italy, his limbs cushioned on the grassland or the forest circuit of a well-heeled residential estate to the north west of Rome, outside the village of Olgiata. There, behind high wire fences and 24-hour security, were ten square miles of woodland and a rolling golf course where, at the club-house, you might see Sophia Loren's mother taking coffee. It was on this estate that an old school-teacher friend of the Coes had an apartment; and, for the only four months of his life, he escaped the English winter weather to become a full-time athlete, training morning and afternoon and in between times working with disciplined fury at a nearby gymnasium. This was his preparation for one of the most rigorous races he would ever run.

PC: The record-breaking of the previous season was a shade unnerving. Seb and I were in contact, mostly by telephone, and I kept referring myself back to the training programme. Was it correct? I was worried whether it was right for him. If it was, then keep going in exactly the same way up to the Olympics, but be sure never to go over the top. We could have made the common mistake: if what you are doing is good, an increase of it must be better. In other words, if the larger part of his work was anaerobic, larger than any other in his field as a proportion of overall work, I could have stepped up the 800 repetitions and finished with a damaged athlete. Intensity is more important than volume, provided you have a safe, genuine working base. Seb was in tune with my philosophy, it wasn't just a matter of being a trusting son, but sharing in the calculations.

Chris Brasher likens the burden of expectation on Coe to that of Bannister at the 1952 Olympic Games in Helsinki. "An additional burden on Roger was that although Britain had won the war, there was still food rationing. Here was our star who was going to revive

Britain's glory. I remember that he was in such a state before the final in Helsinki that he couldn't even pee, and there was the whole nation back home waiting for him to prove that Britain was still a major power! That was one of the reasons why subsequently he *had* to do the four-minute mile. An additional burden on Seb was that he and the team were there against the wishes of the government and Margaret Thatcher". In the words of Svein-Arne Hansen, the Oslo promoter, "There was only one event in the Moscow Olympics – Coe v. Ovett. Norway boycotted the Games, but I was there. I'd tried to get them in the same race at Bislet beforehand, but not surprisingly failed. I think Steve was being protected by Andy." Which was fair enough. Both had run at Bislet, Coe at 1,000 metres, Ovett in the mile. Coe's run had come first, and he set a new world record of 2:13.40, and for half an hour or so he was the simultaneous holder of four world records. Then came Ovett, and again the expectant Bislet crowd was not disappointed. Dave Warren, who would be representing Britain with the other two over 800 metres in Moscow, had been prevailed upon by Norman, somewhat against his wishes, to make the early pace for Ovett; Norman being the kind of man you couldn't refuse. Ovett tucked in behind Warren, while behind him Cram and Graham Williamson were hell-bent on settling the one remaining Olympic place for Britain in the 1,500 metres. Sadly for Williamson, running in borrowed shoes, he was below his best. Cram came in second some way behind Ovett, who with 3:48.8 clipped a fifth of a second off Coe's time on the same track a year before. The tension as Coe and Ovett headed for Moscow was mounting to breaking point.

When I look back at the sense of expectancy, not just in Britain but around the globe, surrounding the Olympic confrontation between two phenomenal runners, it is easier now to understand how Coe came to make his historic blunder. I remember noticing while talking privately with him some weeks before departure, that he had permitted himself, not without justification, to enter a state of mind in which he genuinely did not think he could lose. "In the 800 metres, I don't think there is really a serious challenge", he had said. "Not one. James Maina of Kenya might be a medallist if the Kenyans go. He is one and a half seconds slower on paper, which may not be much physically, but at that sort of pace, it's considerable psychologically. If the race is fast, there will be nobody else who knows what it's like under 1:43. I've been there before, and I know it doesn't hurt, and that I'm in better shape than last year. I think there are one or two who will give Steve some bother in the 800 metres if it's fast. In the 1,500 metres, it *should* be between Steve and me. I think Masback and Scott (if the Americans go) and Coghlan and Straub of East Germany will be in for third place". The Americans did not go: and Coe would be imperceptibly overhauled beforehand, in the battle which takes place in the mind, by the aura of his rival.

Peter was likewise in a slight state of mental confusion, on his own admission. "Whatever happens to an athlete on the day is a reflection on the coach, other than at a time of illness," he says. "It's lovely to break records, but what was *I* doing breaking records on the eve of the Olympics – was I peaking him too soon? Will he maintain it under Olympic pressure? Do you try to progress, or hold on to what you've got? I had a table of progress . . . and we'd got there a year early. It was the most difficult tightrope to walk in training, the frequency with which the stimuli were applied. It was a time when we had to be together, in the same town, totally monitoring everything all the time".

Brendan Foster makes the salient point that for Ovett at this moment, record-breaking had a clearer rationality. "It was immaterial, whatever Steve may have said before, he *had* to get into that area [of records] for his own need, to show himself before he got to Moscow that he was as good. Athletes are the least objective of people, even when they think they are. You cannot find yourself on the warm-up track alongside a guy who you know has run seconds faster than you have. Not when you're expecting to win. You have to be flexible". Foster speaks as a man who set a British record of 3:37.64 when finishing seventh in the Commonwealth Games the day Bayi broke the world record: and ahead of Foster national records were also broken by Walker of New Zealand, Crouch of Australia and Jipcho of Kenya. Yet Frank Dick makes the counter point: that the mental security of world records is not necessarily enough, as was to be shown by Coe. "You have to have the bullets for all eventualities," Dick says. "Coe and Ovett were both animals in Moscow. It's not speed that counts, but the instant changes of pace, and reaction to them". The ordinary viewer, indeed the ordinary club athlete, can have no conception of the environment that envelops the competitor entering the Olympic arena. It is this factor more than any other, real on the one hand and at the same time partially the product of the competitor's own perception of what an Olympic Games means, that destroys even great athletes.

Until you get there [Derek Ibbotson, the former mile record-holder says], you've no idea what's required, mentally. Towards the end of my career, I could still beat people on the track who could thrash me in training. That was Pirie's problem, he always had to prove himself to himself with the fiercest training session just before a race, and then would be drained on the day. It was lack of confidence. The great thing going for Coe *was* his speed. The finest thing you can have going into a race is knowing you have the fastest basic speed. If you're simply stronger, you know you've got to drop them early, like Dave Bedford. That's how I beat Delany in '57 (when breaking the record in London). He was Olympic champion from the year before, and proclaimed in America as "King of the Boards", the man with the "Blow-torch Finish". I thought, I'll get him blowing, and I went for it from 300 metres out in a very fast race. We'd gone through 800 in 1:55, then the quickest ever first two laps in a four-lap race.

I knew Seb from Yorkshire, where they used to say when he was a teenager that he'd burn himself out, but those were mostly people who didn't know too much. I've never met anyone who had talent that didn't train hard. You can't win major races without it. Peter Elliott has trained harder than anyone, but he began with less talent. What worried me about Seb was his seeming lack of tactics up to that time. Ovett would have been a great runner in professional handicap races. Perhaps the suspect quality in Seb was because of his lighter build, maybe he was looking to stay clear of trouble. I'd thought he would win both races, even against Ovett, if he got himself in the right position. He was a superb athlete, with the perfect stride pattern, like Brian Hewson. Yet the mental business of going to the bank again and again takes enormous emotional strength. I used to joke and laugh a lot, but that was my way of not getting up-tight, quelling the nerves. The ones who says they never get nervous are lying. Herb Elliott would never say a thing, would just shake your hand, totally introspective within himself, never uttering a word.

Foster's expectations were the same as Ibbotson's. He would have bet money on Coe to win both events. "If you looked at him in '80, he had everything going for him, with that devastating acceleration. In two years Coe had developed so much – he'd not only developed Ovett's kick, but he had the endurance to spread-eagle the field in Oslo the year before. If you looked at Ovett in '77–'78, you said, "let's bottle this and keep it". Bedford was another with his money on the lightweight for both, though majority opinion said Coe for the 800 and Ovett for the 1,500.

The heat and semi-final stages of the 800 metres had passed uneventfully, producing the following finalists in draw order (with qualifying time and personal best):

Nikolai Kirov (USSR)	1:46.6	1:45.6
Steve Ovett (GB)	1:46.6	1:44.1
Agberto Guimaraes (Brazil)	1:46.9	1:46.0
Detlef Wagenknecht (GDR)	1:46.7	1:45.9
Dave Warren (GB)	1:47.2	1:46.2
Jose Marajo (France)	1:47.3	1:43.9
Andreas Busse (GDR)	1:46.9	1:44.8
Sebastian Coe (GB)	1:46.7	1:42.4

SC: I've never known pressure like it. I thought people had exaggerated, but they hadn't. There was no comparison. I'd felt pressure going into the Europa Cup the year before, but it just wasn't the same thing. It began after the semi-final. I remember catching Peter's eye at dinner, and he must have sensed that I was uneasy, because he smiled and said, "Don't start *now*". I had the worst night's sleep I've ever had, just lying there listening to my own heartbeat. It was the same the next day . . . I suddenly felt ungainly. That morning, I saw Kenny Mays of the *Daily Telegraph* and he'd said with a friendly leer, "Well, 7.30 tonight, the moment I've been waiting for". The moment *he'd* been waiting for! It was just the kind of well-meant comment that tightens your nerves another turn.

In the afternoon, Coe had again been unable to sleep, which was unusual. Peter sensed something was wrong, but was at a loss to know what to do.

PC: I had to ask myself afterwards why, of all times, I did not prepare him properly – *if* I hadn't? I'd always said that if he lost, it would be my fault. That's why, when he did, I was ashamed. I had sensed for a while beforehand that he was detached, almost inert, but I was alert to the danger of putting *more* pressure on him. He doesn't like me to bother him in the hour before a big race. Our work together has by then been done, and he's locked into himself with mental preparation.

Later Seb could only remember feeling utterly empty. As they waited in the tunnel to go out for the start, Ovett said to him: "It's stupid to think we're doing this here for nothing, when we could turn pro-fessional and fill a stadium on our own". It was cooler than it had been in the past few days, and the flags around the rim of the stadium were stiffening in a strong wind, which did not penetrate down as far as the runners. The floodlights were on in the half-light of the evening. The moment the gun went, Coe moved off, in the outside lane, as though it were the start of a 10,000 metres race. He looked as though he were running in soft sand. At the lane break, it was Guimaraes of Brazil leading from Kirov, and as they approached the second bend Ovett was badly boxed when other runners converged in front of him, com-ing across from the outside. Coe had made no attempt to close on the leaders.

SC: I remember the gun going and feeling sluggish, running without convic-tion. I came off the lane-break with no awareness of anyone's position. I was thinking of *nothing*. Going into the second bend I was probably in my best position in the race, fifth or sixth, with Ovett just in front of me.

Ovett now vigorously handed off Wagenknecht. The six-foot four-inch East German lost his balance, veered outwards, and in turn impeded Marajo, who almost went down. A few strides further on, Ovett swerved to the right, and again Marajo was impeded. Coming into the home straight the first time, Guimaraes was still in the lead, the entire field still bunched together within three strides. Coe was loping along at the back, like some stowaway, Ovett caught with a wall of runners in front of him. Approaching the bell, Ovett tried to force his way between Wagenknecht and Kirov – and failed. As Guimaraes went through the half-way in 54.5, Ovett was sixth, and Coe last.

SC: I was conscious of where I was, but still had a total lack of urgency. What I had no awareness of, until I later saw the video, was how badly positioned Steve was at that stage. It was a chance to have made a decisive move, yet I did nothing.

Round the third bend Warren accelerated to the front. The race was developing in precisely the shape that Andy Norman had predicted in tactical discussions with Ovett beforehand. "There's no natural leader there," Norman had said. "Guimaraes, who doesn't know the European scene, will probably find himself in the lead in something around 53. If Coe goes before the bell, and you're boxed, you're dead" – Ovett was, Coe didn't – "Warren will probably put in a burst out of bravado, and Kirov will go from 280 out, as he always does. Take Kirov and *go*, don't slow and wait for someone else's kick, keep at it. Kirov will come back at you wide, and make it difficult for Coe if he's not then ahead". Such was Norman's prescience, he should have been doing David Coleman's job for the BBC.

Down the back straight Kirov and Ovett followed Warren and both of them went by with 200 metres to go, Guimaraes and Wagenknecht another two strides down, with Busse, Marajo and Coe another three metres further back.

SC: Down the back straight I stupidly still felt OK, unaware that Kirov had surged until he turned into the final bend. Into the final bend I still hadn't been buried, yet continued to hang back.

It was allowing himself to be boxed at that moment by Busse and Marajo that finally cost Coe the race. By the time he changed gear and started to go past people, he was some twelve metres, or about six strides, adrift of his rival. Coming off the final bend, Ovett made his move past Kirov. Way back, Coe was at last responding, ripping past Busse and Marajo, then the fading Wagenknecht and Guimaraes. With forty metres to go, he was third and still gaining on Kirov and Ovett.

With twenty metres to go he passed Kirov, but now his phenomenal sprint was spent and he could close no further. By ten feet or more the gold medal was Ovett's in 1:45.40.

"Seb might still have been OK had Kirov kept the lead and had Steve waited off the final bend," Wilson said, "but approaching the final straight Steve opened up very hard indeed. A big gap yawned, and I turned my back because I simply couldn't watch. It was too good to be true that Steve should win an Olympic title so easily". Mitchell's view, watching at home in Loughborough, was that Warren's 100-metre burst after the bell was the phase that had fundamentally finished his friend's chance. Peter's belief that his son had to be so bad to lose, to a degree he could not conceive, had been given substance.

SC: Entering the final straight, I knew that I'd probably blown it, that it was going to take a fantastic effort to come back. Suddenly I was going past everyone. Two went, and I was fifth; two more, and I was third, but wondering if I was even going to get a medal. I had no idea how fast I'd run the last 150 metres. I'd grown accustomed to taking liberties in one or two races in the previous year, to running wide from the back and now, in the most devastating way, I'd discovered you can't do that in an Olympic final. With thirty metres to go I knew I was not going to win, and the extraordinary thing at the finish was that my first reaction was a huge feeling of relief rather than disappointment. That it was *over*.

On the medal rostrum, still mentally blank, Coe shook Ovett's hand conventionally. Clive James in *The Observer* wrote that Coe looked as if he had just been handed a turd. The public perception, at home and around the world, was that Coe was less than gracious in defeat, but he was seeing and hearing nothing; not even the Olympic hymn as the Olympic flags were raised, instead of the national anthem and Union Jacks – (part of the terms of the British team's participation in defiance of their government's instruction). Besides disbelief at Coe's ineptitude, the media were afire with speculation on whether Ovett had run so physical a race that he might be disqualified. Ovett would admit on television: "If anyone was guilty of doing more than their fair share of pushing, it was probably me. I can be called the worst of the bunch". Ovett had won in the same time as he had achieved when finishing *fifth* in Montreal.

It was a fairly rough race, and relatively slow [Harry Wilson says]. I've never spoken to Seb and Peter about this, though my attitude with Steve was, if it's like that [rough], get in there and look after yourself. Seb might have attempted to steer clear at the back or front of races, maybe as a result of being bundled out by Wülbeck in Helsinki. If you'd asked me beforehand, I would have said Seb for the 800 and Steve for 1,500. Steve had moved away from the 800 as his first event. His training veered towards the longer race, as his two-mile record against Rono in '78 had proved. Steve thought he could win *both*, because of the three-day gap between the events. *I* thought it was a hell of a load, particularly if the fifteen is your main event. The 800 was proof that you have to be positioned right. From the beginning of the back straight the second time, you've got to be there. You should only have *one* man to overtake. If Steve was in the right position, I didn't think anyone could beat him. Once the competition began I thought, yes, maybe he could take both, because he was saying, "I haven't had to do anything yet". I could see why he was confident. Yet I do remember, that until he was fifty yards out I couldn't believe he was going to win the 800 so easily. When I turned away, I said to Ron Holman, our long-distance coach, "Tell me when he's passed the line". When I look at the film now, it must have been hard for Seb to stick in there to get second, because he would have known at ninety metres that he wasn't going to win. It was good that he kept going as he did.

SC: It was a double setback. Not only had I lost the race, but there was this seeming proof that he couldn't be beaten. Plus the fact of his unbeaten sequence over 1,500 metres. By Tuesday, however, the sharpening process with Peter was beginning to work, the deep breathing I needed which I'd never had during a race. Peter knew I was tough enough to take the severe training between the two events, as well as the next three races and that this was what was needed. The worst pressure on me had been from my own friends, who took the 800 so much for granted. For Ovett, the 800 was only ever going to be a bonus. Now the public perception had changed. Peter certainly had not believed I could lose, either, unless I ran appallingly. I *had*. Steve dominated races, physically, and won races that way – and he still thought he could do so four years later in LA, but didn't realize that the event had moved on so much by then.

The semi-final of the 1,500, in which I was boxed in the final bend, and had to produce a really fierce burst to get clear again from Fontanella of Italy and Marajo, proved my kick was back to peak, even if the run was unintelligent. What was coming back was the belief that I could make a mistake and still win. It almost *helped* to have won in a race where I hadn't got it right. There had been races in the past where I'd done that on purpose, almost for the hell of it. The crowd of press and photographers waiting for our departure from the Village for the final was like a Cup Final at home, watching the teams depart from the hotel. And it wasn't just the English press. Throughout the Games, the British camp had been the first port of call each day at the Village even for many of the foreign press, "what did they have for breakfast?", wanting their slice of this little bit of sporting history. My view of Steve by the day of the final had altered a bit. It wasn't that the ghost had been exorcized completely, but the first race against him for two years had released some of the pressure on me. Historically, of course, the drama was heightened by our confrontation coming in the glare of the Olympic Games. For me, it would have been better to have got it out of the way earlier. I was still a developing athlete, while Steve was a complete runner. I knew, whatever the result today, that I would get *better*. My doubt had been, could I beat him at this stage? Could I change in four days? I don't think I went into that final with any more belief that he could be beaten – but I was feeling better about myself. I now had a clear focus: that I had to be relaxed, and that if I lost, it had to have been in a great, spectacular race. I *did* feel capable of a great race now, win or lose. I wasn't going to get out and overtly sacrifice my chance of winning to make it historic, however. I was realistic enough still to remember that I was an 800 runner, with a weapon of finishing speed that was several seconds faster than his.

Ovett was also, in his way, feeling that the pressure was off: never mind that there was more attention globally on this single race than any other in Olympic history.

Here we go again, I thought [Ovett relates]. I was relieved, the way the first event had taken the pressure off. The expectation level had been and still was extreme. I wouldn't want that again. It was almost distasteful at times, and it was often intrusive. After the 800, I somehow felt my job was done. I don't want to take anything away from Seb; I gave it (the 1,500) everything, but I had turned off a bit. After the 800, I wanted to go home, call it quits. I'd had a hard heat, in which Straub ran 3:37, and I beat him on the run-in, which was unwise. A matter of pride! I was beaten by two guys in the final, and that's it. I'd been surprised, in the 800, that with 150 to go I could hear there was no one there, and was thinking, "where's Seb?" I always treated the 800, from '77 onwards, as a nice lead into the 1,500. But we had it slightly easier in those days, because the depth was not so great. I could use the 800 as a dry run. That's how I treated them. If you weren't running 1:43/1:44, it wasn't difficult. Nowadays, runners hedge their bets. Seb and I didn't because we were good at both.

Foster emphasizes the irony of the problem created by Ovett's unbeaten sequence of 43 races: that to maintain this, he had to win his heat and semi-final quite unnecessarily, when they were his fourth and fifth races. "I was in the village in Moscow, and sensed Steve was getting physically drained," Foster says. "As for Seb, he might have *retired* if he hadn't won". Norman's pre-race reading was again as accurate as a computer-aimed missile.

We knew it would again start slowly, that there wasn't a leader [Norman says], and that Straub would pick it up at 700 out. That was his way. I told Steve,

"Whoever is in front with 300 to go will win". Steve was well aware that Straub was as strong as an ox, and I warned him of the possibility of Coe being in front with Straub in between them on the last lap. Steve was thinking, "I went away from Coe in the 800, I can do it here". But I told him, "Coe will have fear and hatred driving him on". When Seb led with 150 to go, I walked out. I knew it was over.

During the intervening days, Foster had been chiding Coe: pull this one out, and you can go on to greater things: lose it, and you'll be sitting around for years wondering whether you're going to be another Ron Clarke or Dave Bedford [record-breakers who failed in the Olympics]. Meanwhle, Brasher and Clarke, convinced of Coe's potential, were busy debating the tactics that might bring him victory, and sent him a note expressing encouragement and giving their advice.

One evening we sat long over dinner and drew up a plan for Seb [Brasher says], because we wanted to keep alive this duel between two of the greatest middle-distance runners we had ever seen, a duel which fascinated the world and which was doing so much for the sport. We knew that Seb was the hunter: that nobody could set a pace fast enough to drop him. And we knew also that he was the fastest finisher. That had to make him favourite. We wrote to him, outlining the tactics we suggested: relax on the pace, move into position, and strike . . . remembering that he who strikes first is generally victor. We said, "The only person who can beat you is yourself". We also urged him to unleash his kick in the semi-final in order to let his opponents see what he could do: and that he had to take his chance, because life does not give you many. When we watched the semi-final, and saw another blunder in the last lap, we said to each other, "He hasn't got a tactical brain. He's had it." Mind you, he wasn't as bad as Roger [Bannister], who was awful. In the 800, it was as though Seb had been sprayed with nitrous oxide. It was the mental resurrection in those six days that makes him such a great athlete.

Straub, meanwhile, was making *his* plans. "He had finished seventh behind Ovett in Prague," Bernd Diessner, his coach, recalls. "At that time I did not consider him an outstanding athlete, and I had to tell him that he needed much more and faster interval running. The breakthrough had come in 1979 when, running almost alone in a minor race at home in Potsdam, with no rabbit, he had run 3:33.68. It was as much psychological as physical, though. The confidence came from interval running at longer distances, 6 x 1,000, say; or maybe 3 x 1,000 at 2:35, a single 2,000 in 5:20, then 3 x 1,000 at 2:35, with five minutes' rest between each one. We had to make a plan for both Coe and Ovett. I knew that Jürgen was fighting for a medal, and that he had to reduce the early pace. We thought Ovett was the stronger, even if a little tired, but knew Coe had the speed. Yet Coe was at the beginning of his career, maybe experience would play into Ovett's hand.

"The pace of the first two laps, a leisurely 2:05, was the perfect way for Jurgen for the race to be run. After three laps, I hoped that maybe he could win, though we were more than satisfied with the silver. The result was a surprise, but on the day Coe was the best. There was no space in the last 700, with the way Jürgen ran, for anyone else to make a tactical mistake. There was no time to recover. Jürgen made no mistake. I had never supposed," – a shrug of incredulity – "the possibility of such a finish". Norman's view is that Straub might have become better than even Coe or Ovett, "if they'd let him out of East Germany more often. If you don't know the strengths of other runners, it's difficult to gauge races, but part of the East Germany psychology then was to keep their own runners in a shell".

Dave Bedford still gets the shivers when he contemplates Ovett's closeness to athletic immortality in these Games.

Before Moscow, whatever Steve's self-belief or lack of it, he will have woken in the middle of the night wondering if he had the ability to beat Coe [Bedford says]. Move it on a few days, a few weeks, and his hand is so close to touching the golden apple, he must have felt its glow. I wonder at the end of the day not whether he had the bottle to pick it up, but whether he had what is called the "visualization", of thinking through it beforehand, "What if I win the first one?" I don't think Steve had seen it as an entirety, whereas I think Seb had.

Ibbotson recalls: "Before the 1,500, I thought that was it, that Coe would be mentally crushed. It's in those circumstances you find out if you're a man or a mouse. He'd been found lacking, how's he going to beat the unbeatable Ovett? Maybe Steve was slightly more relaxed than he should have been – but there was a great chance for him to have given Coe a stuffing".

The line-up for the final would be:

	Qualifying Time	Personal Best
Jürgen Straub (GDR)	3:39.4	3:33.7
Jose Marajo (France)	3:39.6	3:35.1
Andreas Busse (GDR)	3:43.5	3:37.1
Steve Cram (GB)	3:43.6	3:35.6
Vittorio Fontanella (Italy)	3:40.1	3:38.3
Sebastian Coe (GB)	3:39.4	3:32.1
Jozef Plachy (Czechoslovakia)	3:40.4	3:37.2
Steve Ovett(GB)	3:43.1	3:32.1
Dragan Zdravkovic (Yugoslavia)	3:43.4	3:38.0

There was a huge contingent of East German supporters at one end of the back straight, right by the start line. Coe and Ovett completed their warm-up exercises in front of them, and as they coasted back to strip for the start of the race, they passed the Nero-like figure of Norman, standing alone in shirt-sleeves with his arms folded, down in one of the photographers' dug-outs. The nine finalists, stripped and sleek, were led single-file towards the line, now on an invisible leash. They lined up, jostled, re-grouped . . . and the gun went. Straub and Coe went straight to the front. It was a pedestrian pace, but there was very little barging for such a slow procession. Straub ran with his head down, as though looking for guidelines on the track; he was locked into his own private world, he knew what he had come to do. As they came off the first bend into the home straight, they were grouped in twos: Straub and Coe, Marajo and Ovett, Cram and Busse, Fontanella and Zdravkovic. On they went, cautious, contained. Down the second back straight, Cram had moved up alongside Ovett, ahead of Marajo. Other than that, there was no change as the pack, still unbroken, moved sedately to the 800 metres mark in 2:04.9. It was now that Straub made the move which would convert the race from a stroll into a remorseless burn all the way to the line: the start of the longest Olympic finishing sprint ever, with the intention of dropping Coe and Ovett.

SC: Suddenly I realized Straub was going for broke. I knew that no one could take over that kind of pace, not that they would want to. I had to follow him, and instinctively guessed that Steve would be tracking me so as to have both of us in his sight. He would know that I was the one to follow, that Jürgen had sacrificed his final kick by making his bid so far from home. When Jürgen went, he opened a gap and I had to fasten on very quick . . . and it just kept getting quicker. I felt comfortable. Suddenly it was single file, and I was running free in a lane of my own. I knew that sustained speed of this sort would play into my hands. I'd always been confident, arrogant if you like, that I could maintain this speed longer than anyone. I was out in the Derbyshire hills again, but this time it was Jürgen's back ahead of me, and not my father's car. And I was in a position to make the next break.

From the amble of the first two laps, 61.6 followed by 63.3, Straub was lifting the third to a searing 54.2. Up in the grandstand, Peter was convinced the race was as good as over. No-one but his son, he felt, could sustain such a pace and still retain a finishing kick. "It didn't look that fast, because the front three were all such superb stylists," Peter says.

At the bell the order was, strung out in a line: Straub, Coe, Ovett, Busse, Fontanella, Marajo, with young Cram, competing in an

Olympic final at nineteen, trying to hang on in seventh place. Ovett, many television commentators were saying, was poised for victory. At 1,200 metres (three laps), Straub lowered his head for a final assault, and Coe had to respond. Into the final bend, the climax of the race, Coe was at his shoulder. They were into an area where the months of conditioning and training would be called upon – "sprint, drive, work the arms". With 180 metres to go, Coe put in his first kick that carried him past Straub: there was daylight between them, he could hear Straub's feet receding. What he did not know was that his kick had almost exactly coincided with Ovett's bid to overtake him; and now Ovett saw the gap between them stretch to another stride-and-a-half. The "split" times would show that Coe, even within such a ferocious last 700 metres, was accelerating the whole way from 180 metres to 50 metres out.

SC: I put in another semi-kick coming off the bend, and took a glance back on either side. Jürgen was still just in vision, with Steve in line behind him so that I couldn't see him. I was now running for the tape, with the mental agony of knowing I had hit my limit, of not knowing what was happening back there behind me. I tried to drive again at 40 metres out, and knew I had nothing left if anyone challenged. The anxiety over the last 20 metres was unbearable. A few yards past the line I sank on to my knees, it was such a bloody marvellous relief.

More than 20 million people in Britain had watched that hypnotic three-and-a-half-minute race on television. Derek Johnson, a silver medallist at 800 metres in 1956, and chairman of the International Athletes Club, summed up succinctly: "It was the greatest finish to a 1,500 metres since Jack Lovelock's in 1936. To kick twice at that pace was something I had not believed possible". Coe won the gold medal with a last 800 metres of 1:48.5, the speed with which he had won his first heat in the shorter event. It was the fastest last two laps ever run at that time in a four-lap race, the last 200 metres in 24.7, the last 100 metres in 12.1 for a winning time of 3:38.40; some six seconds outside his world record.

"At the end of the third lap," Wilson said, "you'd have said that, with any normal opposition, Straub would have done enough to win. At 200 metres out, he was a yard or two clear of Seb, with Steve another couple of yards down. It was starting to look difficult for Steve . . . who had all his normal finish pulled out of him and couldn't quite close the gap on Straub, who'd never beaten him before". Straub had held on for the silver medal in 3:38.80, Ovett taking the bronze in 3:38.99.

Half an hour later, with a feeling of satisfaction more acute than he

had yet known, thinking that he could now retire at any point with a
sense of fulfilment, Coe was at the press conference and talking about
moving up to 5,000 metres for 1984. As many recounted, his battle
over six days in Moscow had been more with himself than with Ovett.

The day after the 800, meeting him in the village, he seemed like a mesmerized
rabbit [Brasher recalls]. The expression on his face was "what am I going to
do?" – a little boy lost. Nobody could help him, he had to help himself. It
could have been a burial. There's no other expression. Straub could not have
done better for Seb on the day, turning it into an 800 metres race: a warm-up
followed by a fantastic long finish, hanging on, hanging on. And then
accelerating for the line. I wouldn't put it in the same class as Herb Elliott's in
1960. Herb came out of an Australian winter into the European summer, not
believing he was fit. With immense courage, he went from 600, saying catch
me if you can. I asked him afterwards whether he'd not been worried about
Rozsavolgyi, the talented Hungarian, coming back at him, and Herb merely
said, "Who's Rozsavolgyi?" I think Herb was in a class of his own.

Ovett, the Rozsavolgyi of 1980, reflects: "I was running as hard as I
could go at 150 out, and Seb was going away from me!" Hildreth, who
in the previous week's *Sunday Telegraph* had stated that Coe had "no
chance on earth", now called it "a sublime final". Bedford says: "As
an athlete, I know how difficult it is to come back overnight. When
you are beaten badly you usually have to go through a period of re-
appraisal before you win again at this level. It's not like other sports,
where you can blame other people. In that situation, the 800, there was
only one man to blame. But to have gone into the 1,500 with such a
chink in your armour . . . I can't think of any sport in which you could
have to do this, even less so was there the chance for Seb to succeed.
His training, coming up to those championships, must have been *so*
good".

Cram admits that he was fortunate to have made the team – in
preference to Williamson – and even more fortunate to have gained the
experience of reaching the final.

Making the team was my aim that year [Cram says]. With all the attention
surrounding Coe and Ovett, reaching the final for me was very valuable. Yet I
learned more off the track than on it. I was lucky to be able to spend a lot of
time with Steve, he and Harry helped me a lot. In the first round, there was no
one in my heat I even knew, but I was able to scrape through. I was in Steve's
semi-final, and Harry said I should try to stick on Steve's shoulder or I'd be in
trouble, and I squeezed through by a fraction of a second. In the final, I was so
overawed when the gun went, I was left for dead. I was in cuckoo land, caught
up watching Seb and Steve, so that I remembered nothing of the race, racing-

wise. At the finish, coming in eighth, I didn't have to ask who had won. I looked at Steve, who smiled, but it wasn't the smile of a winner. I didn't know at that point he'd come third.

The main lesson I learned was on the warm-up track. I saw that Seb and Steve were human, especially Steve, when before that it had seemed that nothing could touch him, but in Moscow, before the final, Coe was silent and controlled, in his own world, while Steve was chatting but not really relaxed. We sat under a tree for a while, and he was clearly nervous, talking about "if" he won a medal. I knew at that point in my own mind who was likely to win.

Hedley reflects on the value to Cram of having run almost anonymously in the Commonwealth Games in Edmonton and in Moscow. "In Edmonton, he didn't survive his heat," Hedley says, "which was delayed by the arrival of Trudeau, the prime minister, with Prince Philip, and afterwards Steve was in tears. He was nobody then, and in Moscow he only just got through his heat and semi-final. But it taught him so much. He realized that even the great runners had fear".

An indication of the objective, almost detached, manner in which Coe and his father analysed training and performance was that, when celebrations had died down, and they were able to assess the season as a whole, they could come to the conclusion that it'd been a *poor* year.

SC: The build-up was not what we would have liked, even with a 1,000 world record in Oslo. I had sciatica, from a pelvic injury, so that although I was *fit*, in one sense, I was only getting through day by day, before and during Moscow, with the help of physiotherapy, primarily from Helen Bristow (now married to Neil Allen of the *Evening Standard*). *The* race of 1980, as a race, was winning in Zurich, beating Scott and Walker, who'd been absentees because of the boycott. There were those who claimed they might have split me and Steve, taking the medals. Winning in Zurich that night was important to me. Though I may momentarily have felt I was the best in the world in Moscow, the feeling didn't remain. I've never had the luxury of thinking it would be true a month down the road, even when I was confident of beating *anyone* in '81. I did treat every race as a cup final.

Mel Watman has warm memories of that night in Zurich, the evening when Tatyana Kazankina of the Soviet Union ran the still-existing world record for 1,500 metres of 3:52.47. "I thought Seb might have run 3:28 that night," Watman recalls, "but he got caught up in a marvellous race, and decided after two laps that the priority had to be to run to win". Coe's time was 3:32.19.

The most traumatic day of Coe's life was behind him. "Moscow brought home to him for the first time in several years the extent to which he *was* vulnerable to his nerves", Angela Coe says. "It was the first time it had happened at international level, that he couldn't cope with it, that it was somehow outside himself. I don't think it ever happened to him again".

IV · Ovett

SC: Assessing Steve Ovett's athletic career, you have to talk about longevity. Quite remarkably, he's been competing, at or near the top internationally, for almost seventeen years. And *enjoying* it. I didn't go on as long as he has. Assessment for any individual has to be on *performance over time*. In the last few years, Steve's not produced medals, but he'll only give up when he loses that inner sparkle. When people talk about Steve Ovett not being the same in the championships of '83–'84 as he was in '80, remember you're considering someone running *ten* years after his first championship medal. It's like looking at Muhammad Ali. As a fight fan, I remember Ali's fights with Frazier and Foreman, with Liston and Quarry, but not so much some of the later fights. When someone has a long career, like Steve, the inevitability is that younger people, watching in his later years, will have no idea how stunningly brilliant he was in his prime. My assessment of Ovett might seem dismissive of those who came after him, of Steve Cram and Peter Elliott. But in energy and physical presence – and I've met them all on the track – I can never feel for anyone else the way I feel for Ovett. If you talk to Scott, Walker, Wessinghage and others, at a certain stage in Steve's career his appearance on the track was, for them, like being the proverbial rabbit caught in the glare of a car's head-lights. He could galvanize the public, and convince a group of contemporaries that the race was only for second place . . . and the athletes *accepted* this. It was *this* feeling that I experienced in Moscow, and the only difference between the 800 and 1,500 for me there was that I didn't have *any* alternative. I was driven by a fear of him, by fear of repeating my own failure.

Brendan Foster often used to remind me in my early days that it's medals, not records, that count in cold retrospection. By that judgement, when you consider Ovett, he has gold medals at Olympic, European and Commonwealth championships at *different* distances. Besides that, there's European silver and Olympic bronze, as well as a hat-full of world records, by a runner who was not out of the top three of the British ranking-list in a decade. To ask what more he could have done, you're pushing analysis to extreme margins. His accident in '82, injuring his thigh on railings when out training, was the beginning of problems. Yet he broke the world record for the 1,500 in 1983, and but for his leg would have been challenging for the gold medal in the European Championships in '82. I suppose, being hypercritical, he might have maintained his 800 speed for longer than he did, in order to assist his 1,500 running – not in order to race 800 in main championships – though that's an outsider's observation; and I don't like criticism of *my* preparations. Yet I think it might have helped Steve, after 1980, to realize how far the 800 had moved on, might have persuaded him *not* to run the 800 in LA, to have determined his plans from a more practical, informed position. You can't get away from the importance of basic speed. To the end of my career, I was working with 400 metre sprinters at the Haringey club in London. The length of time I was able to compete at the level I did was conditioned by commitment to speed-work, both in training and competition. There's no reason why, with Steve at the age of 28, we shouldn't have got three medalists on the rostrum for 1,500 metres in 1984. But that's a tough assessment.

Steve's confidence has been questioned by some athletes. Whatever way you look at it, he's never tended to look fully at ease in world record attempts. His initial reaction to my record-breaking was: 'I enjoy my running, why hurt myself?" Brendan's view of Steve was that he never *learned* to hurt himself, whereas I was prepared to find out. In support of what I am suggesting, Steve said in Prague that, if he'd seen the clock at the end of the first lap, with under 50 seconds, "I'd probably have walked off the track!" What determines the limit of an athlete's performance is the inner conflict, the doubt about your abilities. This can be either limiting *or* lifting. You won't find out about yourself if you go into races sure that you can win, however much that certainty may be justified.

It was always *big* news if Steve or I lost, when we were at our peak, more than if we won. That carried its pressures, conditioned us mentally in a quite different way from most other runners. After my error in Moscow, for the next four years, according to David Coleman, I was "tactically naïve". Steve, after two or three outstanding 1,500 victories, was a "master tactician". Yet I have seen Steve run some inaccurate tactical races, and only get out of difficulty by sheer brute force. So much judgement is a matter of public perception related to current environment. In 1971, Andy Carter won a European 800 metres bronze in Helsinki, and came home a hero. When I gained a silver medal in the European Championships in 1982, I was seen by many as some kind of failure . . . the same with Steve when he took only fourth place in the World Championship in '83. *We* were the only people who fully knew the extent to which we had or hadn't failed, with the knowledge of what our condition was, going into the race. Yet I found that there were pseudo-psychological studies of me appearing in the media, and of my family, with every kind of false analysis. Meanwhile, the sport would move on, whatever Steve or I or anyone else was doing.

Between 1979 and 1981, for instance, with his cat-and-mouse tactics with me in Prague, over whether he would or wouldn't double up, Steve annoyed and irritated me: while what he thought *I* was, as a person, maddened him. Mostly, however, during a period of intense media interest, whenever we were asked to comment on each other's races, actions, preparations, we didn't say much. You'd read a lot of column inches about our perceived rivalry, but little of it was attributable to comment from either of us. Today, it's going the other way, athletes are making every kind of comment about rivals, they're far too willing to be critical. Just think of the crossfire that Cram, Elliott, Crabb, Morrell and others have indulged in during the last few years. I'm delighted to say that ever since Los Angeles, Steve Ovett and I have had the highest regard for each other and have been good friends.

Steve Scott's appreciation of Ovett has been there from the time they first ran against each other in Jamaica in 1977. "He had so much talent . . . and so little confidence," Scott recollects. "It was disgraceful! Among fellow athletes, he was cordial and social, would always go for a run with you, but I thought he had *low* self-esteem. There always had to be someone there stroking him: his mother, Harry, Andy, Rachel his wife. He was always saying, 'God, I hope I don't screw it up tomorrow.' At first I thought this was all phoney, it was only later I realized it was a confidence problem. That was evident in the way he picked his races, kept other people out. I'm convinced he did that. He wasn't in the same bracket as Cram or Elliott, who would go for a race with the attitude: 'Beat me if you can.' It was because of insecurity, in my opinion, that he ran so many races tactically."

Frank Dick sensed the element of doubt in Ovett, and as chief national coach he had years in which to observe a great runner operating in areas of maximum pressure.

Steve found it difficult to believe how brilliant he really was [Dick says]. Seb projected a total, "allowable" conceit of himself at all times. There was almost a haunting fear in Steve, not believing in himself. There was all the cocky waving to the crowd, yet I felt this *reflected* the element of disbelief. You never saw this in Seb. This may be a purely personal perception. Maybe it wasn't a weakness in Steve, but an unusual form of modesty. For Seb, from early on, his life-plan was clear: for instance, "This is how I have to treat the press", he seemed to be saying, in preparation for his later career. Ovett changed like night and day the moment he started his clothing company in 1982. He changed who he was. In any great achiever, there has to be a rough edge, and after that time, Steve's rough edge had gone.

Seb's real strength emerged in Moscow, the ability to turn things around in his head: his tenacity, the ability to organize his thoughts. That said, it was difficult for Steve, having won the first event, to retain the aggression to do it again, to be motivated in the same way as if he'd lost the first event. Part of Steve's reputation was indeed physical, and once he'd established that, people gave him space. Steve always wanted to be seen as his own man. Inside all these great athletes, there's a desire for the public not to believe another athlete is better than they believe *they* are.

It was better for Coe and Ovett to be apart, and in my opinion it was not damaging for the sport for them to be rivals in different stadiums. It was probably *better* for British athletics, because that way there were many achievements, separately, by two runners, instead of one or two meetings together, against each other, and probably at a slower pace. Yet in 1982, I

Father and son, face to face, in the unending search for excellence.

Runaway victory in the Europa Cup final, 1979, a week prior to a third world record in 41 days: L to R, Wulbeck (WG), Rechetnyak (USSR), Milhau (Fr), Grippo (It), Bayer (GDR), Baron (Pol), Zivotic (Yug), Coe.

Third of a unique three: breasting the line in the 1,500 meters in Zurich (3:32.03). A legend is made.

Left Floating, it seemed, more than touching the ground: Coe leads Scott (US) in Oslo en route to the mile record, second of three in '79. (3:48.95).

As proud as coach as father. Peter and Seb attending a Sports Writers' Association luncheon prior to Moscow.

Weight-training for aerobic stamina at winter hideaway training camp in Rome, early 1980.

Second is nowhere: without focus, without emotion, Coe trails Ovett at the finish of the 800 meters in Moscow.

Dispirited loser with his silver medal alongside Ovett and Kirov (USSR).

A nightmare of anxiety as Coe strains for the line in the Moscow
1,500, ahead of Straub (GDR), Ovett and Busse (GDR).

Coe sinks to his knees in relief, barely aware of Straub's congratulations.

The boy next door: admiring young neighbours gather outside the Coes' house in Sheffield as he displays his medals.

Head and shoulders uncharacteristically go back in the searing
finish of an improved 800 world record, Florence '81 (1:41.72).

Florence: "Those split seconds while you wait for the crowd
reaction, not looking at the clock, just listening for the noise, the
crescendo which tells you have done it, the tailing away which
says you've failed."

In Peter's opinion, the best of all: overtaking pace-maker Rob Harrison (GB), Oslo,' 81, when improving 1,000 record (2:12.18).

Regaining mile record from Ovett, Zurich, '81, Coe celebrates with Mike Boit of Kenya, a rival so often at his heels (3:48.53).

Exultation. Mile record broken for third time in nine days, Brussels '81 (3:47.33) within two days of Ovett's record in Koblenz. From where came the strength in that slim frame?

Sickness, defeat, elimination. Laid low by glandular infection, Coe finishes fourth at 800, Gateshead, '83, withdraws from world championship. L to R: Cram (6), Wuyke (Venezuela) (4), Elliott (7).

Cram takes the first World 1,500 title, ahead of Scott (out of picture), Aouita (549), third, and Ovett, hidden behind Cram, fourth.

The long road back: Coe hill-climbing above the Thames at Richmond Hill in the winter of 1983–84.

Nearly down and out: Coe stumbles in clash with Williamson (57) in 1,500 Olympic trial, 1984.

Elliott (18) at Coe's shoulder at the bell in Olympic trial 1,500. Eliott won: Coe was selected.

Silver medalist Cram looks pensive at missing the medal that mattered to him most.

Left Will I, won't I? Anxiety in the final straight as Coe reaches out to retain Olympic title, Los Angeles.

Proud and happy to win for his country in LA.

The smile of relief as much as triumph on the rostrum with Cram and Abascal of Spain.

Coe, third, congratulates Cram on taking his mile record in Oslo, 1985 (3:46.32). Gonzalez of Spain, centre, was second.

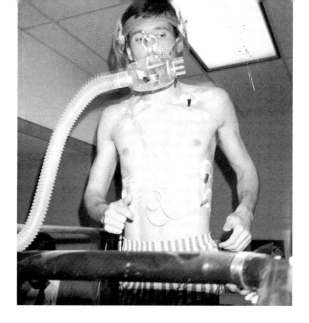

Wired and tubed for physiological testing at Dave Martin's laboratory, Atlanta, '85.

Overleaf Spontaneous adulation, studied response.

Three Brits in a line: Coe inches ahead of McKean (351) and Cram for coveted 800 title, aged 29, in European championships, Stuttgart, '86.

would have liked Ovett have shared in the world record for 4 x 800: what a quartet we had that day at Crystal Palace, Elliott, Cook, Cram and Coe.

Harry Wilson defended Ovett's robust tactics. Confronted with this issue by the press, Wilson answered: "What do you want me to teach him? To let somebody else win? In middle-distances, you reach a situation where you either push or you lose the race – what's your alternative? There's a great deal of physical contact anyway . . . I like 800 metres and 1,500 metres precisely because they are aggressive races. A runner has to learn to survive . . . you have to be alert enough to look after yourself."

The avoidance of one athlete by another, which drew much criticism within Britain, was not restricted to the rivalry between Ovett and Coe and their pursuit, between 1978 and 1984, of separate routes other than the main championships, in which the composition of the field was beyond their control. "Avoidance" became a common occurrence with the steady rise of commercialization, and the wish by leading competitors to preserve unbeaten runs, to protect their commercial status. In certain instances, of course, it may simply have been a matter of looking for a quiet life.

Ovett's "avoidance" of Coe at the Coca-Cola meeting in 1978, allegedly keeping him out of the two miles, found an echo at the same meeting the week following the Olympic Games in Moscow. Again they ran separate distances, Coe the 800 metres, Ovett the 5,000 metres, in which he was beaten in the last stride by John Treacy of Ireland. Foster thinks they should have raced each other, though that would have been a tough emotional assignment at the end of a hard season, and immediately following the traumas they had just undergone.

I believe they would agree now they should have raced each other more often [Foster argues]. Obviously Olympic titles were more important, but there were times when they should have given the opportunity to a wider audience in Britain, to enable Dads to take their kids for something to remember; so that instead of taxi drivers in London saying, "I was there when Chataway beat Kuts at the White City", they could be saying, "I saw Ovett against Coe".

As Mel Watman points out, with regret, they had only three races against each other when both were at a peak: one in Prague and two in Moscow. Yet Ovett was not the initiator of "avoidance". In 1977, Juantorena had refused to run against Boit at Crystal Palace. Juantorena had just completed an exceptional 400/800 double in the Montreal Olympic Games . . . though in the absence of the Kenyans, on account of the boycott. Juantorena did not want his achievement tarnished a short time later, and it was coincidental that Ovett added to the controversy of that evening by refusing to accept Boit in the mile. Brian Hewson, the promoter, was obliged to accommodate Boit in a separate, and meaningless, 800 metres.

So regular, indeed, did "avoidance" become, that some promoters would imagine a request for it when none existed. Following the Coca-Cola meeting in 1980, and then a 1,500 in Zurich, Coe closed his season with an 800 in Viareggio. Included in the field was Don Paige of America, a boycott absentee from Moscow. Paige's coach came storming up to Peter, claiming that a request to exclude Paige was "unethical". Peter answered that he and his son never objected to anyone. Paige ran, and beat Coe by a whisker.

Ovett takes a sanguine view about the accusations of avoidance, as much as about press criticism of his extrovert and at times perverse behaviour.

It wasn't as simple as one guy not being willing to run against the other [Ovett says]. When you're aiming for peaks, you don't run every weekend, you're not a commodity for public consumption. Situations were being created by pressure from promoters, as much as anything. It was all cloak-and-dagger. We were amateurish. Seb and I could have made a lot of money on the track. There were opportunities, but I didn't have anyone financially representing me, the way Seb did when he joined IMG at the end of 1980. Andy Norman suggested to me I *shouldn't* join IMG, to prevent them having the two top athletes and cornering the market. I made errors of judgement: I think we could have organized ourselves better. It was the time the sport was changing, towards becoming professional. If Seb and I had acted together, it would have forced the sport to make changes that might not have been good for it; the governing bodies might not have coped. The benefits might have been only financial.

As for the press, I did try to talk to them in the early days, but some of them just wanted glib one-liners, they were telling me what I should say. Why the hell should I accept that? I didn't need to cultivate an image. You can never live up to the expectations the press puts on you, the way they did with Bedford. If my behaviour caused them problems, they should revalue their attitudes. And the business of Seb being the "nice guy". I couldn't believe that people wanted this (polarization). It didn't upset me so much as my family. They wanted people to know the way I really was. It was annoying the way things were warped. It *did* polarize. This suited the media story. In one way it was to the sport's benefit, I suppose, the heightening of interest. But a lot of the press output was poor, undeserving of the effort by the athletes.

Antagonism towards Ovett from the press had first begun in 1975, when he expressed a lack of interest in the European Cup final to be held in Nice, and said he'd rather hitch-hike to Athens for a holiday with his girlfriend. He offended the press sense of patriotism, and was branded, unreasonably, as arrogant and immature. In the event, he did compete in Nice.

The increasing hunt by promoters for records and head-to-head confrontations did bother me as a coach [Harry Wilson says]. Your first concern is with performance, you are performance-orientated in your training schedules. Yet I came to realize that runners have financial ambitions as much as anyone else, that maybe athletics *was* no more purely for performance. It affected every coach and athlete of that calibre, the way you planned a season. You had to take into account extra races, that were diverting your performance. It had become the same as actors, the Richard Burton Syndrome, going for the film with the big fee, irrespective of the script. By 1981, record-breaking had become a fact of life; the independent actions of Seb and Steve affected each other. Here were two who could beat the world. It was inevitable that there would have to be a series between them, yet it never came off. For the first time, Steve had become interested in how fast he *could* run. I told him he'd never yet found out. Andy was managing his races and knew the financial ropes, yet Steve was still happy to run *slow* races and win tactically! He'd attempt records more by request than inclination. Promoters were offering huge sums at that time, larger than now (1991) in relative value. It was a no-way-out situation: when promoters said that they would provide the pacemaker. The best thing that happened to Steve, after the Olympics, was that he left home and got married.

The marriage factor is discussed by Coe elsewhere in the book. For Ovett, tensions at home had been rising with his mother's coolness towards Rachel, his girlfriend, as recounted in his autobiography; intensified in Moscow by her son's sign-writing messages with his finger, via television, to Rachel back home, 'I.L.Y.' – I love you. It reached breaking point when they returned home. Gaye had stamped out of the stadium when Steve had lost the 1,500. Happily the family is now reunited with the arrival of grandchildren.

SC: My situation before Moscow was enviable yet unenviable. Had I gone to Moscow as a European bronze medallist, and not the holder of three world records, the pressure would have been more on Steve. As it was, there was no sense, in an Olympic year, for us to seek a confrontation outside Moscow. It's an easy thing for others to decide from the side-line. There's so much more to planning, than whether or not to run against another opponent. We'd come from opposite ends of the spectrum: initially, Steve a young 400 metres runner and I a cross-country runner, but subsequently the roles were reversed, with me running the shorter distance. I was therefore quicker than him at the *start* of almost *any* season. At what point, therefore, would either of us wish to tackle the other? He wouldn't want to tackle me early in the season. That's not *avoidance*. An Olympic year is psychological as much as physical. It's like the Motor Show: you don't pull the dust covers off a new design before the show's opened.

There was never too much of a problem for me about opposition. In fact, I've never changed distance on the day before an event, because I was always planning *that* distance on *that* day, because that was what I *needed*, in my tactical planning of the year with Peter. In 1984 at Zurich, for instance, there was a hell of a race at 1,500, with the creation of a separate mile event for Aouita, not originally scheduled, because he wouldn't race in the 1,500.

Brasher's annoyance, repeatedly expressed in *The Observer*, is that in a golden decade of four great runners, Ovett, Coe, Cram and Elliott, plus Thompson, Wells and others, the government, in conjunction with British sport, failed to build a stadium worthy of the greatest races . . . which were never run in Britain. "We're bottom of all developed countries, when it comes to stadia," Brasher says. "I can quite see why runners will not make a hole in their commercial worth by a single race outside the Olympics or the World Championships. The four-yearly showdown of the Olympics is probably too long a gap, because some athletes' careers don't last that long."

The intention of the Coes, in 1981, was for a year of switching off, of being free from conformity, of enjoying racing on a schedule of their own determination. The public was about to see a cavalcade of record-breaking, in which Ovett would have a major, coincidental role. It began with an indoor world record by Coe, erasing four-tenths of a second from Carlo Grippo's time, with 1:46.0, running against Busse and Wagenknecht in a match with the GDR at Cosford: the first world record by a Briton at home since Bedford's 10,000 metres at Crystal Palace in 1973. In June against his own expectation from the state of his training, Coe ran his phenomenal time of 1:41.73 in Florence, lowering his 800 metre record of two years before by half a second; helped by a promising young Kenyan, Billy Konchellah, who made the running for the first 400 metres. Konchellah would have his own glory in the World Championships of 1987 and 1991.

SC: I could feel the night air becoming chilled. As we went through the bell, I heard Maeve Kyle, the British team manager, shouting "49, 50", so I knew it was fast. I didn't feel as good as in the first record in Oslo, but that was because I was running half a second faster. When you get to the bell in a record run, which I now knew it would be, the thing that is screaming inside your head is "keep working". You know that the rate of fade is going to be greater than usual, that if you lose concentration it will be worse. It gets to the point where you are listening to your own footfalls, dimly trying to decide whether the interval is lengthening. From 420 to 500 metres, I was able to lift the pace marginally, opening a gap on Konchellah, but was having to shout at myself mentally to maintain rhythm. One of the most exciting feelings, when you're going for a record, is when you hit the front: the exhilaration of knowing, like an actor or comedian, that you have your audience on your own, exclusively, all the way to the tape. The response of the crowd at that moment is like nothing else. In a stadium such as Oslo, Brussels, Zurich or Crystal Palace, they know the situation, what you're going for, and the reaction coming out of the darkness is a magic moment, a surging push in the back. It rewards the entertainer which I think is there in any top athlete. As you cross the line, there are those seconds while you wait for the reaction: just listening for the noise, the crescendo which tells you you have done it, the tailing away which says you've failed.

The average of Coe's best *five* times was now 1:43.27, itself faster than any other man had run the distance. Juantorena would have been fifteen yards behind.

From Florence to Oslo. A month later, Coe returned to the scene of former glories, the intention having been to run 800 metres. In the light of the Florence time, there would be more chance of a record, for which a Bislet crowd was waiting, through an attempt to improve his time for 1,000 metres. On arrival, however, it became apparent there was a thin field for the 1,000, and Coe requested a switch to the mile, in which Ovett was running. The answer was "no". Allegedly, Norman had said, on behalf of Ovett, that a promise had been made to the IAAF not to pre-empt the Golden Mile in Brussels, to which both Ovett and Coe were invited. A quick check with the IAAF contradicted this.

With pacemakers provided for the 1,000, Coe went for it. He passed the 800 mark in an astonishing 1:44.56, inside the time that day for the separate 800 metres race; and though he began to lose drive, his head going back and his rhythm deteriorating, he lowered his record by more than a second to 2:12.18.

SC: For the first time ever in a race, I was aware of the clock as I came into the finishing straight. With 50 yards or so to go, I could see it winking alongside the photo-finish camera, "2:05, 2:06 . . .'. The clock was going faster and I was going slower. It seemed that my feet were only barely leaving the ground. It was the toughest of all my records.

Ovett duly took the mile, but with a time (3:49.25) two-fifths of a second outside his own record of 1980. He had been optimistic of success, for he was in perfect condition. Three days before, in Milan, he had run a 1,500 metres in 3:31.95, half a second outside his time in Koblenz the previous autumn, when he had taken *that* record from Coe.

PC: Ovett, in my opinion, was the more complete runner, out of the trio of him, Cram and Elliott. I'd seen him win an intermediate English schools 400: waving *then*, and losing tenths of a second in the process. It was all so easy for him. He was big when young, and stayed big. You can't have more than forty unbeaten races over four laps, mostly against world-class opposition, without being exceptional. He had this startling finishing burst, and he ran creditably when he switched to the 5,000. He was able to dominate. He had many arrows in his armoury, but wouldn't do more than he *had* to, until he got drawn into the record-breaking sequence. He had a much finer style than Cram or Elliott, a better foot-plant and heel flick, a nicer arm action. It was a magical change of pace, matched only by Seb and Aouita. Ovett was more interested in head-to-head, in winning, until he saw the attention being paid to records, and realized that he had to respond.

It's not unreasonable to say I did a shrewd job with Seb. Shrewdness goes hand in hand with honesty. Although I got him through *relatively* successfully in the Olympics, as a result of his endeavour and character, I had a very different athlete in '81 compared with '80. In '81, there could be several bites at the cherry, getting the emphasis at the right time. I had the opportunity for correction; what we didn't pull off in one race, we could get right in another. This was a blissful year for an athlete who couldn't have been more confident, during a period that was less stressful. The basic training that year was identical, with only shifts of emphasis for a longer season: not one peak but a sustained spell. That's what the Board have never understood, the precise target of an Olympic year or a World Championship and its difference from an ordinary season. Seb had been tempered in the fire of '80, and come out of it stronger.

Taking Seb and Steve at their peak, I'd give Seb the edge, not just because he was faster, but because he had the stronger nerve. Steve was young when he went to his first Olympics, but didn't make the most of it. If Seb had been to Montreal, maybe he wouldn't have messed up Moscow. In 1985, Cram emulated Seb's "long burn" in the Moscow 1,500. Seb against Ovett would always be a close-run thing. No matter what pressure Ovett was under, he was always running beautifully, a marvellous sight.

It was this subtle difference, evident in Peter's words, that was apparent to the ordinary club runner. Ovett ran for the exhilaration of running, Chris Brasher believes, whereas Coe ran to be *good*, with an introspective search for excellence. "In the perspective of the club runner, he identifies *far* more with Ovett," Brasher says. "Ovett is a runner first and last. There's no other epitaph than 'the man who loved running'. Once, he'd prepared for a 1,000 record attempt in Edinburgh; there was a plane strike at Gatwick, so he goes home, catches the club bus, runs in the Dartford half-marathon, wins, as an unofficial entry, and lets Barry Watson take the first prize of a television set."

Winning the AAA Championships 800 metres in early August, Coe sliced a large area of skin off the outside of the ball of his right foot, the consequence of a blister that had first appeared six races previously when he broke the record in Oslo. An additional problem was that, already under some criticism from the Board for suiting himself in his race schedule, Coe was due to run a week later in the Europa Cup final in Zagreb.

SC: If it was the last time I was able to stand up that summer, I just had to go to Zagreb with the British team. I had to accept that I would have to sacrifice my own aims, if necessary, because I could not possibly withdraw from Zagreb, and then turn up to run for myself in record attempts in Zurich and Brussels. It was the doctor's opinion that I ought not to run again for the rest of the season.

He flew to the Swiss mountain training-centre at Macolin, high above Lake Neuchâtel, where he spent the week training gently with his foot strapped, on pine-needle-covered forest paths; his work on the track limited to one session of 300 intervals with Mike Boit before flying on to Zagreb. Against his father's advice, and encouraged by the author – I had a similar experience when boxing, immediately prior to an important football match – Coe ran in Zagreb with sticking plaster applied directly over the bare flesh, rather than with plaster over a dressing. The policy was successful; in a conveniently slow race under a scorching sun, he held off a challenge from Wulbeck and Beyer to win comfortably. He returned to Switzerland, the foot having been protected for the climax to the whole summer.

In Zurich, he was to attempt a double world record: the mile, and with his time at the 1,500 metres mark also officially recorded. The two records were currently held by his rival. He succeeded over the longer distance, while failing, oddly, at the shorter, thereby demonstrating how different is the psychology in the approach, physically, to two distances differing only by 109 yards. He would encounter the paradox of being dissatisfied with a world record.

SC: It might sound arrogant, but it wasn't a particularly good night, I didn't run that well. I was way off, approaching the 1,500 mark, and I only rescued it (the mile) in the last straight. Mike Boit and I both achieved the objective, for he took the African record; but looking at the video, the main impression was of Cram running so well behind the two of us, an instinct for where he should be. You could tell he was dramatically improving, and was soon going to be a threat. He ran under 3:50 at the age of only twenty. At the time, I felt mentally done in. I'd lived ten days with the worry of the blister, and thought that it could be the last chance for a record that year, because Brussels might be, first and foremost, a race. I'd missed the 1,500, and didn't believe I'd done enough to protect the mile record even for the rest of the season.

Part of the problem in Zurich was that Tom Byers, who had volunteered to make the pace for the first three laps, was suffering from a cold. Pete Petersen, his coach, was expressing doubts about Seb's request for the first 1,200 metres in around 2:49. "I don't think anyone could do that, *and* keep going on schedule," Petersen said. In London, it was planned to interrupt the Nine O'Clock News on BBC to include the race, such was now the impact of the record-breaking British pair.

SC: I accept that I put pressure on myself over the weeks beforehand, but when the day arrived, the tension in the hotel near the stadium was overwhelming: a feeling of the sky pressing down, the walls crowding in on me, the kind of expectancy there is said to be a few hours before a world heavyweight title fight. The dimension of the meeting adds to the mood beforehand, with over a hundred of the world's top athletes all there together, the biggest event outside the Olympics and the World Championships.

Byers would try to take the pace as far as 1,000 metres, then Boit for as long as he could thereafter. In the dim half-darkness of the warm-up area, the collection of great runners began circling, separately, introspectively, like seagulls circling before a storm. Walker was there, grimly purposeful; Scott, who had become a father a few days beforehand; Cram, conscious that he had wasted the chance to win an important 1,500 in Zagreb; Wessinghage, padding round with his athlete wife a stride behind, a familiar sight on the athletics scene. Coe was preoccupied, his shoulders hunched the way they are when he is not relaxed. Tiny autograph hunters kept infiltrating the warm-up area, scurrying out from under Coe's feet as he floated past, oblivious. The conditions, as they went to the line, were perfect; but Byers involuntarily allowed the pace to slacken fractionally below par for a first 800 of 1:53.6, yet still ahead of Ovett's schedule in his record the year before. Coming off the fourth bend, Byers' head began to roll.

SC: I realized Tom was fading, but wasted the next hundred metres wondering whether he might pick it up again. By the time I decided to go, the hesitation had cost me a second. At the end of three laps, the time was a second outside Ovett's, and the chance for the 1,500 record had gone.

The 1,500 metres went by in 3:33.27, almost two seconds outside the record, yet Coe found the strength to sustain his run round the last bend and into the final straight, to reclaim the mile record in 3:48.53. The time at 1,500 should have meant the mile record was lost, but Coe's finishing speed saved it. Ovett's final 109 metres when setting the mile record in Oslo had been 16.1; Coe's was 15.3. Walker had finished faster than anyone, having left his effort too late. Coe, deaf to the applause, was clearly disappointed, though Andreas Brügger, conspicuous in scarlet blazer, was busy acknowledging the acclaim like a circus master. Byers apologized to Peter, and received a friendly rebuke. "Was the record broken or not?" Peter asked the young American.

A match-race, between close rivals, is better than a record, Brügger argues, providing the pace is respectable. "For the kind of meeting we stage, we want runners racing at somewhere near their potential. We don't want winning times of 1:48 or 3:38, there's no interest for the spectators in that. We have a knowledgeable crowd. You'll find them applauding because a record has been broken even before it's announced. But what they most appreciate is a fine *race*, and for that you still have to have somebody to make the pace. For 1,500 metres, you probably need not one pacemaker but two for a chance of the record, *and* you need runners prepared to make the effort – a Coe, Cram or Aouita. The ideal is when you have two pacemakers as far as 1,200, and then *two* runners who are agreed to pick it up from there to the finish. But they need to have talked about it beforehand."

In Coe's view, the problem in attempting the two records simultaneously was mental, not physical, but Harry Wilson disagrees. Wilson argues that when going for the mile, the runner can nearly always raise a little extra pace over the last 100 metres, whereas if extending himself for the 1,500 *en route* the effort has to be made from 1,400, which leaves a long way, 109 metres, to the finish of the mile. He thinks the barrier is physical rather than mental.

To give some idea of a record-breaker's schedule, this was Coe's programme, between Zurich and his mile in Brussels nine days later:

Thursday, 7 miles before breakfast; *Friday*, home to Sheffield, a warm-up followed by 5 x 800 in under two minutes, with 90-second intervals; *Saturday*, 9 miles cross-country in the morning, 4 x 300 in the afternoon; *Sunday*, 6 x 200 in the morning, 10 x 100 in the afternoon; *Monday*, 10 miles on the road; *Tuesday*, 15 x 200 in 28.0 with half-minute recovery, in the morning, 9 miles through the woods in the afternoon; *Wednesday*, a fast 5 miles in the morning, hill-climb accelerations in the afternoon, followed by four miles; *Thursday*, rest day and travel to the race; *Friday*, 25 minutes jogging and strides in the morning.

He was fortunate that his foot had held out.

In the meantime, Ovett was heading for Koblenz, scene of his 1,500 metres record in 1980. He was due to run the same distance now, but rumour had it he wished to switch to the mile, in pursuit of Coe. Other runners arriving the night before could discover neither which races were being run, nor in which they could take part. Petersen could obtain a list of the field for neither 1,500 nor mile. Scott was refusing to pace Ovett, Wessinghage wanted to run 5,000. On race day it became apparent there would be both 1,500 *and* mile, Scott winning the first in 3:31.96, to beat Ryun's fourteen-year-old American record of 3:33.1. Officials scrambled to mark a starting line for the mile only minutes before it began. Scott had been perilously close to Ovett's world record; now Ovett, given the early pace by Bob Benn and James Robinson of America, reduced Coe's mile record of the previous week by thirteen hundredths of a second: 3:48.40.

Coe, unsurprised, saw Ovett's time come up on the television news. Throughout the summer season, there had been regular headlines announcing "It's on for Brussels" – a confirmation that Coe and Ovett would meet in the fourth IAAF Golden Mile. Ovett had directly confirmed this to the press when running the mile in Oslo. Now, he suddenly found an alternative appointment, running in a minor international match for England in Norway. Ten years later, he says the decision was Norman's; Norman maintains it was Ovett's.

When Coe woke in Brussels on the Friday, he was feeling fresher and more relaxed than the previous week in Zurich; and knowing that his training had produced fitness of a higher degree than he had had all summer. Byers, recovered from his cold, was determined to compensate for what he regarded as a lapse in Zurich, and would lead the first three laps to a time of 2:49. Scott, following his record in Koblenz, reckoned Coe would be pacing *him*; the smiling, enigmatic Boit, one of the most enduring competitors of any era, would be in there making it hard for everyone.

The line-up was: Boit, Byers, Coe, Coghlan, Flynn (also of Ireland), Khalifa (Sudan), Masback, Maree (both US), Robson (Scotland), Scott, Walker, Wessinghage. Sydney Maree, a black South African who had just acquired American citizenship, was approaching the peak of his career. At the end of the first lap, Byers led from Coe, Boit and Coghlan, with a four-yard gap between them and the other nine runners.

SC: The fact that I was running to win, rather than to break the record, gave me a comfortable feeling. I followed Tom, but was aware of Mike (Boit) in my shadow. Into the second lap, I had no consciousness of the record. Mike and I were well clear of the rest by now, with Tom doing his job out in front, and he was spot on at 800m in 1:52.67. Going into the fifth bend, there was a near-disaster when I clattered into the back of Byers. It must have been my fault, momentarily losing concentration. I didn't feel I was going to fall, but the margin must have been small. At 1,000 metres, the end of the third back straight, Peter shouted "yes" and I knew that meant something good. I went past Tom into the bottom bend sure that it would take something special for anyone to get past me now.

At the bell, Boit was hanging on three strides down. Coe needed a last lap of 56.5, for he was now half a second outside Ovett's equivalent in Koblenz. Critically, the 32-year-old Boit was still pushing him hard, though Coe felt more relaxed than in any other race that summer, producing possibly the smoothest last lap, when under pressure, of his whole career. In my own experience, I would say that he never looked more elegant, at top speed, than on that memorable night in 1981. In perfect cadence, he flew round the final 400 metres with almost no rise and fall in the head and shoulders, pulling ever further away from Boit, until he crossed the line for a new record in 3:47.33.

It was his third mile world record in three races at the distance, his fourth world record of the summer, and his eighth in all, excluding the indoor 800 metres; and the most ever achieved by a British athlete. Peter was beside himself with glee, brimming with pardonable self-satisfaction, after so much advice beforehand that the split times he had requested in the pacing were too ambitious. "It was as sweet as anything, and I knew he was going to do it," Peter said.

SC: It was a feeling I only had two or three times in my career, that night. I did feel unbeatable, and was toying in my mind whether to run from the front – a thought I had later, in the Olympic Games in Los Angeles: that my condition was good enough to lead from the start. Yet both times I was still slightly cautious. I was feeling really strong; and I'd been doing in training what annoyed my colleagues, whether intentionally or not, *surging* for half-a-dozen strides. So that Steve (Mitchell) would say to me, "You're a bastard to run with", and then tell John Caine, another friend from Gateshead, that it was no use complaining about it. I was doing the same thing during that race in Brussels, deliberately, into the last lap, because I was aware Mike was there and still very strong. When I could hear him right behind me but with no hard breathing, I knew I was into a race, never mind any record attempt.

I'd expected Ovett to run in Brussels. I'd always planned to be there, and he was committed to it, too. Two nights before, I'd been sitting in the office of the *Sheffield Morning Telegraph*, with Alan Hubbard, when an agency story came up on the wire that he wasn't running. Wilf Meert, the promoter, would say Ovett had *agreed* to run, but Norman arranged this fixture in northern Norway, where the temperature must have been about 5 degrees centigrade. Why did he?

That was a wonderful summer. I had a good time socially, was enjoying life, having an easy time at Loughborough. I was glad not to have anything as all-consuming as an Olympic Games, though unless you treat an Olympics as consuming, you've no chance. Frankly, at the time I probably thought less about my records, about their significance for the future, than Peter did. They meant a huge amount to me on the day, but Peter was more clinical about them. What I did think, after the Brussels record, was that I could do without the World Cup soon afterwards. Yet that was the nearest to championship running, and if I lost it would have been another arrow for those who suggested I could only break records rather than win championships. That was *still* a hole in my armour.

The Brussels record had been a rare climax to a spell of nine days, in which Coe and Ovett had exchanged the mile record three times. Norman's view, years later, is that he assumes Ovett "didn't think he could win it, or didn't want to tow Seb to a new record. He thought Seb would take it, but I didn't." This opinion has to be tempered against the fact that, by 1985, the relationship between Norman and Ovett had cooled. This is not to say that Norman has lost his eye for a direct line to the evidence. He remains unhappy to this day about Ovett's *waving*.

If there's time to wave [Norman says bluntly], there's time to take another second off your time. Steve's weakness, given his brilliance, too often was that he didn't *bury* people. By the next week, there was the chance for someone in the race to say, "I almost caught Ovett that time," and to raise their confidence. The press used to say Steve was a great tactician, but have a look at some of the races. The best tactician ever, in my opinion, was Boit: he'd get in there, get behind the pacemaker and then slow it down for his own purpose, letting the pacemaker get away from the field before other people realized, as much as to say, "I'm not ready yet."

Sometimes, I used to say to Steve, "Why not be friends with Seb?" but he wouldn't have it. I guess you could understand that, at the time.

Ovett defends his absence from Brussels. "I was cavalier, I just ran" he says. "Maybe Andy did take over at times, but that was to my benefit. I didn't look further than saying yes or no. I was calculating about my running, but not about negotiations. I wasn't involved with promoters. Maybe Seb thought about this more, discussed it with his father. My parents supported me, but were not involved. For Seb and me, it wasn't as simple as just lining up, any more than it would have been for Lewis and Johnson in 1991. IMG didn't contact me."

Following the apotheosis of 1980, Coe had placed his affairs, or at least some of them, in the hands of Mark McCormack's International Management Group, a world-wide organization handling the commercial interests of a multitude of sports performers and celebrities, and others. Coe's relationship with IMG is discussed in a subsequent chapter; but, after the records of '81, IMG had attempted to co-ordinate for the next year a series of three head-to-head races between the two rivals, dove-tailed into scheduled IAAF meetings, at Crystal Palace, Nice and Eugene, Oregon. The announcement was made in May, 1982. Ovett and his wife went to London the night before, to be on hand for the press conference. Early that morning, Ovett went for a run in Hyde Park, and there stretching his legs was Coe. Ovett would later write in his autobiography:

Here were two men who were supposed to hate each other's guts, passing office workers looking on in disbelief. We ran for a while, both surprised by the coincidence, wondering what a photograph of us together in that situation could have been worth in Fleet Street. Seb asked me how married life was, I wanted to know what he was doing at Loughborough . . . While the media have always been quick to point to the differences between us, no one has ever brought attention to the uncanny parallel of our lives. The main aspect which strikes me is that Seb has a dominating father, while the strongest influence in my family came from my mother. In both instances, you could argue that their part in our lives went beyond that of normal parents. Seb's father took a very public part in the affair – in fact, my first memory of Seb is not so much of him but of Peter, this rake-like figure with angular, gaunt face and eyes peering over the top of his glasses, ushering and fussing around Seb, almost in the manner Zola Budd suffered when she arrived in Britain in 1984. Fathers who coach their sons are fairly prolific in athletics, but no-one has attended to the needs of the athlete with such constant attention as Peter Coe. He always seemed to be on hand, with spikes and tracksuit at the ready, before and after races, and attending press conferences. That sort of proximity, which you normally associate with ice-dancers and their coaches, would embarrass me.

The schedule drawn up, at a farmhouse in the middle of Northamptonshire, between Norman and Robert Jackson of IMG, was for the following series: 3,000 metres at Crystal Palace on July 17, 800 metres in Nice on August 14, and a mile in Eugene on September 25. Interwoven around this, both runners would be hoping to win gold medals at the European Championships in Athens and the Commonwealth Games in Brisbane. Suddenly, there was a year that would be littered with Coe against Ovett. It was not to be.

The previous December, Ovett, while on a training run in Brighton, his home town, had lost concentration on a familiar corner, and caught his thigh on some church railings when taking too narrow a line on the pavement. He punctured the tendons attaching the muscles to the bottom of his right femur, underwent an operation, and had not fully recovered fitness until shortly before the scheduled 3,000 metres in July. By then, Coe was out of action with a stress fracture, suffered during a 2,000 metres run in Bordeaux. No sooner had Coe recovered, than Ovett tore a hamstring in August, putting him out of the running for the major championships. Coe ran at Athens, but suffered a surprise defeat. The IMG series had disintegrated.

SC: The races that were fixed for the two of us were in meetings open to the rest of the world. I'd rather have gone for three 800s or three 1,500s. What I suggested was an 800, 1,000 and 1,500! Steve initially asked for a 5,000, and I said I'd accept a 3,000; knowing that even if he was the two-mile world record holder, effectively the same distance, he was going to find the 800 difficult at the other end of the scale.

Roger Bannister stresses the extent to which an injury such as Ovett's was likely to affect the rest of his career. Bannister had a similar, though less serious, injury when training in the dark on Harrow School playing fields, running at full speed into a pile of building blocks, which left a concrete splinter in his shin bone. "The chance of either winning or losing in major races turns on a hairsbreadth," Bannister says. "We're talking about a minute fraction of one per cent. In the medical profession, physiologists and neurologists" – Bannister's own fields – "are working to margins of five per cent."

For Ovett, the injury was undoubtedly a turning-point in his career, never mind the natural talent that still carried him to a further two Olympic finals and a Commonwealth gold medal. "It was a dark street, and I was going flat out," Ovett recalls. "My knee caught the railings, and I passed out. It's been a major factor in my life since then. I was six months in plaster, with all the rehabilitation which that necessitates. You're in trouble if one leg is ten per cent adrift, never mind *wasted*. A consequence was that I've had back problems ever since, and an imbalance in the legs." It was a cruel mischance that undermined such a glittering career, as serious and maybe even more so than the medical problems that would be suffered by Coe in the coming years.

SC: Steve was back for the 3,000 race, but ran poorly, and the winner was

Moorcroft. Dave was within an ace of Rono's world record, on the night of the France–West Germany semi-final in the World Cup in Spain. I had a stress fracture of the fibula; Steve ran in Nice, by the time of Eugene I was running again, but was under the weather after my failure in the European Championships. By then, I'd already decided to pull out of the Commonwealth Games in Brisbane late that year.

It was a summer of problems. I had difficulty fitting in a qualifying time for the 800 metres in the European Championships, running a specially arranged private trial in Nottingham, organized by Frank Dick, only eleven days after I'd started training again following the fracture. At that point, I decided not to go for the 1,500 in Athens. The Board were difficult over my Nottingham qualifying run, even though the timing was authentic.

Coe ran a fast 800 metres in Zurich, where the emerging Cram was also in outstanding form when winning the 1,500 in 3:33.66. Absurdly, the British Board now required Coe and Cram to appear at the Talbot Games at Crystal Palace for expedient commercial reasons. Peter Coe accused Dr Bill Evans, the chairman of the Board, of "flushing a championship medal chance down the drain, and doing six weeks damage to my athlete". Evans replied that the decision was all to do with "who runs athletics". Seb Coe retorted: "When you find out, Bill, please let the athletes know, we've been trying to find out." It was a foolish if inadvertent blunder; six years later, Evans would be one of those who voted to keep Coe out of the Olympic Games in Seoul.

Under pressure from Thorn-EMI, new sponsors of the Talbot meeting, exerted through Evans, Coe ran at Crystal Palace; and unnecessarily did so again, only a week before the European Championships, for the benefit of the Heinz Games, together with Cram, Garry Cook and Elliott, in a successful attack on the 4 x 800 metres world record. Though he was not to know it for some days yet, Coe was suffering from a glandular infection, and his fast relay leg drained him of the strength he would need in Athens. There, after moderate times on successive days in qualifying for the final of the 800 metres, he was beaten by Hans-Peter Ferner of West Germany, taking the silver medal in a pedestrian 1:46.68. The legs were empty. Half-way down the home straight Ferner, whom he had beaten with ease in Cologne a fortnight before, went past him. Coe could not respond, and was beaten by a man who had never even won his own national title. Harkonen of Finland took the bronze, Cook was fourth.

SC: Cosmetically, the race had gone well: I was in the right place at the right time, but was missing the normal endurance work in May and June. I'd been getting through on natural ability.

Peter was grim-faced. What he knew, and what as yet had not been disclosed, was that Seb had developed swollen glands. Before the end of the evening, Coe had withdrawn from the 1,500 metres (for which he was a late selection), and within a day from the mile in Oregon. Back home, hospital consultation diagnosed glandular fever; he withdrew from the Commonwealth Games. Ovett had missed Athens with injury, and Cram had taken the 1,500 metres with a commanding run ahead of Kirov (Soviet Union) and Abascal (Spain). In Brisbane, Cram would thrust himself to the forefront of the sport by completing the double, winning the 1,500 ahead of Walker and Boit. The youngster now wore the crown.

SC: I'd run seven races in three weeks, after recovering from the fracture, on no real training background. The diagnosis showed that I must have had glandular fever at some stage, and still had a glandular condition. I'd had repetitive sore throats and tiredness before Athens, where I was heavy in the legs. The symptoms continued into winter. I took a long break, and went back to Loughborough for the start of a post-graduate course. I had a small office in the PE department . . . and was falling asleep in the mornings. Any thought of moving up to 5,000 metres was abandoned almost immediately. We were now getting into a cluttered calendar, with the World Championships dominating the next season. In a straitjacket of events, now more than ever it was going to be difficult to switch.

v · Cram

SC: Steve Cram, like Ovett, came into prominence at an earlier age than I did, with times and performances that caught public attention. He was in an Olympic final at nineteen, an age at which I wasn't even selectable, neither fit enough nor mature enough. My first recollection of him is running in an English Schools meeting in 1978. There was a longer apprenticeship for me. One moment Cram was a steady-based 1,500/3,000 metres runner, beginning to get to Permit meetings where prizes were allowable in the form of payments into athletes' Trust Funds. I remember Cliff Temple writing what a come-down it was for Cram, from an international match one day to a schools meeting another. The next moment he was being selected as third-string for Moscow. He was clearly talented. There'd been a run-off for the third place with Graham Williamson, who fell flat on his face. Steve couldn't have come through at a better time, because there was no pressure on him, the attention all being focused on Ovett and me. On the other hand, Cram might have preferred to have arrived after a longer gap, so that the talent which he brought to the sport could have made its own more separate impact.

Cram had an opportunity at nineteen that I would have loved to have, though I don't say it would necessarily have helped me to avoid the errors I made in 1980. I might have inched into the team for the 800 in 1976 if I'd run 1:47 at Stretford a bit earlier than the beginning of August, the trials having been in June, when I'd finished way down in the 1,500. We sent Steve Ovett and Frank Clement for the 800 at Montreal, and no third-string. You can't beat the process of gaining Olympic experience: the travelling, the food, the Village, the buses, the queues, the warm-up track, all of that when there's no public expectation of you. Brendan was close to Cram, living round the corner as he did, and I think it was he who coined the nickname "Bambi". Steve flowed, but there was a slight ungainliness. By 1982, *he* was now under pressure, going to the line in Athens having suddenly become, within 24 hours, Britain's main representative in the 1,500 with all the responsibilities. Williamson fell again, taking a couple of people with him; Cram looked round, started sprinting, and took the gold medal in style. He had *arrived*. Yet we should have expected this of him, because when he finished third in Zurich the year before, he'd revealed such a capacity. Now, boarding the plane for Brisbane, he finds himself famous for the first time; and at the age of barely twenty-two he's won two of the top four championships available to a British runner.

I could reasonably point to '82 as a year in which Steve Ovett and I should have been in contention for one or both European or Commonwealth titles. Cram would undoubtedly have been a handful, but I was only twenty-five and should have been at a peak. Yet there I was in '82 losing the 800 final in something over 1:46. You still have to go out and *win* titles, and for his age Cram was winning them in the most commanding way. He was competitive, aware, and wanting to turn over both Ovett and me. He had the right frame of mind, believing that he *would* have done it with the talent he had. That we'll never know. There are no soft Championships, whatever the field, and Cram won in Athens and Brisbane. It was splendid that he was there to continue the line for Britain, maintaining what was to be a continuity in the 1,500 in major championships from 1978 to 1987.

By 1984, I knew he was the guy who could take my title, so there was a degree of Cram-watching on my side. You never wish injury on another runner, because you know it could happen to you next week, yet I couldn't help wondering why Steve was chasing competitive racing when he was experiencing injuries. By the reckoning of Peter and me, you eliminate injuries in training, not racing. So, in the build-up to Los Angeles, I felt I was doing it right. You do look around for reassurances from other areas, you watch how rivals are handling themselves in interviews, anything that gives a guide to their mood. Do I think changes in Steve's approach in 1984 could have changed the result? Probably not. I'm simply observing aspects of his approach to championship races. I think these were even more evident by 1986.

Steve Ovett was more like me than Cram was. Cram by now was moving around with an entourage: Jimmy Hedley, his coach, Andy Norman, Brendan Foster and a crowd of Nike people, and a hive of television men: not to mention John Hockey his agent. He wasn't in the Village in '84, he was with a whole group in a hotel, and in my opinion he was not properly focused. A friend from television was telling me how Steve had to be advised at his hotel to get in the shade, away from the swimming pool. He was relaxed, well adjusted, but there was a change in his mood by 1984. Perhaps that's hardly surprising when you're European, Commonwealth and world champion, and only months away from completing the quartet. I wasn't intimate with him, but I was beginning to suspect the way he handled himself before big championships was not geared the way I would do it. In '84 he had sporadic problems, injuries during his build-up. His training was good, seemingly, but he was breaking down in races. He and Steve Ovett came to Loughborough to run for the AAA, and the three of us did an interview with Ron Pickering, and Cram was the least relaxed. I knew something was wrong. He ran 1,000 metres, and Ovett the 800, qualifying for LA. Cram was less forthright than he had been in '83, less sociable, and I read an interview in which he said he now understood that it's not always possible to be out and about before the big championships, that he realized my attitude of being tightly focused and even appearing stand-offish was maybe *necessary*. But did he respond?

Cram's best season was '85, a year when nothing went wrong for him. He was at the height of physical maturity, and I'm sure it was his intention to wipe me off the record book in the mile. He did. I was behind him in third place on the day. Individual athletes go into seasons with very different perspectives.

Cram had no difficulty focusing in 1985 in a way he didn't in '84. John Walker has said that all great athletes have a season in which they don't put a foot wrong, and for Steve it was '85. Besides the mile, he ran 1:42.88 when beating Cruz in Zurich, and set a 2,000 metres record of 4:51.39 when lowering Walker's time in Budapest. Things looked pretty impressive for Steve in '86 until the European Championships in Stuttgart; and after that, illness and injury have dogged his career right up to the present time, which is a shame.

There's been an element of over-racing in his schedule. I've always believed that less is more. Whenever you race, you should be making a statement. That is why, say, I would run *1:44* in a county championship. You should only race when it's important: an experiment or benchmark within training, or *en route* to something else. A race for me has never been run without a specific purpose. Sometimes, to bring on a particular aspect of fitness that cannot be achieved in training. You never forget that the name of the game is to be *mentally* competitive. Road races in winter are partly fitness background, and partly the maintenance of mental *discipline*. Making yourself *do* it. I've always taken the attitude that if someone is willing to pay you to run, that's splendid. But it has *never* been more than a by-product of my racing. I suspect that at critical moments in Cram's career he may have accepted races that were *not* a part of his primary objective. Steve might come back to me to say he preferred week-by-week racing, whereas I got satisfaction from clinical approach to championships. He would be right about that for me; and only he can know the truth for himself. He was the first great athlete to come through almost a whole career when it was a professional sport. I went to university in 1976 needing to establish a place on the job market. There were no race-fees being offered then.

Life at the top in athletics now is a totally false one: cheap this, free that, discount flats, fill-your-tank-free and sign an autograph. When it all stops, you have to pay. That's why if I've wanted something, I'd pay for it.

When Dave Moorcroft was achieving England's first 1,500 metres victory (at the Commonwealth Games at Edmonton) since Bannister's triumph over John Landy in Vancouver 24 years earlier, young Cram, aged seventeen, had been eliminated in the heats; but two weeks later he was showing the benefit of experience with a personal best of 3:40.1, a new UK age-17 record, in a junior international against West Germany at Crystal Palace. Born in Gateshead in 1960, Cram did not have initial success, though at the age of thirteen he came second in a Northumberland and Durham cross-country event. The following year, he was third in the English Schools junior cross-country, and fourth in an English Schools 1,500. He began to work seriously with Jimmy Hedley; and to ease off his ambition to be a footballer while retaining a fanatical love of soccer. By July 1978, a month before the Commonwealth Games, Cram was establishing a world age-17 record for the mile, with 3:57.43 at Crystal Palace. His elimination in the 1,500 heat at Edmonton, in 3:44.8, in ninth place, was a disappointment, yet it had given him the opportunity to take a look at such formidable runners as Bayi, Dixon and Kip Koskei of Kenya at close quarters.

By 1980, Cram was setting the fastest mile by a teenager, half a second better than Ryun's 1966 time. By 1981, aged only twenty, he had 3:49.95 to his credit, yet was still only ranked third in Britain. For two years, he had been in almost every important race: eighth in Moscow, eighth in the Golden Mile at Crystal Palace behind Ovett, Scott and Walker, and fifth at Zurich behind Coe, Scott and Walker, all in 1980; sixth in the mile in Oslo, and third in Zurich behind Coe and Boit, in 1981. By 1982, the pressure from Cram on the rest began to intensify: a mile in 3:49.90, in second place behind Maree in Cork, an 800 metres victory at Crystal Palace, against Spain, Japan and Kenya, in 1:44.45. The latter ranked him third on the UK all-time list behind Coe and Ovett; he had gone through the bell in 51.4. It was after this race that Cram said provocatively: "I think Ovett and Coe can no longer consider themselves having a divine right to win races."

A month later, in Zurich, his winning time of 3:33.66, ahead of Todd Harbour (US), Scott and Walker, thrust him into the front line of international recognition. Even before the European Championships, Cram had become a runner against whom no one could be confident. It was in Athens that he was to establish the pattern of all his finest victories: making a long drive from before the bell that would drain the finishing kick for those in pursuit. He made his break with 600 metres to go: almost unintentionally, when Williamson, moving to take the lead, was spiked by Abascal and tripped on the back of Cram's shoe. Cram took off, never to be seriously challenged, though he began to tie up in the home straight as Kirov and Abascal tried to regain ground. Cram's time was a medium fast 3:36.49, and it was a much slower final that he won in Brisbane for the Commonwealth title. It was a forgettable race, with much pushing. Cram almost went down in the last lap, caught up with the Australians Hillardt and Scammell and Walker of New Zealand, who had been trying to push between the Australians for much of the third lap. Cram swore at Scammell, then overtook Boit, the leader, and with a fine turn of finishing speed became the first since Bannister to achieve the European and Commonwealth double.

Coe, attempting a return to form in 1983, and preparing for the first World Championships in Helsinki, had begun well enough during the indoor season. At Cosford in March, he had lowered his own 800 metres record to 1:44.91 in a match against the United States; and a week later, in Oslo, established a new 1,000 metres indoor record with 2:18.58, finishing barely out of breath. By the beginning of June, news was filtering through from overseas which suggested that, in a forth-coming Permit meeting in Paris, one of the first to be staged under the new system of professional trust funds, he might have to run close to world record time if he were to out-stay a 23-year-old Moroccan. Said Aouita had just become the ninth fastest man ever in Florence: 3:32.54. He would be in Paris, as would the formidable Gonzalez of Spain. The dilemma for Coe was that June was earlier than he would have wished to produce a peak, the World Championships not being until August. Aouita, a former World Student Games champion, had been training at altitude in Mexico, and had run his time in Florence with a last lap of 54, faster than any last lap in any world record at 1,500 or a mile.

Coe was pre-selected at 800 metres for Helsinki, and was required to qualify for the longer distance. "It's a humbling sport," Coe reflected at the time, looking ahead to Paris. "You're lucky to take out a fraction of what you put in. In a sense, Athens was good for me. Every sportsman needs to be brought up sharp now and again. I'd had three marvellous years since 1979, lucky to avoid serious injury. It would have been bad for me, and for the sport, to have come back from Athens with the 800 gold medal after only four weeks of make-shift preparation."

I had endeavoured to warn Coe, to prepare him for such set-backs, when sitting on the crowded bar floor of a suburban Rome hotel at about two in the morning, back in September of 1981. He had just concluded his best season with victory in the World Cup; and instinct had told me that an athlete operating at his supreme level could not expect indefinitely to ride free of misfortune. It was bad enough in 1982, with a stress fracture and then glandular fever; now, he was about to encounter a situation far worse. In June the crisis was still two months away. Running in Paris, jostled by the pack soon after the gun, he caught a foot on the inner kerb, and tumbled almost headlong into the long-jump pit. By the time he recovered, the field was twenty metres further on. With a stupendous effort, Coe regained the leaders, and fought Gonzalez stride for stride down the finishing straight, losing by three-tenths of a second. Deducting two seconds for time lost off the track, never mind disruption of rhythm, Coe's time of 3:35.17 seemed good enough in the circumstances. Aouita had not run. In Oslo, four days later, Coe reassured himself with a really fast 800 metres in 1:43.80.

Elsewhere, Cram and Ovett were struggling to prove *their* fitness at 1,500 metres for inclusion in the team for Helsinki, Cram delivering a scathing attack on the selectors for alleged favouritism towards his two rivals. Coe and Ovett had both said that they wished to double-up in both events, which would leave Cram and Williamson disputing third place for the longer race. Cram felt that the two superstars were going to be selected for what they had done in 1980 and 1981, while he was being given no credit for his victories in 1982. A row developed over Cram and Ovett both wishing to run the same 1,500 metres at Hengelo in Holland, Ovett muscling in at an event which Cram had expected to use for no more than proof of fitness: not as an occasion for confrontation with a rival. Cram took the option to run the 800 metres instead, with a not-so-fast 1:46.36. He was into a phase of injury worries and unable at this stage to find true form.

Ovett was also in trouble. In his first serious race of the year at Oslo, he had run just inside the Helsinki qualifying time with 3:38.81, in a rough race in which Abascal had fallen following a collision between Ovett and Flynn of Eire. Ovett's form continued uncertainly; he failed to finish in the AAA Championships 800 metres, and was not nominated for that in Helsinki. Busy pressing for inclusion at the shorter distance was Peter Elliott, who had run a fastish time when finishing second to Coe in Oslo; while adding to the pressure on Coe for inclusion in the longer event was Williamson, third the same night behind Ovett and Gonzalez.

Fresh anxiety was just around the corner for Coe. In the Talbot Games at Crystal Palace, he was defeated over 1,500 metres by Dragan Zdravkovic, last in the Moscow final. Zdravkovic passed Coe in the final fifty metres. Coe said afterwards he felt "shattered", but would still be running the following week, in the invitation mile at the AAA Championships. It had not, as yet, become public knowledge that there were inconsistencies in Coe's training sufficient to cause doubt for him and Peter. Coe denied that financial considerations made him run the following week, saying that he wished to protect Robinson's, the sponsors, who had planned the meeting for many months. With Scott also committed to the Invitation Mile, my understanding is that a large slice of the US television fee would be going in the direction of Coe and Scott, particularly with IMG involvement. But I accept Coe's word that he would not have run unless he felt he needed the race. There have been enough occasions when he has pulled out of races when there has been money to be made.

The British Board, meanwhile, was in as much confusion as anyone. Prior to the AAA Championships they announced that Cram, Ovett and Williamson were selected for the 1,500 metres; and promptly withdrew the announcement. This seemed to mean that Williamson, who had better 1,500 times for the season than Cram or Coe, might be obliged to run-off for a final place with Cram . . . if Coe were to produce front-line form in the Invitation Mile, to which neither Cram nor Williamson was invited. Cram, his season disrupted, privately did not expect to be chosen.

Feeling himself pig-in-the-middle of a controversy that was not of his making, Coe resolved the situation unilaterally. Four days before the Invitation Mile, he withdrew his wish to be considered for the longer distance. His statement to the domestic news agencies would have put shame on any organization less insensitive than the Board. It read:

> I consider I am morally obliged to take this action for three reasons. Firstly, the public debate by selectors in the press on the selection policy, without reference to athletes, presented a one-sided picture. Secondly, the impression that's created in the press and public was that I was receiving special consideration at the expense of other athletes. Thirdly, the continuing argument of the relative merits of individual performances in different races, in which mine were not always the slowest, rather than the head-to-head selection I have always sought, put me in an untenable position. If I was selected it would be under a cloud. If I did anything other than win in Helsinki, I would be open to accusations that another athlete should have been selected. I feel it has become a matter of personal integrity not to permit a situation to continue, in which other athletes were complaining that I was in some way influencing their decision on which races they had to run. This has never been so. Over five weeks ago, I said publicly that the British Board must not let selection for the 1,500 metres drift on until it becomes too late. This they have done. I was willing to meet anyone head-to-head, and consider I was the one who was being avoided.

Coe's statement came the same day that the Board had said he, Cram and Williamson should have a showdown in the Invitation Mile. Up to that point, Cram had been avoiding meeting Williamson head-on. It was another example of the Board failing to do their job: make selection on their own judgement.

SC: I'd been having difficulty putting training sessions together. I didn't complain to Peter, because you tend to believe that you're going to be OK. At my level, one is used to being in some pain, to be permanently tired during severe periods of training. Yet things were so bad at this stage that if I wanted to sneeze I had to get down on all fours because of the pain shooting down my legs from my abdomen. I had not as yet told Peter about these pains. Peter must have had his suspicions because, by July, Robert Hague, the endocrinologist, was coming to training sessions, though I didn't know why. We'd tried every kind of change: easing off a lot just before a race, though I was still having to struggle. Part of the problem was that Peter was calculating my difficulties were mental rather than physical.

On top of all this I was annoyed to have Brendan ringing up Steve Mitchell and suggesting it wouldn't look good if I kept Cram out of the team. That was hardly ethical; and it was about that time that I decided to withdraw from contention for the 1,500 metres. I've never gone into any championships if I didn't think I could do well. Yet even after the defeats by Gonzalez and Zdravkovic, I wasn't giving Peter the full picture. He was being philosophical, saying, "We're still short of finishing work." My fast 800 in Oslo had been run on mental resilience rather than on physical ability. That was the race when, if I'd been truthful, I would have said the game was up. Yet when I lost to Scott in the Invitation Mile, I was still thinking I could cure the pains by physiotherapy; in fact, this was aggravating the pains, which were glandular. I thought the pains were emanating from my back and the problem I had had the previous winter, which had been put right by Eddie Franklin, the Chelsea football physiotherapist whom I'd been using since moving into a flat in Fulham.

Although running a well-judged tactical race in the Invitation Mile, and being in a perfect position to strike at any time in the last lap, Coe was unable to respond to an early kick by the 26-year-old Scott, who won by almost ten yards in 3:51.56. Coe beat Williamson; yet when he had called upon finishing speed, it wasn't there. His last chance to prove to his own satisfaction that he was fit, before going to Helsinki, was in an 800 metres at the Gateshead Games.

SC: I rang up to ensure I could run. I needed to justify my place in the Helsinki field, but with Cram making a return in this event after injury, and Elliott looking for a sharpener, I was heading into a cauldron. The local press headlines were "Trial by TV". It's the only time I've felt an alien in an English stadium. I felt unwelcome. I wasn't there to defeat Cram or Elliott, but was looking to establish my own form. I ran a sound tactical race, was clear around the final bend, went to accelerate as in the recent mile . . . and nothing happened. Cram, Elliott and Wuyke of Venezuela all went past me. In the warm-down area, Peter lobbed my training shoes to me. The papers wrote that he'd lost his temper and thrown them at me! The BBC News team shoved a microphone at me, and Peter told them: "There's nothing he can say." That was reported as my father refusing to let me comment. It was media take-over time.

Peter and I finally had to recognize that something must be seriously wrong. I was given an introduction to Carl Nicholson, a consultant at Leicester; the next day I was admitted to hospital for a biopsy on the gland under my arm, which in the event they removed. A disease called toxoplasmosis was diagnosed, and for the next eight weeks I was on a course of tablets that made me feel terrible. The idea of maybe never running again was less overriding than the wish simply to feel *well* again. I hadn't really felt well for a year and a half, since before Athens. Even getting in and out of the car had been painful, and for much of the '83 season I was on pain-killers. Mechanically, I literally couldn't *move* properly. I didn't become sure that I could run again until springtime the following year.

After I came out of hospital, I went to stay with Steve Mitchell in Loughborough. The press behaviour was disgraceful. Journalists would try to talk their way into the house by deceit, the way two of them had managed in the hospital! Neighbours were asked by photographers if they could borrow the bathroom to get a better camera angle on Steve's house. We made a getaway, to another residence, and were pursued down the motorway. Every kind of press speculation about me was going around: that I was suffering from anything from excessive use of performance-enhancing drugs to AIDS to leukaemia. Although Carl Nicholson said he saw no medical reason why I should not run again when cured, he couldn't give any assurance that I would be fit for the Olympics the following year; and I already realized I would be missing some of the important road-work during the winter. I didn't put on running shoes again until after Christmas. Five months were lost. On a book-signing trip to Dublin, following the publication of a training book by Peter and me, I was so sick I couldn't complete the engagement.

If Cram and his home crowd had been ecstatic over the defeat of his legendary rival, never mind that they were initially unaware of Coe's debilitating condition, the press would put the situation in perspective. Many of the headlines proclaimed "Coe Loses" rather than "Cram Wins". Ovett had said afterwards: "It was a strange experience, watching Seb's race. We'd been so close, in athletic terms, over the years, that it was almost like watching myself losing. I can only admire him for appearing in those recent races. He's put himself on the chopping block four times, and chosen not to hide." Coe makes the point that if ever there was a reasonable case for avoiding anyone, then this had been it. "If I'd not scratched from Helsinki that day, the selectors would have had the right to de-select me."

If the race was a disaster for Coe, it had been, proportionally, by no means impressive for Cram, with a time of 1:45.03. It was, however, some proof that he was on the way to regaining the quality of the previous year.

PC: Cram's record is a very good one, but when he buckles, he buckles badly. Did he over-race? In general, if you are good enough to stand on the track, you're fit. I think Cram had a basic biomechanical problem, which meant his racing programme should have been curtailed. If you decrease racing, you can decrease training, and thereby reduce stress impact. His problem was foot placement, though whether this could be corrected by orthotic inserts or exercises I don't know. In motion, Cram looks marvellous from a side view, but often looks ungainly head-on, especially when he starts to roll like Zatopek. When he's fatigued, he's calling on other muscles to help take the strain, and this adds to the temporary impression of tiredness. At 800 metres, Seb always had the edge on Cram, other than at Gateshead, but otherwise their respective best times were within fractions of each other. In Cram's favour is that he's won a World Championship and two European 1,500 titles, which is pretty good.

For Seb this was a chaotic year. There had been fluctuating symptoms, without identification. Initially, we were not looking for illness, so we searched the training programme to see what might be producing the fluctuation. Seb was always such a good athlete that even finishing in third place he was showing fast times. But what was wrong? I'm not an authoritarian coach, so if the athlete wants to push, I go along with it, even if I'm worried. Seb was doing this in '82, going harder in training than I wanted. If '82 was undulant, then '83 was downhill. The pattern was consistent: running out of steam in the last 200 metres. We should have been looking sooner for illness.

Jimmy Hedley has an explanation of Cram's repetitive calf injuries over the years; and questions whether his injuries have been compounded by the number of races he has run.

The problem with Steve is that, more than most, he runs off his toes [Hedley says]. This means that he has developed huge calf muscles, like a footballer. They're big because of the power he is developing. He gets more propulsion from his calf than other runners do, so ironically his strength is his weakness. He has regularly encountered muscle tears when running at his limit. It's the power that enabled him to run as fast as he did over 800 metres (in the same way as Snell). When he ran 1:42, I couldn't believe it. At the stage he got down to 1:46, I didn't think he could improve on that. He didn't have the *ability*. When you get to 1:42, you're talking about 200 in 21.8: yet Steve's a winder-up, not a sprinter.

Steve Scott is an admirer of Cram's attitude to racing over the years.

He's so sociable and at ease, and I like him more than any [Scott says]. He doesn't intimidate other runners, he's fun to have around, and can be one of the lads, yet he races extraordinarily. He's never been afraid to take on anyone, and he's run a lot, hasn't he? What does anyone run *for*? To be the best? Cram has *fun* out there. If he's not known for his all-time accomplishments, maybe that was not what he was looking for. I think we have shared a lot of common goals and attitudes . . . but he was able to do it a lot better. The first battle between me and Cram was in '82, losing to him in Zurich when I was otherwise unbeaten, having broken the US record with a time a fraction outside Seb's then world record of 3:47.33. At that time it looked to be Cram taking over from Coe and Ovett.

The following year, I was supremely confident going into the World Championships in Helsinki. I felt that I would be able to handle the race any way it was run. I had the most confidence for any race I've ever run. The heats and semi-final went fine. In the final, it began extremely slowly, and was a matter of who made the first move and when. Aouita went first at around 500, before I expected, then Cram coming up to the bell. I had to go outside Aouita on the final bend and couldn't reach Cram. In my pre-race plans, I'd never calculated Ovett as a factor. I should have been first to move, as intended, and when I didn't do that, I should have reacted more quickly. Yet having said that, '83 was my mental peak. I was physically stronger, in my home Olympics the next year, but was mentally shot.

Helping Cram to plan his campaign against the world in 1983 was Brendan Foster. He was to play a critical strategic role beforehand. They had been running together since Cram was a boy, side by side around the Jarrow roads, and an affection had developed in the older man. It had been Foster, hard-pressed by the seventeen-year-old during the Emsley Carr Mile in 1978, who had nudged the selectors into picking the boy for the Commonwealth Games.

Steve took his opportunities [Foster reflects]. In '82, if both Ovett and Coe had been at their best, Steve probably wouldn't have got there. When Coe dropped out in Athens, what Cram gained was immense. Prematurely, he was a champion. By Brisbane, he seemed unbeatable, running the last lap in just over 52. Now I began to think, "this fellow could beat the other two at their best." Yet I'd seen Williamson run away from Cram when they were juniors, and at that time it had looked as if the young Scot would be the next star. The beauty of Cram was that he knew how to use his talent: to wind it up and wind it up, getting faster and faster, until no one could halt him. Up in the commentary box in Helsinki, I'd had a good view in the heats of the way others were running, and had noticed Aouita regularly moving out into lane three approaching the bell. So my advice to Cram was to get to the bell before Aouita, and make it a final sprint of more than a lap, to draw the sting out of the Moroccan. It was that move, incidentally, which probably cost Ovett a medal.

A first lap of 64.9, slower than that of Mary Decker in the women's final, and an 800 metre time of 2:07.7 – slower even than the amble of Moscow – was the prelude to a sizzling finish by the big kickers. As Foster had forecast, Aouita made his move down the penultimate home straight, and Cram was on to him in a flash, closely followed by Scott and Abascal, with Ovett boxed at the back. The bell was passed in 2:49.4. Aouita, his head no higher than Cram's chest, was throwing in everything, with a personal third lap of 54.8. Yet he could not drop Cram, and into the final bend he was consumed by the devouring strides of the 22-year-old Geordie. Behind Cram, Scott was driving himself to overtake Aouita in the last few metres. Cram's winning time was a moderate 3:41.59, but he had run the last lap in 52 seconds. Scott took the silver, Aouita the bronze, with Ovett beaten into fourth place. Misjudging his tactics, caught at the back of the field when the critical move came 450 yards from home, Ovett had run the last lap in 51.9, faster than anyone. He was left saying: "It was the worst race of my life."

In an early biography, Cram recalled:

I knew nothing about Ovett being boxed. I've run my race and I haven't a clue what happened. Everyone was probably saying how terrible Ovett ran, but I'm going round doing my lap of honour, thinking I've run the greatest race of my life. It *wasn't* a great race, one of the most disappointing races of the Championships. I was just the guy who ran the right race. Picking up a Union Jack and waving to the crowd was the most enjoyable part of it, the immediate five minutes afterwards because you are still on such a high. What happens after that, for the next hour or two, is a gradual anticlimax.

An unseen hand in helping Cram bestride the athletics world at this moment had been, perhaps, Andy Norman. It was he who had suggested, and made possible around Europe, Cram's repeated races at 1,000 metres which had developed speed with endurance.

In the month after the World Championships, Cram, metaphorically, was making hay while his sun shone. He ran *nine* races. After a fast 800 at Oslo, he then ran brilliantly to win the Van Damme Memorial in Brussels, with a 1,500 metres in 3:31.66: two seconds off his personal best, three-tenths of a second slower than Ovett's world record, and third fastest all-time behind Ovett and Wessinghage. Yet, as for Coe at Zurich in 1981, there seemed to be more disappointment than satisfaction. "It was just what I *hate* about chasing world records," Cram said. "I'd run a personal best, yet everyone was coming up to me saying, 'Bad luck, Steve, better luck next time.' They all feel you're bound to be down because you've failed to beat the record, yet you're delighted at running faster than ever before. It's all ridiculous." Demonstrating his willingness to meet anyone, anywhere – most of the time – Cram had a thrilling finale to the year in the Coca-Cola Mile at Crystal Palace. A stirring battle between him and Ovett ended with victory for Cram by a stride in 3:52.56. The two of them slugged it out over a last lap of 54 seconds, with Ovett unable to dent his opponent's fractional lead when positioned all the time within striking distance. "It was a great race," Ovett said, "and I enjoyed it a lot more than I did Helsinki."

As he moved towards 1984 and his second Olympic Games, Cram wrote:

I've got no long-term plan to be the greatest ever 1,500 metres runner and go down in history – that's one of the reasons why I haven't gone around chasing world records. I just want to do well whatever race I'm in. My motivation purely comes from then and there. I've no great ambition to achieve immortality in athletics. I would be disappointed if I didn't win an Olympic title, simply for the reason that I'm capable of winning it. You have to realize your capabilities. If your potential is Olympic champion, then you have to hope you achieve that. I think it is important not to allow any personality clash to come in the way of athletic competition. I psyche myself up by wanting to get the best out of myself. I try to forget who the other people are in the race. It's just me against eight or nine others, not me against Steve Ovett or Seb Coe. If you concentrate on individuals, then the likelihood is that someone else comes through who you are not watching. I don't like rivalries. I look to get on with everybody because that means I can enjoy my athletics much more. Of course I'm hungry to win. Once you have reached the top you want to stay there. As the saying goes, there's only one way to go once you're at the top. If I want to stay there, I have to win in LA. It's only an excuse for me if I can say to myself, "Oh well, I've always got 1988."

Whatever the causes, Cram was to have problems similar to 1983 in his preparations for 1984. How he adjusted his preparation was a matter for the discretion of him and Jimmy Hedley, yet Derek Ibbotson observes:

I can't understand why Cram switched from climate to climate. He had too many races. There were times he raced when he should have concentrated on getting it right in training. He raced too much for money, and didn't need to. It was the same with Dave Bedford. When Dave was at a training camp in Switzerland before the Munich Games in 1972, he suddenly went off to Finland because he'd had a good offer. When he came to Munich, he got stuffed. I said to him: "If you'd won the Olympic 10,000, you'd have been made."

VI · Mission

All he wanted was to get away [Steve Mitchell says]. Within a few days of coming out of hospital in Leicester, we'd driven down to Italy, where Emma and Nick, his younger sister and brother, were on holiday, a few miles north of Rimini. It was a good time, marvellous weather, and no-one to bother him. If the television from Helsinki came on, he wouldn't watch. It had hit him hard, because it was the first World Championships, and it stung his pride not to be there. Yet, you can't be sure . . . the break away from competition *could* have done him good, never mind the illness. We didn't talk that much about the disappointment. The thought of the Olympics the next year motivated him in a quite different way. Had it been a European Championship I'm not sure he would have recovered to the same extent. Considering the crisis in his life, I thought he handled himself pretty well. We were training together quite hard during the winter of '82/'83. When he suddenly started to get beaten in the summer, why no-one thought he might be unwell is beyond me, when I consider it now. *He* thought he'd over-trained, while Peter, checking the records, insisted everything was normal. Why didn't we think again? In the talk between Seb and Peter, '83 was always planned as 800/1,500 back-to-back series. I thought he would have a better chance in the 1,500, and I remember Foster ringing up and moaning about Cram's misfortunes in mid-summer.

Given the emotional burden being borne by Coe during the winter of '83/'84 – doubting his health, doubting his whole athletic future – many might wonder whether he was at a disadvantage being unmarried. The bottom line is that, given his nature, for him it was probably an advantage. It allowed him to maintain an exclusivity of purpose that is denied in many instances to those who have the responsibilities of married life, even if there are the benefits of sorrows shared being sorrows halved.

Luiz Oliveira, the Brazilian coach who is the only man to have had three runners beating 1:44, believed Sabastian Coe's unmarried state was a substantial factor in his enduring quality as a great runner.

Marriage is all right in team sports [Oliveira says], but less so for the individual. The responsibilities take a lot out of you. Marriage reduces your ego, though that factor does not apply in the Muslim culture. It does in Western societies. It affects a man's whole life. Naturally enough, wives want to accompany you, and that reduces you. International races are not a recreation. It's one of the main problems with American runners, they take their wives and girlfriends all over Europe. Not only is it bad, temperamentally, for their running, in the majority of cases, but it's absorbing money from the sport unnecessarily, the cost of it all. Athletics is not a holiday.

Coe's view is emphatically the same. There were always girlfriends in his life: sometimes embarrassingly so, when they closed the door behind them and went scampering off to trade their confidences to some disreputable newspaper. Yet Coe knew that marriage for the prominent athlete was unavoidably a compromise.

SC: Marriage maybe altered the direction of Steve Ovett's career. I don't want to pour cold water on marriage, or to be simplistic like Bill Shankly, who boasted of taking his wife to a football match on his wedding day. And you couldn't put Dave Moorcroft in this category, because he was married within weeks of leaving college in 1976, and six years later was breaking the world record for 5,000 metres and getting close to the 3,000 record. The first thing you'd see after a race would be Dave together with his kids. But certainly it wasn't right for *my* mentality during my running career. The situation for an international athlete, I think, is that relationships outside the sport have to be *un*demanding. You only have a few years to reach your objectives. If you have a relationship with a woman it has to be one in which there will be no challenge to your saying you will be away for the next eight weeks. If you look at marriages in sport, that have occurred between an athlete and wife or husband, that is the pattern. The partner yields and accepts. Where the athlete marries an equal partner, it can be more difficult. Athletes don't want disruption, questioning of their actions, because their life has to be theirs. That's why you don't want partners at races. If I'd married in my twenties to someone offering a challenge, someone who was strong and certain of themselves, I risked losing momentum in athletics, precisely because you have to invest in relationships and long-term commitments. That's a selfish thing to admit, I realize that. I was tackling Stuttgart [European Championships] when I was thirty, where in other circumstances I could have had children aged four or five. I had girlfriends, but never lived together with anyone. It was always clear that I was not interested in settling down.

At a New Year's party he gave in 1984, for friends and in thanks to those in the medical profession who had been providing moral support for the past four months, Coe was introduced, by a mutual friend in television, to Jane Williams.

We were happy the way we were [Jane says]. I had no plans, it suited us both, the way our lives went. When Steve Cram and Daley got married, Seb would say humorously, "Oh well, that's that!". So the way we were was fine with me, we each had our own space, our own houses. Those early months of '84,

Seb needed an awful lot of encouraging, he'd lost so much confidence. He was jolly, for much of the time, but no-nonsense, never mincing his words about his anxieties. What he needed was somebody cantankerous, not sympathetic. Somebody who would quickly dismiss poor training performances and say, "That's in the past, it's the future that counts." This is what he got from John Hovell, the photographer who's been a coach for so many years and was deeply involved at Haringey. John's help that winter was pretty important.

John was there, always willing to help out, working to Peter's schedules. What impressed me about Seb was that there was never any complaint about the hard work, he was more than willing to put in the time, sometimes more than necessary. He couldn't bear being around the house, and would do extra training, saying, "Don't tell Dad or John." I weigh eight-and-a-half stone, about 120 pounds, and Seb would do his hundred daily knee-lifts with me sitting on his shoulders, to save going to the gymnasium. I'd balance myself with my hands on the walls, which left finger marks, and one day my mother asked, "What on earth are those?" I'd hold Seb's feet while he did a hundred pull-ups, lying on the ground. "How many's that?" "Seventy-eight." "OK, another twenty-two."

He never talked about what would happen if LA went wrong. That wasn't in his calculations, though I had no concept beforehand of what was involved, how huge the whole thing was. He was conscious of every twinge and every sniff. Just before the AAA trials, he tore some fibres and was really worried. I think the Middlesex Championships at Enfield in the middle of May were the turning-point, when he ran 1:45.2. He had all the lads and his colleagues round the outside of the track, shouting split times: Steve, Malcolm, John, the rest. That race did him an enormous amount of good – when he wasn't busy asking what the score was in the Cup Final. He could be so humorous, but the public don't see this, in public he's so serious, keeping up the considered, thoughtful appearance. At club championships, at get-togethers, he's one of the boys, and it's not an inverse snobbery, it's spontaneous. In LA, you'd find him much of the time out-of-hours chatting with the hockey team, say, or the wrestlers.

When he was beaten by Elliott in the trials, we were all pretty sombre, but John Hovell snapped everyone out of it, including Seb. "Right, then, who's getting the drinks?" Seb went off to Chicago, taking Peter's schedules with him, but essentially he wanted time on his own, plus the time-zone acclimatization. He was so meticulous. He left behind the money for a ticket for me, and called regularly during three weeks with Joe Newton, the friend of his and Peter's with whom he was staying in Chicago. Separating from Peter was important, I think, though I didn't know Peter very well at that stage. Seb had decided, however, that he had to do it *his* way. It was not until he was in the Olympic Village, doing 200 metre repetitions, that the confidence was really there. He'd been in the doldrums when beaten by Elliott. He was desolate. My mother heard on the BBC that he'd been selected, and when he happened to call me, I said, "You're in." He could hardly speak.

By April, Coe was beginning to feel refreshed after each training session, instead of incessantly tired, as he had the previous year. Once then, going home with Peter after training, he had fallen asleep in the time it took Peter to boil the kettle for coffee. He had been having to stop off at service centres on the motorway between Loughborough and Sheffield because he was falling asleep at the wheel. Once, pulling in for ten minutes, he had woken up an hour-and-a-half later. And then there was the press. The denigration continued throughout the winter of 1983–84 and on into the summer. When he was asked about his hopes for recovery by the *Daily Star*, and he replied that there was nothing he could say at this stage, an article followed saying that he was "as approachable as Frank Sinatra on a bad night" and that he was "a tormented athlete who knew that the game may be up". All this under the by-line "Another Star Exclusive". The only exclusivity seemed to be that he had nothing to say to the *Star*.

SC: The first thing I shouted after I crossed the line in Los Angeles was "Who says I'm finished now!" I wanted to do it as much for Peter as for myself. There was a body of *coaches* who thought Peter's principles were beginning to unravel, people who were sure I'd paid the price of previous years – "What can you expect when you run those 800 repetitions?" With what seemed a certain glee, John Walker was writing beforehand that I no longer frightened middle-distance fields, that I was no longer invincible. What I wanted from LA was not just a medal, but to run really well, to show the press and the athletics world, who were taking an inordinate pleasure in my difficulties, that I wasn't finished: that I could not only get back to international standards, but prove them utterly wrong. The period between May and July in 1984 was the only occasion, when I was fit, that failure bred failure, and this was on account of my own loss of confidence on the race-track. I had to decide that only I – not Peter, not my family, not my girlfriend – could determine how I ran. That was why I decided to get away early to America, not just for the time-zone acclimatization to the eight-hour difference between London and Los Angeles, but to come to terms with myself. All the training schedules were agreed with Peter, the race plan was straight-forward: the series in the 800 bringing me towards a peak in the 1,500. As Peter always said, riders in the Tour de France don't start on the first day at a peak, they build up during the race. What I needed to sort out before LA was my own *mind*: and I was the only one that could do that. Between an athlete and his coach, perhaps especially father and son, there is a tension which can go from you to him, and then be reflected back on you, emotionally even more charged. Of course I needed Peter, but I could not go on inflicting things on him hour by hour.

PC: It was like a company project. The investment was massive. It *had* to work. Was it a show of strength, or folly? If it worked, it would be seen as a great success: if it failed, as an even bigger folly. I was committed firstly to getting Seb to LA, and then to getting it right for winning medals. If you study your runner, you know he needs a certain number of races after reaching the basis of condition, in order to reach a peak. Seb needs about seven or eight from about the time of the Middlesex Championships. There was only one race other than the Olympics to worry about in '84, the trial. Some people understand the principles, most don't. After Elliott beat Seb in the trial, John Rodda wrote in *The Guardian* the next morning: "Coe will get better, Elliott will not." The really fast 800 in Oslo, immediately following the trial for 1,500 at Crystal Palace, with a very fast last 100, was all part of the planning. I knew from the time Seb ran 3:54.6 for a mile so easily in early July that it was all coming back. At the trial in June – a pseudo-selection thing to create importance for the meeting – Seb hadn't run a race for three weeks. If you look at the schedule before the first heats of the Olympic Games, he had a mere five races plus a relay leg. The Olympic racing was planned irrespective of any other runner, entirely designed around his own development day by day. It was not in any way geared to Cram, and there were so many different sounds coming out of the Cram camp. The separation thing, his going to America without me, couldn't have happened more simply. We were sitting in the car after one of the races, and I said, "If you don't want me to crowd you, it may be as well to start now." That was what he wanted, and perhaps he was reluctant to shout it out. *He* felt he *ought* to be on his own.

Coe had announced, at the time of a road relay at Cranford, Middlesex, in March, that he wished to be considered for the double in LA. He was running his first competitive event since the defeat at Gateshead. Subsequently, he was pre-selected for the 800, but would have to enter the trial for the longer event. His 1:45.2 in the Middlesex Championships had ensured his early selection for the 800, but as with the World Championships the previous year, there were four trying to find room in the 1,500: Cram and Ovett, with the credentials of their performances in Helsinki, Coe and, this time instead of Williamson, Elliott. The trials for the 800 had taken place earlier in June, Elliott having won himself selection then; now he ambitiously planned to expand his range to the unfamiliar four laps. Elliott was not to be treated lightly. Aged twenty-one, he had won the European indoor silver medal the year before, and was an outstanding fourth in the World Championships at 800 metres. In thirty races at that distance, he had 20 times beaten the Olympic qualifying standard of 1:47.

SC: Both Elliott and I were in the 1,500 trial under false pretences. We were both told the winner would go to LA . . . and he didn't. We were there simply to put bums on seats, to help fill the stadium and for the benefit of television. It clearly was *not* a selection race, in the way they told us privately. I'd probably have entered the race anyway, but I didn't need the additional pressure. I could understand Elliott's attitude when he won the race, though given the way we ran on the day, as a selector you wouldn't have picked *either* of us.

It was an unmemorable, slow and rough race, with runners barging into each other among a field of twelve. In the first lap, Coe was pushed by a young Frenchman, Laventure; and on the second lap, entering the home-straight, he nearly went down, lunging sideways after seemingly being buffeted from behind by Williamson. Elliott was spiked in both legs, and ran a tactically unintelligent race in a vulnerable position behind the leaders. Eamonn Martin led the first lap and Laventure the second, in a fraction under two minutes. Down the last back-straight, Elliott went ahead, followed by Coe; after the final bend Coe made his move, came through on the inside to lead by a couple of strides, and seemed to have the race won. Elliott clawed his way back, to become the first man ever to beat Coe at both 800 and 1,500 metres. It was only Elliott's fourth race at the distance. The time, 3:39.66, 13-hundredths ahead of Coe, proved nothing, though Elliott loudly proclaimed his right to the place for LA. Thankfully, the selectors saw it differently. Elliott was to say later: "I knew what was likely when I saw Andy Norman talking to Coe after the race." What in fact Norman was saying to Coe was "well, now you can just concentrate on the 800." However, Elliott's supposition was in principle correct. At the selection meeting, Norman's intervention proved decisive.

The selectors decided to leave it to the council of the Board [Norman recalls]. It all went a bit quiet, so I said to them, "We're talking about winning, and out of the four of them, Coe, Ovett, Cram and Elliott, who would you put your life on to win – Elliott?" The chairman, McAllister, agreed with me. The argument was over.

Elliott was as loud in his protests afterwards as he had been in his claims before the announcement. Whether or not his words were reported accurately, in numerous interviews he was quoted as saying: "If I had been born south of Watford, maybe it would have been different. I'm just a working-class lad. If I had a university degree, it might have made a difference. My face doesn't fit." Etc. For a nation obsessed by class distinctions the contrast between the graduate Coe and the carpenter Elliott was too good an angle to waste, in what was a genuine controversy: it was conveniently overlooked that Coe had spent much of his life running in the same county as Elliott.

As Coe set off for Chicago, part of the advice-background on which he was acting came from Dave Martin in Atlanta. Martin had been in Helsinki, and returned home via London to have a long talk with the Coes. Up to that point, in spite of regular correspondence, Martin had been volunteering little advice, following the old adage: "If it works, don't fix it".

I had fed some input, physiological information, some biochemical background [Martin says], and things had been going so well for three years: the records, the benefits of professionalism. Seb and Peter didn't see our treadmill in Atlanta as a secret of success, though the exchange of correspondence continued. Post-'83 I emphasized that sport was a game, that they had to look forward, not back. If Seb had toxoplasmosis, then I'd better study the physiological effects of this. I wrote to Seb that rest was as important as medication, that there could be a residue of the virus for years which might not affect performance, but needed monitoring. In LA, I was next door with the Belgian team. It was clear to me when I saw him that Seb was back in shape.

If Coe was still under a veil of uncertainty, the season was as problematic as it had been the previous year in the build-up to the climax for Cram. Ten days before he was due to leave, there was a fresh injury problem, this time a twisted ankle. He came into Foster's office to say that he didn't think he could go to LA. Foster gave him some old-fashioned advice. "If you don't go to LA, then you won't get to the final. If you do go, then maybe you'll make the semi-final. If you're in the semi-final, you could qualify. And then?" Hedley thought that Cram was improving day by day in LA, but had finally run out of steam.

Athletically, Steve should have been delighted with his performance out there [Foster says]. He gave a fine demonstration of the athlete he was, and gave Seb a great race. What was remarkable, and for me made this Seb's best performance of all, was the times in those seven races – that level of performance day by day in the heat was unbelievable. The others who went for the double, like Cruz and Ovett, ended up in a heap.

Cram's final try-out in Gateshead, in front of a handful of friends, was conducted in testing conditions of wind and rain. Sharpe did the pacemaking for two laps, after a week in which he had selflessly applied himself in partnering Cram during training. Cram had to pick up the running on his own well before the last lap, and pushed himself to record the moderate time of 3:39.9. It was enough to convince him that it was worth his going. He would not, he considered, have to run near a world record; and his mental stability was as important as his physical condition. He felt that a capacity to run a fast last lap should be enough to put him in contention, though he was prepared for the possibility of defeat. If he won, it would be against the odds.

I knew people were saying that I'd won the European, Commonwealth and World titles, but not the Olympics [Cram says], that this was something I *had* to have. Yet I lost, and could still sleep soundly. By the end of the season I was running well, with a time of 3:33. In life, *timing* is everything. For me, that year didn't work. The previous year, everything was right. You just move on. When I arrived in LA, I had nothing under my belt to give me confidence. Three weeks of steady running and some track work-out in America put me in a better frame of mind. I was concerned beforehand mainly about Scottie, Abascal and Cruz. I was thinking Cruz was the man to beat after his 800 victory, he seemed to have so much strength, but then he pulled out. I'd thought the final would be fairly pedestrian, and was planning for that kind of race. I'd done some speed work, and wasn't geared for what happened, the way the race was run. I wouldn't have supposed beforehand that Seb would have wanted that, either. My preparation was geared to a quick finish rather than a long run. If you'd told me three weeks beforehand that LA would be won in under 3:33, I'd have laughed. I think Seb's performance in those seven races was superior to 1980. I'd no complaints. The way Seb came out of those seven races was astonishing.

Walker, while warning Cram of what he might expect, was giving Coe almost no chance.

The opposition is breathing right down Cram's neck [Walker had said]. I was probably four seconds better than my opponents going into the Montreal games. When you get into the races, it becomes totally different. You start fearing opposition, athletes you've never raced against . . . I can assure Steve Cram that he won't be able to get rid of that pressure, though I think it could be even greater on Coe. He's been out of it for two years . . . I believe somebody who's been out of that winning position for two years will have been badly affected psychologically . . . I was aware of Cram warming up in the World Championships. He's got such a casual attitude, but good speed as well . . . everyone will be watching Cram in the Olympic final.

Peter Elliott, restricted in his ambition to the 800, had his expectation impeded by an injury to his foot. He prepared on a track that was too hard, and cracked a bone. "He *was* racing too much," Wilf Paish now admits, "but how can a coach say to an athlete, 'turn that down' when an agent offers £2,500? An athlete needs an agent to get races." Elliott had joined Paish in 1980, but theirs was never wholly a happy relationship during the two years before Elliott won the trial for the 1982

Commonwealth Games; Paish, however, was reluctant to enter him for the European Championships. Elliott went on holiday to Benidorm, came home to find himself thrust into the 4 x 800 record bid, and with no form, decided to pull out of the European Championships. With Coe and Ovett unfit for the Commonwealth, Chris McGeorge was picked rather than Elliott.

That was the start of my problems with Wilf [Elliott says]. It was Wilf's idea I should go for the double in '84, and I had total belief in what he said. I was training so hard. I'd be up at six, work at the steel mill from seven-thirty to four, then drive to Leeds for a session with Wilf: do an hour's work with weights at Carnegie College, then back to the track for some sprints, and drive home to Rotherham feeling like a zombie. The 1,500 trial against Seb was even billed in the *programme* as "Apprentice takes on the Master". When I won but was not selected, I was really disappointed – though when I look back, I was peaking in July and he was just starting out for the Olympics. That's what counts. At that age, I was naïve.

There is something fascinatingly harsh about an Olympic Games, as though all the animals in Kruger Park were rounded up and put in cages, and then released in front of an audience to see which animal is left standing at the finish. An Olympic Games can be cruel: that is partially why there is nothing quite the same. Waiting in one cage, in 1984, was the quite exceptional Joaquim Cruz of Brazil, bronze medallist at the World Championships: the twenty-one-year-old son of a poor carpenter in a near-slum suburb of Brasilia. Oliveira had been coaching him since he was eleven, though he had been involved as a youth as much in basketball as athletics. He was sixteen before he received his first pair of spikes, and immediately improved his 1,500 metres time by twelve seconds. Equally to be feared was Earl Jones from Eastern Michigan University, just twenty, and running faster almost week by week. In the US trials he had shared an American record with Johnny Gray of 1:43.74, though Jones had been beaten by Cruz earlier in the season. Coe, Ovett and Elliott were about to enter unknown territory; Coe's world record three years previously was not likely now to give him much protection. Besides Cruz, Gray and Jones, a formidable range of runners was gathering for the two-lap event: Marshall, the third American, who had run under 1:44; the two Kenyans, Koskei and Konchellah; Ferner, the European champion; Fall of Senegal, and Guimaraes, another of Oliveira's athletes who had featured in Coe's record run.

The series of heats and semi-finals over three days was exceptional, becoming steadily faster. The winning times in the second round by Cruz, Jones, Konchellah and Koech of Kenya were fast enough to have won medals in Moscow, while in the semi-finals Cruz ran 1:43.82 and Coe 1:45.51. After the semi-final, I drove Seb and Peter back to the Village, before returning with Peter to downtown LA, where he caught his regular bus back to a friend's house at Long Beach. Father and son had not talked that much on the journey down the Santa Monica–San Diego freeway to Westwood. There was not that much to say. Each knew that the pattern they had devised was taking shape. Now it was up to the athlete. Before Peter caught his bus, he sent his son a message on the video computer system which his son would be able privately to "key" open, with his personal identification number, the next morning in the Village. Peter thought that, while in Seb's opinion the man to track would be Cruz, Gray might be the one to watch. Peter's message said, in essence, "Remember it's seldom a two-horse race. Watch out. Love, Dad." The draw for the final, in lane order, was:

Earl Jones (USA), 1	Johnny Gray (USA), 5
Donato Sabia (Italy), 2	Joaquim Cruz, 6
Sebastian Coe (GB), 3	Steve Ovett (GB), 7
Billy Konchella (Kenya), 4	Edwin Keoch (Kenya), 8

Ovett, bothered by a respiratory condition for some time prior to the Games, only just made the final, literally throwing himself across the line to make it in fourth place by six-hundredths of a second. He was in distress after the fastest time he had run since the European Championships in Prague. Elliott had scratched from his semi-final because of his injury, too painful now even to begin to sprint.

In the first fifty metres or so of the final, Jones and Sabia were fractionally ahead of Coe, though out of the lane break it was Koech and Cruz leading from Jones, with Ovett fourth, a position he held going into the second bend ahead of Coe. Down the home straight, Coe went past Ovett to be third at the bell in 51.3, a stride-and-a-half down on Koech and Cruz, and with Jones at his shoulder on the inside. Coe was shadowing Cruz, holding his position until the final bend. At the same moment as Cruz kicked, 140 yards out, so did Coe. Cruz was surging clear, and Coe's kick pulled him fractionally away from Jones, who was moving wide to go past Koech. Ovett's bid had died at the end of the second back-straight, while Gray also was out of touch. I had been asked beforehand by friends, keen to place a bet, where I thought Ovett might finish: and had replied that it was less a matter of "where" than "whether". Ovett would trail in last.

Off the bend and into the final straight, Coe glanced behind inside, but the only threat was there out in front: and pulling still further away. Cruz had settled the gold medal between 130 and 70 metres out. Down the straight, Coe and Jones battled in front of Koech, who was fading badly. The last ebb of Coe's kick edged him away from

Jones, but Cruz was home by a clear four and a half metres. The Brazilian had lowered the Olympic record to 1:43.00, and was the first from his country ever to win an Olympic track title. Coe's second silver medal at this distance was the first reward of his incredible recovery.

SC: One thing that final proved to me, apart from the likelihood that I was getting too old for the event, was how uneducated, athletically, the Los Angeles public was. By the time of the medal ceremony for the 1,500, almost the whole crowd had gone, and so had most of the security staff. British spectators were able to walk into the middle of the in-field. The fact was, *no* American had featured in the medals. At the finish, I'd put my arm around Steve in commiseration, and said, "I think we're too old to be playing with fire" – not realizing how bad a shape he was in. A few minutes later, down in the tunnel leaving the track, he was down on his hands and knees, looking very ill and ashen white. I was really concerned, and he didn't answer when I asked if he was OK. I went to get him a drink, and could see that he had cramp in his hands. The medics, who had panicked out on the track, now seemed quite uninterested when he was out of public view. I thought he was having a heart attack, and eventually they rushed him to hospital. The next day, British team managers pleaded with him not to run in the 1,500, but I knew enough about Steve to expect that he would, though I felt worried for Rachel. For two days, she was walking around in extreme anxiety.

Cruz's gold medal was bringing him acclaim: and problems. Instead of being able to have a quiet meal and an early night, in preparation for the 1,500 metres, he had no food and was kept up until three in the morning waiting for a telephone call of congratulations from the President of Brazil, Figueredo. By the day of the 1,500 heats, he had a sore throat, but was unable to take normal medication because of fear of being positive on a drug test. "He won his heat in 3:41, but I had to scratch him from the semi-final as he was getting worse," Oliveira says. "That did me a lot of damage in Brazil. I was criticized by the athletics federation, called a mercenary. It was said I was afraid he would tarnish his image and thereby lose money in Europe. Yet if he'd been healthy he could have won a medal."

Andy Norman says that his advice to Ovett had been *not* to run the 800 metres in Los Angeles, but to concentrate on his main distance.

Steve had disagreed with the whole idea of the World Championships the previous year [Norman says]. He had this notion that it was another competition got up by "you and your mates" to generate money, whereas I assured him it would become one of the main events of the athletics calendar. For Helsinki, the *women* on the Board council kept him out of the 800 metres. For

LA, I was opposed, too. I tried to tell him, "It's no longer a tactical race, the Americans will run 1:45 and look over their shoulder and laugh." But I think his wife was maybe pushing him to do both events, because she felt he could have won the previous year when the title had been taken by Wülbeck.

Indications of the respiratory problem which Ovett was to encounter in LA had been there the previous winter, upon his return to England from Australia. There had been a cough which kept him and his wife awake at night, and eventually bronchial infection was diagnosed, a course of antibiotics costing him two weeks training in the middle of May. In the heats and semi-final of the 800 in LA, he had experienced a numbness in his forearms, with his thumb and forefingers locked together, and was unable properly to shake hands at the end of the race. He had chosen to ignore these serious symptoms, suggesting to Rachel that it was on account of the heat, and he had better start taking more fluids. For his breathing difficulties following the fast semi-final he had been given the same inhalant spray by the British medical department that had been used by the hockey players. In the final he admitted to being close to fainting.

I'd been fine and was running exceptionally well during preparation in San Diego before the Games [Ovett says]. Some of my training times were the best ever. I was on a high, even though I was training harder than ever. When I went to LA, the climate hit me like a brick. Within hours, I had the symptoms of a viral attack, but my mind wouldn't accept it. I couldn't believe my luck that this should happen, and I thought I could run through it. I carried on purely *because* it was the Olympics. Not that I think you should die for the Olympics, especially when you have a family. But I didn't think it was as serious as it was. After the 800, I promised Rachel that if I had a problem in the 1,500, I'd run off the track. I'd felt that the tests I had in hospital were by American doctors looking for a cause which would *exonerate* smog. Clinically, things were uncertain; the doctors could not guarantee that after three rounds of the 1,500 the same occurrence would not happen. But they seemed to think I could not do myself any serious harm. Frank Dick came to my house in LA to try to persuade me not to run, and I sensed that the British Olympic Association were probably taking a soft option: that if I withdrew, then no-one would be ruffled, apart from me.

I wasn't against Steve continuing [Harry Wilson says]. Beforehand, I'd thought if he scraped into the final of the 800, he would have done well. The training in San Diego *was* better than ever, and I felt more confident about winning the 1,500 than at any time since '81. The pins and needles and chest pains started just before the 800 heats. You get accustomed to colds, but when an athlete loses sense in his arms after repetition-training, you know something's wrong. I sympathize with Steve, wanting to go for the one per cent chance in the 1,500. It was difficult for Rachel to understand, though I'd worried when his pulse was still 160/170 an hour-and-a-half after the 800 final. We talked over the 1,500 and Steve said, "What if they do three laps in 62 seconds, then I'm in with a chance." It's like the boxer saying, "I may land one punch." Seb must have felt the same when he had a cold at the Commonwealth Games in Auckland: "Things might turn out for me." I don't think a coach can *make* an athlete either train hard, *or* stop him. They have to decide for themselves, so that afterwards there can be no recriminations.

The first semi-final of the 1,500 metres was potentially the more severe, with ten of the twelve starters all serious candidates to reach the final; only the first four, and the four fastest losers from either race would qualify for the final. Coe was lying a comfortable second behind Abascal coming off the last bend. Over the last fifty metres, Coe eased as Scott moved through to take second place. Coe failed to notice that both Chesire of Kenya and Wirz of Switzerland were accelerating from behind and about to pass him on either side. He lunged at the tape to hold third place by two-hundredths of a second. Had he been fifth, he might have been eliminated, if his had not been the faster heat. In fact, though he stood rigid with anxiety to look up at the re-run on the huge television screen and see whether he had made third place, the first seven from this heat went through. Ovett was in Cram's semi-final; Cram would win, and Ovett, second into the final straight, would hold on to fourth place at the line, once more in distress and taken to the medical centre for attention.

SC: Prior to the final, at no stage did I ever feel I was anything but, at worst, Cram's equal. He'd had an injury problem, but I knew he was now fit, and therefore dangerous. What encouraged me was that in my opinion Cram has sometimes misjudged his racing programme prior to championships. So that when I was training in Chicago, and not racing, running the way I needed, and Steve was still busy racing, saying that this was what got him fit, I felt that I was right and he was wrong. I'd been so eager to get to LA and get into it. The mood was so different from Moscow, which I'd never been eager for. That had been a *reluctant* show-down.

Following the semi-final, I had driven back slowly in the darkness to the University of California at Los Angeles (UCLA) with Coe. He was calmer than I had ever seen him before, prior to a major race. It was almost as though he were going on holiday, rather than running in an Olympic final which was the climax of a year of superhuman effort and determination to rescue his reputation. On arrival at Westwood, he jogged up the steps into the Village, and I could sense that it was the gait of a man who would sleep untroubled.

The finalists who would go to the line the following day were:

Joseph Chesire (Kenya)	Jim Spivey (USA)
Sebastian Coe (GB)	Omar Khalifa (Sudan)
Steve Scott (USA)	Peter Wirz (Switzerland)
José Abascal (Spain)	Steve Ovett (GB)
Andres Vera (Spain)	Anthony Rogers (NZ)
Steve Cram (GB)	Riccardo Materazzi (Italy)

SC: I never saw Cram in LA, apart from in the stadium, because he was outside the Village in a condominium down the coast. I often had lunch or trained together with Walker, Abascal and some of the others. It was a slightly strange situation, in that both Cram and I were with the same shoe company, Nike, who hardly took any notice of me in LA, as though I was something of an embarrassment. Nike had clearly estimated that Cram was their man for the future, and that my endorsement now mattered little. Shortly after the Olympics I decided to switch to Diadora, the Italian manufacturers.

For Scott, to win an Olympic title on his own doorstep was the dream of dreams. He lives just down the coast from Los Angeles, and for seven years he had been moving among the best of the world's runners on equal terms. He had already shared in many outstanding races, and had taken the silver medal in Helsinki, the previous year, behind Cram.

Not having been able to compete because of the boycott in 1980, I had an inflated idea about what the Olympic Games were going to be [Scott reflects]. Day by day, with the approach to the Games, I became as tightened as a spring. If I'd had the same mental relaxation as I'd had in '83, I might have pulled it off . . . maybe not beaten Seb, who was fantastic that day. I was able to handle it all, up until the *final*. I don't think I slept more than an hour the night before: the anticipation, the anxieties, the adrenalin pumping through me all night. To be the leader in the second lap, which was my plan, I had to have the relaxation to hold it, and control it up front, with the pressure of being there in front of a home crowd. I was afraid of Cram more than Coe, because of the way the year had gone for Coe. There was no way you could perceive Seb having the kind of Olympics he did. In discussions with Len Miller, my coach, I had said it had to be Cram to look out for. I know how to pick 'em, don't I! I feel Coe's was the best performance I've ever seen, considering the facts – his illness, his second victory, his ability *totally* to focus on a single event. He never raced as much as the rest of us, he only ever raced for a purpose, and cared little for minor events.

Scott was a talented golfer and recreational javelin thrower, who had come into athletics as a former baseball pitcher. Besides his silver medal and his defeat in London of an ailing Coe the previous year, his mile in Oslo in 1982, 3:47.69, a stride outside Coe's record, was testimony to his talent. At twenty-eight he was at an ideal stage of his career for this moment. Before the Games, he had been saying: "Hardly anyone is thinking about Coe and Ovett anymore. They're just faces in the crowd. Anyone of eight in the final could win." In an interview with *Track and Field News*, Len Miller said: "There isn't any single factor that is most outstanding about Steve except what I call resilience . . . the ability to come back from a disappointing performance or defeat with renewed dedication, enthusiasm and confidence. I've seen a lot of potentially great athletes sidetracked by defeat. But with Steve, it seems that with each defeat he becomes more steadfast in his determination." Scott had been defeated often enough by Coe, Cram and Ovett. This should have been his moment.

"The excitement was the opportunity of a clean sweep by Britain," Bedford recalls. "They all had problems: Cram his injury, Ovett his breathing, Coe his illness, yet the chance was there. It was an incredible possibility for the sport in our country." Frank Dick was in two minds about the outcome. "I didn't know which way it would go," he says. "For Cram to have won he would have had to go for a long burnout, his usual style. But that would have been a brave thing to do, especially against a background of injury, and knowing that Coe was a terrier who was fit. It's a huge decision, to take over at the front: that's your *statement*, and you've nothing left to draw on." Derek Ibbotson was convinced Coe would win. "After a series like the 800, I just couldn't see anyone beating him," Ibbotson says. "Maybe that's Yorkshire bias, but I felt that Seb's speed would give it to him, once we'd seen he was back to his best. It was extraordinary that for such a light runner he had such strength. He must have had a phenomenal training background." Mel Watman reflects: "I couldn't understand anyone wanting Elliott instead of Coe at that time. Coe ran the 800 as well or better than he was likely to. The 1,500 was one of the greatest of all Olympic runs. I expected it to be, because I have always thought there was a different, *special* quality about him." Svein-Arne Hansen says: "When you look at how exhausted Cruz was after four races, the series of seven by Coe was something incalculable." "It was," Chris Brasher says, "perfection."

SC: I went down from the Village for the final in a car with Harry Wilson and Luiz Oliveira. We chatted on the way, at the end of which Oliveira said that he was going to scratch Joaquim because he had a cold, and Harry said, "It wouldn't have anything to do with being *knackered*, would it?"

As the runners went to the line for the start, briefly delayed by the medal ceremony for the 4 x 400 relay, in which Akabusi, Cook, Bennett and Brown had taken the silver for Britain behind the USA, the western end of the stadium was already in evening shadow. Looking at Ovett, there was no hint for the moment of all the traumas of the past week. There was a magnificence in his muscular profile, an echo back to the days of the ancient Olympic Games, with the strong face, barrel chest and slim hips. If you looked a little closer, perhaps you could detect a slight pinched anxiety in the eyes. Coe might have been about to run alone: withdrawn, focused, introspective. He knew how he was going to run, whatever anyone else might do.

The early pace was made by Khalifa, a former Loughborough student and a consistent runner at international level. Close behind him at the end of the first lap were Chesire, Coe and Scott. Ovett and Cram were lying seventh and eighth, trailing Abascal. Materazzi had stumbled and almost fallen on the second bend.

Down the back straight the second time, Scott, conspicuous in a vivid red vest, made a sudden twenty-yard surge, carrying him past Khalifa, Chesire and Coe. Here was Scott's plan to make it a fast race dramatically taking shape. Cram and Ovett were still in the middle of the pack. Around the third bend, Coe closed on Scott, passing Khalifa and Chesire, with Cram closely following on his heels. Along the home straight for the second time, Scott led, with Coe running wide in the second lane, Abascal having taken up fourth place just ahead of Cram. After 700 metres, with two laps to go, the order was: Scott, Coe, Khalifa and Abascal, Cram, Ovett, Chesire. Ovett had just made an unavailing effort to gain ground.

As the runners moved down the back-straight for the third time, Scott having maintained his lead to the 800 mark in 1:56.8, it became apparent that Scott was ailing. Going into the fifth bend, Abascal, a shy man from Santander, who spent much of the year training in Catalonia as a member of Barcelona Football Club, rounded Scott to pick up the pace. He knew he had to maintain the level of his challenge if he were still to be in contention at the finish. Coe and Cram, as though on automatic pilot, slotted in behind Abascal. Scott's bid for glory had come and gone, though by extending the second lap he had invaluably helped set the stage for Coe.

Coming into the straight towards the bell, Ovett was running wide in fourth place but visibly struggling, the fierce pace draining the remnants of his strength with every stride. At the bell Abascal, Coe and Cram moved in line-astern, two yards separating each from the next man. Abascal was three-tenths of a second up on Coe, with a time of 2:39.0. Scott was now disappearing behind Spivey into sixth place. As Ovett entered the sixth bend, fortitude gave way to common-sense. The chest pains were returning, and with them recollections of his wife's pleading beforehand. He gently ran off the track, as the field in front of him surged away towards their moment of success or failure.

The crescendo of the race was being reached as the runners approached the last bend. Coe and Cram fanned out, in line-abreast, to take Abascal. Coe was unaware as Cram summoned all that was left, in an attempt to pass the man who still stood between him and ultimate acclaim. As Cram came into peripheral view over Coe's right shoulder, Coe gave him a half-glance, kicked . . . and was gone. On the crown of the bend, Coe again looked behind down both sides, and saw that there was now only one man to beat.

Into the home straight, Coe led by two metres: and now he gave his third kick. Cram was unable to respond as Coe moved further away, balanced and rhythmic. Cram tried all he knew, just in case Coe's surge should falter, but now Cram's limbs were flailing and his face twisted, his effort distorting his flow rather than assisting it. On the run to the line, Coe stretched his lead to six metres, setting a new Olympic record of 3:32.53, thereby lowering the time set by Keino in Mexico City sixteen years before. Way behind him, Chesire and Spivey, streaming past Scott, had failed in a vain bid to wrest the bronze medal from Abascal. A sad Scott would finish tenth.

Ovett had been carried away on a stretcher, arms and fingers numb, eyes glazed. "The image in my mind as the field went through the bell was for Britain to finish one, two and three," Brasher recalls. "And they *were* one, two and three in the world. Many other recollections are obscured by the memory of Ovett and his courage, knowing that if he did have a serious virus infection, he was putting his life in danger. I've known people who had a virus, went out for violent exercise, and died: for example, Mike Wells-Cole, a British orienteering champion. I coached him. He was doing repetitions on a Sunday afternoon in Richmond Park, went home and collapsed, and was dead."

Ovett, ten years on, remains dispassionate about the experience:

It *was* a shame but, oh well, just another race. Maybe it was horrible to watch for others, though I think that anyone in my position would probably have done the same. If I'd not tried, I'd have questioned myself the rest of my life. I was looking forward to it, the adrenalin was up for the race, I had the old excitement. Other people in other walks of life are ill, and no-one notices. Athletes in a sense are the most unfit people there are, riding a permanent line between super-fit and sick. Most club athletes are ill some of the time, but they never get the publicity. I did promise Rachel that if I had the same problem I'd come off. With 350 to go, my heart couldn't expand, wouldn't work properly, and so I said to myself, "Don't be silly, it's only a race." It *would* have been nice if all three of us could have come down the home straight together, something for the albums. Instead, I had to take the rest of the year off.

While Ovett was busy wondering, down in the medical centre, whether he had destroyed his health, Coe was celebrating the destruction of his critics. As he crossed the line, a momentary expression of intense pleasure turned to a grimace of anger. Looking up at the press and television ranks to his right with a scowl, he bellowed: "Who says I'm finished?" It was a moment of absolute vengeance, of satisfaction, of proof. Yet within half a minute or so, the aggression had subsided, and off he went on a lap of honour, his image of himself re-created, his father vindicated. For a while he would have no space for thinking about the fate of the rival from Moscow who was nowadays his friend.

Abascal was admitting that he had made his run too soon; his coach had said he should wait until he was 500 out, and he had gone at 600. Whereas in Helsinki he had waited too long, this day he had gone too early. Scott was dejected but not broken. He'd run his plan, and had failed it. "I wanted it to be a true milers' race, not a *kickers'* race," he said. "Len and I reckoned everyone would be dead on their feet if I made it fast from the second lap. But the opposite was true: I was dead on *my* feet! The Olympics are pretty nerve-wracking, and now I know why they have them only every four years. If they had them any more often, there would be a lot of athletic alcoholics. I just didn't have it on the day. I gave it all I had. It was a great experience, and I had a great time." Here was an Olympian.

SC: I could remember smiling for the last few strides of the race. The elation changed as soon as I crossed the line to a huge tank of anger, and seven years later I still cannot fully understand this overwhelming feeling. There are points in your life when you wonder about your state of sanity. If I had had a gun in my hand at that moment, I might not be sitting here now. It was anger bordering on hatred. The anger was not aimed at the press any more than at other people, commentators inside and outside sport. It just happened that the press box was there, it was an easy target. It wasn't something I am proud of, and it haunts me still. When great moments in sport are shown, it's always there, on file, and I wish it wasn't . . .

My next thought was "Where's my old man?". I needed to catch his eye. We'd been through a lot together. That last thirty yards, when you're at an absolute limit, is always agonizing, knowing that there's nothing extra you can find. You have to think like a sprinter. Forget the discipline of a middle-distance runner, think like a 200 metre man on a rolling start: arm action, don't let your head sit back, make sure you have a high knee-lift, don't tense the shoulders, raise the arms and hands. That's why speed drills are so important in training. In those last thirty yards, I didn't know where Cram was, what the race had done to him. Looking at the last hundred metres in Moscow, Brussels and LA, I might not satisfy a sprint coach, I might not look like Carl Lewis, but I look more the part than many middle-distance runners.

There was the exhilaration of taking it through the gears on the final 400, and hitting top gear off the last bend. There's nothing more doom-laden than reaching that crown and finding there's nothing there, like Gateshead the year before. When a shape became apparent at my shoulder down the back-straight, a tall white vest, I didn't know instantly whether it was Cram or Ovett. Then I saw it *was* Cram: so I went past Abascal, who was faltering. Maybe I went a shade earlier than I would have wished, but I knew so well that Cram prefers the lead round the final bend, likes to build on that, and that he's *less* happy if he's following you. That was always my game plan: to keep him under pressure and never let him lead. The early pressure was applied for me by Scott, and then by Abascal. When Scott had taken the lead on the third bend, I was comfortable, and was glad, because his speed was providing me with more space to run in, more than if we were niggling around at 3:40 pace. It was like Moscow with Straub: I felt more comfortable at a hard pace than with a big scramble over the last 200 metres, given my small physique. The LA final could have been a Grand Prix, with people in there to make the pace. Khalifa, whom I knew extremely well, who had stayed at Steve Mitchell's house, started it all, and I felt so good. My only uncomfortable race had been the sixth, the semi-final. Once we were into the third lap, even though I couldn't see Cram, I didn't think there'd be any argument about gold and silver other than between him and me, though I wasn't wanting him to appear yet! From the bell, I sensed that Abascal was already at his limit. At every stage, the race was becoming clearer. I had no real sense of the crowd, though beforehand I'd been aware how much they were non-specialists, not under-standing what they were watching, many of them there only for the closing ceremony.

In assessment of what I've said previously in *Running Free*, about record-breaking meaning more to me than championships, I know after LA and Stuttgart, and Seoul, which I missed, that championship series are as different as chalk from cheese. My mistake in Moscow was that I probably was looking at the 800 like another one-off at Zurich. After LA, I really appreciated what the Championship series means, and that was why I was so sad and annoyed about Seoul. On reflection, my feeling that world records were more import-ant to me, which I genuinely believed at the time, were a subjective, almost sub-conscious escape from the claustrophobia of Moscow and the problems that gave me. When I said that previously, I was wanting to get back to what I *knew* I could do well. The significance of what you do in the Olympics doesn't become apparent for some years. The view I expressed in 1981 was, with hindsight, incorrect.

The day after the final I went for a run on the beach, and then off to Zurich, expecting to run against Aouita, who'd won the 5,000 metres. He'd now started to say that if he'd run the 1,500, he'd have won it. Well, he had the choice and went for what I am sure he regarded as the easier option. Whatever he thought of me, he'd lost to Cram over 1,500 in Helsinki. The story of

Aouita, a stupendous runner, is one of careful race selection, right through to 1989. He's a fabulous runner, but we've never known what distance he was going to run from day to day the whole of his career. The astonishing thing about him is that he was within range of world record time at every distance from 800 to 10,000 metres, the widest simultaneous range of anyone since Nurmi.

Final thoughts of LA rest with Jimmy Hedley and Steve Scott. "I was sitting right on the finishing line," Hedley recollects. "I was so upset. Yet Seb came over specially, thrilled as he was, to say hello and ruffle my hair in affection. I'd thought Steve was in with a chance, but Seb was flowing that day. I'd have loved to see them both fully fit at the same moment. The world record would have gone out of the window." Scott says: "No-one was going to beat Coe. He was a man with a mission".

VII · Bonanza

From the late 1970s onwards, money was pouring into athletics: from sponsors, from television, from an enthusiastic public. Increasingly, much of it was finding its way into the pockets of performers. Just how beneficial this would be for the sport in the long-term, only time would tell. By the end of the 1980s, it was already apparent that the flood of money was having a corrupting influence, not only on morality, but on performance. Runners who race every other day will be decreasingly likely to break records. Equally worrying was the extent to which the money was failing to find its way into the grass-roots of the sport for the development of future athletes. At the end of the most successful decade in the sport's history, moreover, Britain still had no major stadium. Priorities could be warped. Following the 1986 European Championships in Stuttgart, there was a firework display at the conclusion of the final domestic meeting of the season at Crystal Palace, during which Frank Dick observed: "They're putting more money up in the air in ten minutes than I have for my field events budget for a year."

More than most sports, performance in athletics has a direct relation to the time and technique devoted to training. A side-effect of the phenomenon of the 1980s – running for money – was inevitably a reduction in rate of improvement at the highest level, as Frank Dick emphasises.

With the rise in the frequency of competition [Dick says], the chances of achievement each year are lessening. If you look at Cram's record at 1,500 metres in major championships, between '82 and '84 his record was first, first and second. If you look at his record between '86 and '88, it has become first, eighth and fourth. The planning for an Olympic gold medal has to be phased in advance over three years, so the athlete must deliberately calculate years "on" and years "off". The need for phasing underlines just how good Coe and Ovett were. It may have helped Seb mentally to be "off" with illness in '82–'83. In both years he was racing right up to the time of the championships which he missed, and therefore was not becoming ring rusty, yet not having the stress of championships. The problem now is that promoters are breeding an era of paced runners, who may not be able to *think* in championships. That's one of the reasons why the Kenyans remain so good, always varying their pace and their kicking. The mental drain in championship racing is huge, as opposed to even-pace, paced running.

The Grand Prix scene may have this effect [Harry Wilson agrees]. It may slow down the record-making progress. You can't have an athlete saying to a promoter, who has a huge crowd and television cameras sitting waiting, "I don't want a fast race." As a coach, you know that with five tough races in five weeks, you have to reduce training. So inevitably you lose the endurance factor. Yet this is one of the *essentials* in middle and long-distance running. I warned Frank Dick several years ago that we, the coaches, couldn't say to our athletes any longer, "The objective is the Olympic Games in three or four years' time." We used to be able to tell athletes to have a year off, to enjoy themselves, to relax. That's vital. But now, if you're full-time, it's your living. It will become the same with the European Championships, with which you would plan a year to peak for one race. Now, that's impossible because of commercial considerations. I'm critical, but I wouldn't want to alter things, because an athlete's talent belongs to him, and why shouldn't he earn a living, like golfers and tennis players?

Roger Bannister, however, adds the important rider that professional athletes are possibly training too much. As a medical scientist, he has the same interests as Dave Martin. "It has not been proven how many hours you have to train to produce *optimum* condition at world-record level," Bannister says. "So much depends on the quality of training, but the consequence of running full-time is that many athletes are expanding their training to fill the time available. If they're not working, they feel they should be doing more."

There is a deeper iniquity in professionalism, of course, than the threat to improvement and record-breaking. It is the threat to sportsmanship, to morality and to the health of the athlete. By performance-enhancing drugs. "Money can be an incentive, it can help develop an athlete's career," Wilf Paish says, "yet it is the cancer of our sport, because it is the quest for money that leads to the use of drugs and blood-doping." And as Dave Bedford reflects, dismayed at the 1990 revelation of a positive drug test on Butch Reynolds, the American world record-holder in the 400 metres:

Reynolds came over as being a nice person. This was a shock. It leads you to ask questions about everyone. I would have staked my life that Reynolds was *clean*. Aouita's talent is awesome, and I just hope he's clean. If I was an official of the IAAF, I'd put every competitor on lie detectors, not drug tests. Lie detectors are reckoned to be accurate.

It would be difficult to tell at how early on an adolescent might become even mentally corrupted by a realization of the possibility offered by drugs for improving performance. Certainly it is true that, following the revelation of Ben Johnson's positive testing in 1988, such a wave of requests for access to drugs from young athletes swept through American clubs that the US federation, TAC, spent £50,000 on a publicity campaign to counter the trend. What is clear, however, is that the making of great athletes has usually been founded in their early teenage years, with their motivation being a simple ambition for excellence: as existed for such champions as Owens and Lovelock long ago, right up to the time of the emergence of Ovett, Thompson and Coe in the mid 1970s. The arrival of the first cheques from sponsorship, endorsements and Grand Prix prizes came after Ovett, Thompson and Coe had already done much of their hard work.

SC: By the end of 1977, there was starting to be "generous" expenses, of £100 or so. Overseas, it was maybe less generous, because I'd not yet achieved anything, and it was especially so for me, as an integral part of what I was doing involved the cost of Peter being there with me. However, by the end of '78, we'd registered a small company, PNC Enterprises, through which we could put all the payments. Although at that time payments for running had yet to be approved by the IAAF – never mind that it had been happening with top runners for fifty years – we kept the Inland Revenue notified of all income, so that there could never be any comeback from them. In 1979, I was breaking world records without any shoe or clothing contract. I was wearing Nike shoes, simply because they were comfortable. My kit was from Viga in Halifax, because they handled the distribution of the then little-known Nike. I'd been given shoes by Adidas in '76, and found them uncomfortable. When I was sitting in the hotel lobby in Oslo in 1979, waiting to go to the track, having just come from the European Cup semi-final in Malmö, I had nothing other than my UK kit, and a university sweat-shirt top. I approached the Nike representative and told him I wore their shoes. "What do you do?" he asked. I said that I had worn Nike shoes in Prague, the first medal for their shoes outside the United States. I felt I had shown a bit of neck approaching him, but got little reaction. Five hours later, I ran 1:42, and the fellow was leaping the fence to get at me before any other sharks could move in.

This was the first break-through for Coe, commercially as well as athletically. The previous year, after running at Gateshead – where a local councillor had been trying to stir up trouble for Brendan Foster, the meeting promoter, over excessive expenses – the police had been to interview Coe and many others for evidence, and had gone away empty-handed.

SC: At that stage, I don't remember the comparison between what I was unofficially getting for a race and, say, the top Welsh Rugby Union player. As the British record-holder, driving to Edinburgh for the UK championships, I claimed for petrol and one meal, and was having to argue with the Scottish treasurer who claimed that petrol was more expensive than a second-class rail fare. My approach to racing was always that the importance of the race came *first*. There *was* money to race abroad, but in my early days nothing at all domestically; and there was a general mood of resentment about expenses among AAA officials. If I went to Switzerland, say, I might go to Macolin for training two weeks beforehand, and the cost of that and the physiotherapy would be offset against the fee of, say, $5,000. There was considerable frustration among British runners. Foreign stars were being paid to come, by British officials who would remove *your* amateur status if you were caught taking anything. It had nearly happened to Dave Bedford at the time of the Olympic Games in 1972. There was no pressure on officials to change, because there were no sponsors and little television. Things only altered when sponsors realized that athletics was a good vehicle, and when officials recognized that if they were going to get the leading competitors to the sponsored meetings, then they had to recompense them.

The generation of Foster, Pascoe, Wells, Ovett and myself bridged the gap. We came into the sport as seniors knowing that financial reward *might* turn out to be there. The idea wasn't new to the sport. On the Scandinavian circuit it had been there for years, back in the days of Brasher, Bannister, Chataway and Ibbotson. Brendan Foster recalls the time when Andy Norman began to take control of the Coca-Cola meeting in the early Seventies. Norman asked, "What do you want?" and Brendan realized he was offering money. It was Brendan who took me aside in '79 and warned that, irrespective of what the sport might think, what was important was a tax declaration: "Have an accountant, and make a tax report." After my 800 record in Oslo, the Nike rep wasn't bothered about congratulating me, only about how soon I could be persuaded to make a trip to their headquarters in Eugene.

I never knew how much Coe was receiving for his Nike endorsement, though it would have been none too difficult to find out. I always preferred to think of him as an athlete rather than a billboard. I would suppose that the Nike contract must have been worth approaching a quarter of a million pounds over four or five years. On the track, he and Ovett were well aware of what they might together have earned from their rivalry between 1979 and 1982, but it was not until 1982 that trust funds were introduced, enabling racing-for-money to become legal. Encouraged by his father – to my mind ill-advisedly, as proved to be the case – Coe placed some of his commercial affairs with the International Management Group, in the wake of his three world records in 1979. IMG had no experience of athletics, knew little of the sensitivity with which an international athlete's schedule has to be planned, and thought that the aggressive, bulldozer approach which worked so well for other individual clients, with tournament pro-moters in golf and tennis, could be similarly effective for Coe. Initially it was. The Coe folio was placed in the hands of a breezy, personable young IMG aide, Robert Jackson. "When Jackson negotiated a fee for Seb's 1,000 metres appearance in 1980, we almost fell off our chairs at the meeting in London", Svein-Arne Hansen recalls. "Seb was the first to have an agent. He was asking for $17,500. But we were happy enough, because we knew Seb delivered, and when he came back in '81, he got $20,000." Coe soon found that the hustling of promoters by IMG was doing his reputation little good, so that he and Peter returned to dealing with these matters themselves. "With agents, it was no longer the same business," Andreas Brügger says. "However, Coe never asked for a specific fee, he left it to us to pay what we thought was right. He did so much for the Zurich meeting that we had reason to pay him well. He was never running endlessly, 25 races a year, but planning carefully, so that you felt privileged if he was in your meeting."

SC: With IMG, it got to the point where I preferred to handle many issues myself. I remained with them until 1986, and left after the European Championships in Stuttgart. I was probably the only athlete of theirs who was never under contract. The only other sportsman who left them was Niklaus, and it cost him two-and-a-half million dollars to buy his way out. It wasn't that there was any lack of commercial ability, but at the time I left, my career was moving in a new direction. IMG had too many people on their books for my liking. If you were a golfer, playing eleven months of the year, going from hotel to hotel, then having them do everything was fine. They have a huge input with most of the golf tournaments. But that wasn't going to be my kind of career. They never handled on-track activities for me, after '81. I didn't want an agent walking into a promoter's office to claim what I was worth. I didn't want people saying things about me that I would not know. I was aware there was an attitude in which IMG would shift commercial opportunities from one client to another, who had perhaps received less impetus in a particular year. I got to hear about a television offer for me only months after it had been turned down. It's for the same reason – that he's attempting to look after the interests of more than a hundred athletes – that in my opinion it is difficult for Kim McDonald adequately to look after all of them.

What Peter and I needed with IMG initially was a buffer from all the demands, the sudden massive interest from abroad. Yet it had reached the point in 1986, at the age of 29, where everything in athletics was a bonus, outside the mainstream of my life. I was sure by then that I wanted a political career. I had sensed that my involvement with the Sports Council from 1983, and then as vice-chairman in 1986, was not harmonious with an involvement with IMG, that there was a conflict of interest between public life and commercial deals. IMG had little understanding of public affairs, of a non-sports profile, of taking on public duties that were "loss-leaders" for later objectives. Hertz have always looked after me with a car since the early Eighties, and I've sat with them round the boardroom table. I wouldn't want IMG in *there*. Nor did I want them involved in the media field. I had many good friends among press and television who could advise me there. So there were too many exclusive areas for it to continue to be comfortable with IMG. If you want to hammer out a contract with C & A, then they're excellent: that's one commercial field dealing with another. But IMG didn't understand athletics: they sent no-one to the championships in Stuttgart in '86.

As with most evolutions, that in athletics inevitably drew its criticisms. To this day, there are many among those aged over forty, and even some of the younger generation, who retain a concept of the Olympic Games as an amateur event. That it has not been so for twenty years or more has been evident to anybody closely associated with it. When Avery Brundage, the then president of the International Olympic Committee, hounded Karl Schranz, the Austrian skier, out of the 1972 Winter Games at Sapporo in Japan, on the accusation of professionalism, he was making an example of one among hundreds if not thousands. As skiing in the Alpine countries is as much an industry as a sport, the names of the leading skiers are as much a brand name within the industry as Ford or Renault. Frank McGhee, a long-standing commentator at the *Daily Mirror*, concluded his coverage of Los Angeles with the condemnation that the motto of the Games had now become "faster, higher, stronger . . . richer". Yet McGhee overlooked that one of the greatest heroes of his career as a journalist had been Muhammad Ali: who as Cassius Clay had emerged as an Olympic gold medal winner in 1960. For fifty years and more, the Olympic Games has been the springboard to professionalism in half a dozen sports, and the IOC was among the first to recognize an irresistible meiosis of ideologies, removing the word "amateur" from their Charter in 1973. The endorsement by the eligibility code for professionalism at the Olympics over the past ten years is further recognition of reality; a process which at the present time Rugby Union is finding emotionally impossible. The new World Cup will force their hands.

The IAAF, once they accepted the necessity, altered their legislation quite swiftly. The proposal for Trust Funds, into which athletes would be able to pay endorsement and sponsorship fees and appearance money – and later prize money – was first debated by the Congress at the time of the World Cup in Rome in 1981 and consolidated the next year in Athens. Andy Norman was one of those speaking decisively in Athens, warning national governing body representatives that, if they continued to turn a Nelsonian eye towards illegal payments and inflated expenses, they would be vulnerable to take-over by a professional circus. The principle of Trust Funds was that they were to be administered by the national federation, taking a minimum ten per cent to put towards coaching and development; and that the athlete, while continuing to compete, could draw money for training and other athletic expenses, the residue of the fund becoming available upon retirement from the sport. Britain is one of the minority of countries to operate the system as intended. In many instances elsewhere, the money has moved directly to the athlete's bank account.

After attending the memorial service in 1981 for Lord Exeter, former Olympic gold medal winner and life-long administrator in the sport, Coe was discussing the question of eligibility and payments with Primo Nebiolo, the IAAF president, when an IOC member, who shall be nameless, interrupted to say: "Surely, you don't want to pay tax!" The cat's-cradle of trust funds was to a great extent resolved by Robert Stinson, a former hurdling colleague of mine at Cambridge University, and subsequent honorary treasurer of the IAAF.

SC: Stinson did an excellent job drafting the regulations. The IAAF had made it clear that they would reject any threat to amateur status that might be brought by national federations. The benefit of Trust Funds, among others, is that if properly operated they provided discipline for young athletes, obliging them to ask for subventions and not to blow their money on stereos and cars. It was devised as a system to get international athletics moving as a unified body, to hold together west and east, the non-professional socialist countries; to enable them philosophically to accept mutual competition. Stinson, and others such as Luciano Barra, have to be complimented on getting that up and running. I think it's important we should maintain the system, and I have no objection about the federation taking a percentage, as long as I have the right to question how it is being spent: to know that it is being used as seed corn, and not on the promotion of another Decker–Budd circus. If the money is going straight to athletes, then the federation gets nothing. Nowadays, there's more autonomy allowed in the managing of funds. You may have an accountant maximizing the benefits for you, but I do think the fund is a safeguard for the protection of the young athlete from his or her own naïvety.

The approach to professionalism by Coe and his father had one fundamental principle: that the money was to be made primarily off the track rather than on it, that concentration on excellence in the latter would hugely multiply the former. It was better to win one major championship title, preferably the Olympic Games, rather than fifty or sixty indiscriminate one-off races, in anonymous cities over three years, for a few thousand pounds a throw. Coe's major income will have derived from Nike (1979–84), Horlicks, ICI and C & A, with a switch to Diadora equipment from 1984. He used his business instinct to grasp the opening as UK distributor for Diadora in 1987, and is now managing director of a company with an office staff of six. A conservative guess would suggest that his off-track commercial endorsements earned him well in excess of half a million pounds. What many will find surprising is that, between 1980 and 1984 alone, he rejected in excess of £300,000 in race fees; even more had he been willing to contemplate the Fifth Avenue mile in New York, worth over £15,000, and three times won by Peter Elliott. Over eleven years, Coe probably turned a blind eye to race fees totalling £500,000.

SC: If I'd gone for more of the money that was there for the taking on the track, I would never have won the second Olympic title. I've always believed there was so much more to what I was trying to do than the money, though I don't deny that the money has been nice. There were times when I would rather go on holiday than run another race for cash. And every race that Peter and I ever planned was scheduled for the requirements of my running development, and not for the money. The same considerations apply to the commercial sector. In 1981, I was offered £100,000 to appear in an advertisement for Brut, but after a series of discussions, I decided it wasn't me. It was the wrong image. I've never been panicked by the thought of the money drying up. I had a degree in economics, and whenever it was necessary, I could go and get a job. I wouldn't race twenty times a year or more just for the purpose of maintaining a larger house.

The unfortunate aspect of professionalism in athletics, compared to, say, tennis or soccer, is that you have to reach a higher standard before you become a real earner. It was possible for players such as Annabel Croft to earn over six-figure sums in a year when ranked outside the top twenty, which is nonsense when you compare that with what Wendy Sly has achieved as a silver medallist in Los Angeles, and the first women's road runner champion in 1983 when she won over 10 kilometres in San Diego. There are talented athletes who are barely meeting expenses. If you're ranked number eight in golf or tennis, you're made: if you're number eight in athletics, last in an Olympic final, you're an also-ran. Yet we as athletes work possibly harder for our success than anyone in sport other than nordic skiers or cyclists in the grand tours. I'm not bitching, but in tennis you're paid to practise. McEnroe and Gerulaitis could go and play a knockabout exhibition and earn £50,000. The fitness in tennis is laughable. I once set up a six-month basic fitness programme for Sarah Bentley, a young tennis player, and she came out of the LTA physiology testing centre at Bisham all smiles: they'd said she was the fittest person, man or woman, they'd seen in over four years! Can you really believe that all male players such as Castle are no fitter physically than Sarah Bentley.

It has to be said, on reflection, that neither of the Coes, father nor son, has ever gone out of his way to endear himself to officialdom in Britain; other that is than by winning medals. Before the European Championships in Athens, Peter was berating Bill Evans and Nigel

Cooper, the chairman and secretary of the Board respectively, for their constant complaints about the state of the Board's finances. "You break the first rule of business," Peter told them. "Never waste your assets for short-term gain. You cannot operate this way." It was the same approach he utilized over 22 years as his son's coach. "Anything between eight and fourteen races is enough for a season," Peter says, "and that's including the early build-up. What are others doing? They're pressurized by promoters, so that you found good runners with potential, like Dave Warren and Graham Williamson, seriously over-racing. I advised Ikem Billy that he should cut down drastically on his racing. Runners squander their talent instead of condensing it. How much authority are they willing to give to their coaches, how much guidance do they really want? I tried never to waste a single lap of Seb's energy."

The role of television in the development of athletics in the past decade has been anomalous. On the one hand, it has helped hugely to publicize and popularize the sport; on the other, it increasingly imposes conditions, exaggerations and demands that can only be damaging. Although there are some sensitive producers, directors and editors working in television, a majority are interested in television more than in sport, in today more than tomorrow, in promoting their own personality as much or more than that of the athlete. In 1985, Independent Television out-bid BBC for the screening of domestic British athletics and in the first year earned lasting criticism for their promotion of a meaningless revenge-match between Mary Decker and Zola Budd: criticism because of the disproportionate £90,000 that the contestants were receiving, meaningless because Decker was at the time so superior it would not be a race. Coe expressed his views on television's handling of his sport in an interview with John Rodda in *The Guardian*:

I think ITV made the mistake of attempting a revolution overnight when actually they had a contract for five years, time to put their style and shape on the coverage of the sport. Frankly, I think there was an air of arrogance about ITV. They were not satisfied with having got the contract and saying, "Fine, we're going to learn in the first year." Considering what went wrong last year, they got a very charitable reception from athletes, officials and sponsors. I'm not sure they'll get the same charity this year.

From a personal point of view there was one plus. ITV covered my club's [Haringey] European Clubs Championship meeting fully and I don't think the BBC would have done that had they held the contract. But on the other side there was the night when TV spent a lot of time hyping my 800 metres race against Steve Cram and then, because of advertisements, missed the first 120 metres of the race. As for the Decker–Budd race, I found the coverage of this event absolutely outrageous. I was incensed by the hype and promotion of it, and I thought it was the most disgusting piece of sports coverage I had ever seen on TV.

SC: I've never been happy with the subvention system of payments for appearance per meeting created by the Board with ITV in '85. In fact I received my best fee in Britain that year, £15,000 for running against Cram at 800 metres. Yet Metcalfe is on record as saying, "The days of athletes deciding when they run and against whom are over, we're going to have a say." What Metcalfe was saying in effect was: "We've paid £11m, we've got schedules to fill, sport is another arm of entertainment, athletics must be judged in the same way as advertising and Coronation Street." So it was obvious to me that the subvention system meant obligations to race: this is what you're worth, these are the events you have to race. It was totally alien. You have to draw the line between the principle of athletes receiving money, and the manner and style in which competitions are run in order to generate those sums of money; so that the sport is not damaged in the way it was after the European Championships in Split in 1990, by a Nike promotion in Munich that was *wholly* a vehicle for television.

The difficulty with so many of the commercial aspects of sport is that attitudes and enthusiasms vary directly with fluctuations in the market. Running shoe endorsement fees have reduced, for the majority of competitors, so much since the early 1980s, when Nike, Adidas, and Puma were, in Coe's words, "throwing money at anything that moved". The fees, however, have remained and become even more astronomic for a handful of leading performers. Boris Becker is said to be receiving $19 million for his contract with Puma – more than the turnover of some sports companies. The agent for Paul Gascoigne, touting him around the shoe companies and exaggeratingly claiming that the player was "better than Best and will be captain of England within the next two years", eventually obtained from Puma a three-year contract approaching £700,000.

The commercial world can have its pitfalls. This is no surprise to Coe, though he was uncomfortably associated with the demise of the Levitt Group, with the inevitable result that some of the mud that was flying unjustifiably came in his direction. This financial services company, formed in the late 1970s to handle mortgages, insurance and investments for clients, was the third largest financial services company in the country, with the backing of such commercial giants as Legal and General, Eagle Star and others. When Coe left the Sports Council, he was approached by Levitt to provide consultancy, in connection with work they would be doing for sports governing bodies. On that basis Coe joined them in 1989. He had been invited previously, but felt unable to do so before he left the Sports Council. From 1989, he worked for them one day a week; but at no time did he either introduce clients, or invest his own money with them. Realizing his inability to continue working satisfactorily for the group on a one-day-a-week basis, that the group had a leadership crisis, and that he was obliged to spend more and more time in Cornwall for the impending election, Coe resigned three weeks before going on holiday in November 1990, in advance of the company's collapse. The sports side of the company had been the only aspect of Coe's involvement, and it was thought that Alan Pascoe Associates were trying to buy into this section of the Levitt operation. Adverse publicity for the group inevitably highlighted the association with it of such high-profile figures as Coe and Adam Faith, whose own finance corporation was half-owned by Levitt. Condemnatory press articles seldom mentioned that such financial institutions as the Chase Manhattan Bank and American Express had also seen fit previously to put their trust in the now ailing Levitt empire.

VIII · Rainbow

SC: In 1985 I made the first attempt to prepare for 5,000 metres. Following a rest after Los Angeles, I embarked on a winter of longer runs, and a series of road races in the following March/April. I was not able to maintain the plan, which had included the possibility of running the distance at the European Championships in Stuttgart, because I was set back quite badly for three or four weeks with a calf injury, immediately following the Middlesex Championships in mid-May, where I'd run an encouraging 1:44.0. Even after I recovered, there was a series of minor niggles, so that I could never put in the solid spell of endurance work that was necessary for tackling the 5,000 to be a possibility. So it became, involuntarily, an off-peak season. I ran into a back problem at Crystal Palace, when stripped for a mile and kept waiting on a cold evening while there were several false starts in a women's 100 metres race. I managed a 3:32 and a 1:43 in successive races within a week, in Zurich and Cologne; second each time, to Deleze of Switzerland and then Cruz, before pulling out in Brussels, during the warm-up for 1,500, with a recurrence of the back injury. There'd been nothing to chase, no championships, but I'd been frustrated with the idea of the 5,000, which I must say had been attractive: the chance of testing myself at something different. Once I knew I couldn't even run an exploratory 5,000, Peter and I then calculated that, with only one winter and one summer to go, I would have to remain focused on the 1,500 and the 800 for the championships in Stuttgart. There are those who will say I didn't have the mentality to be a 5,000 runner, never mind whether my physiology was right. At school, I'd run mostly 3,000, partly because, for competitions, it meant just one day, in and out; not heats the previous day, which there usually were for the 1,500. The principle for Peter, in my young development, was to run over-distance, at 3,000, and under distance, at 800, with the eventual target being 1,500. It was when I started running 800 seriously at the age of twenty that I fell in love with the event.

I think 1985 was an illustration of my not avoiding other runners. I raced against Cram over 800 in Birmingham, in the match against the United States that was one of ITV's first major broadcasts after taking over the domestic contract from BBC. They managed to miss the first 150 metres of our event while still screening advertisements. We were both committed to the Dream Mile in Oslo, which I was more than happy to run, even with the knowledge that Steve had just had a sensational 3:29.67 for 1,500 metres in Nice, setting a new world record in a breathtaking finish with Aouita, whom he had beaten on the line by four-hundredths of a second. That was Cram's year, the best he ever had. Later in the season, he took on Cruz in Zurich over 800 metres and beat him in 1:42.88. Before the Dream Mile in Oslo, I'd lost a bit of training time, and Cram was in wonderful form. I ran under 3:50, while he took a full second off my record from four years previously, running 3:46.32. José Gonzalez was second. Cram's time was still standing six years later.

In the opinion of many, this was Cram's greatest ever run. Steve Scott, who had the reluctant experience of regularly sharing in such events from a rear view position, recollects: "The way he ran away from the field was breathtaking. Until that moment I'd thought Seb's win in LA was the best thing I'd ever seen, but the way Cram burst away and just kept getting faster and faster, was enough to make you want to stop running in order to watch him." "It was," Svein-Arne Hansen says, "the peak of the whole year."

Brendan Foster makes the point that the "window" of great champions, the time at which everything is together for them, mentally and physically, is mostly comparatively short. For Steve Ovett it was 1977–8; for Coe, 1979–81; for Cram, 1984–6. "Coe had a 'window and a half'," Foster says. "Cram's last lap in Oslo was phenomenal. He ran a last 200 of 25.9: usually people are *slowing* at that stage, yet he was still accelerating." Jimmy Hedley loyally defends, as Cram's coach, the fluctuation that has characterized Cram's career. "It took him a year to become used to being the champion of this, that and the other," Hedley says. "It wasn't easy for him. Anything but a win was failure. He put himself in that position. He'd go backwards, start to recover, go back again. He's won everything but an Olympic gold medal. Maybe he could still win that. While Coe was fortunate to have the stimulus of Ovett, Cram was lucky to have Aouita, they were pushing each other throughout that summer of '85. As I recollect, Aouita had better fields when he broke the records in '85 – the 1,500 metres in Berlin, 3:29.46, and 5,000 in Oslo, 13:00.40 – while Steve in his races was leading from the front. Perhaps Steve's best race of all was his 1,000 metres at Gateshead, seven-tenths of a second outside Seb's record."

With Coe hovering in the wings throughout most of the summer of '85, and never getting the cue for a solo aria, the expectation for his challenge to Cram in the double championships year of 1986, Commonwealth and European, was little short of the intensity that had been present in Los Angeles. "I'd had a thrilling season in '85, and in consequence felt very confident for the next year," Cram recalls. "Seb was never one to write off, but the picture had changed now slightly, because for the first time I was going to run both events in the two championships, feeling strong and having had such a fast 800 in Cologne. If I was going to have four major races with Seb in '86, I felt it was imperative to win the *first* one of all, the 800 in Edinburgh. Physically and mentally, I was in outstanding shape in July, at the time of the Commonwealth Games, maybe better than in '85, but never had a chance really to show what I could do. *And* Seb was missing in Edinburgh, with a cold. I won the Commonwealth 800 in 1:43.22, even in those wretched conditions that made the whole week in Edinburgh so miserable. It was a big disappointment for me that Seb was out of action. I was desperately looking for the chance to race against him in *his* event." Cram duly did the double in Edinburgh, devoid of challenge from the boycotting Kenyans, winning the 1,500 with three lazy laps in a raging wind, followed by a blazing last 400 in 51.3.

SC: The early summer had been dreadful, never seemed to stop raining, and Edinburgh had been a continuation of that. I was totally drenched four or five times during prolonged training sessions, and went down with flu. I tried to soldier through the first couple of races in Edinburgh, dragging myself through the semi-final, but though there were a couple of days' rest before the final, Malcolm Reid, the doctor, said I would be stupid to run. I was prevented again from testing myself in Edinburgh against Elliott, and against the new threat, Tom McKean. McKean had beaten Elliott to take the silver medal.

McKean, a stylish Scot coached by Tommy Boyle, was not dissimilar from Brian Hewson, thirty years before: the same easy rhythm, the same turn of speed, only more so. What McKean lacked, it was to become apparent during the course of the next three or four years, was the temperament for the big occasion, a flaw he eventually conquered in 1990. Shy and withdrawn, an outward image also similar to Hewson, McKean possessed a finishing kick capable of startling most rivals. "I'd thought Tom would win in Stuttgart, because I felt Seb was lacking at bit, at that time, but that Seb would be OK in the 1,500," Derek Ibbotson says. "It was his timing in the 800 that was superb, just when McKean couldn't respond. It was a memorable race, with a yard covering all three British runners at the finish."

The reversal of plans, postponing any consideration of 5,000, had not been too disappointing for Coe, for it enabled him to take another stab at that long-frustrated ambition, a major title in his favourite event, following three silvers and a bronze. A key factor in his performance in 1986 was the growing involvement of David Martin.

In November following the Olympics, Seb had his first treadmill test in Atlanta [Martin recalls]. He had the money and the time to be able to travel, and was fascinated with learning more about his physiology. He'd been tested at Loughborough, but no-one had really explained how those data could be translated into training plans. We were experts at doing that. After his visit to Atlanta, I sent Peter a letter explaining our findings, as well as training-pace recommendations. The conclusion was one of having little aerobic difference from other élite middle-distance runners. *But*, Seb had unusual abilities both to produce and to tolerate lactic acidosis. This showed us that his enormous performance capacities were explained by not only a world-class maximum oxygen uptake but also by an above-average tolerance to anaerobic work. In other words, Seb's anaerobic fitness was good even when he was not training anaerobically. Was this the secret to his success? His aerobic qualities were no better than the best, but anaerobically he was very gifted. The reason is probably genetic. The only way to be positive was to have a muscle biopsy, but I advised against this because studying one muscle does not tell you everything – a race is run using many muscles.

The value of the information for Stuttgart was on discussion of his training routine. He was so determined to get that 800 title. What I saw was that while he had a good running and weight-training programme, he may have been stopping the weight training too early. Peter and he had been tapering off weight training before the start of the serious part of the track season, so that he would be fresher at the beginning of his speed work. But big races are at the end of the season, and the 800 is almost a sprint, strength-orientated; and by then his strength was disappearing. I was sure, if he maintained his weight training well into the summer, that strength would synthesize with speed work to do the job. Peter and I came to the decision that if Seb would back off on his volume of aerobic training a little more, and substitute instead extended weight training, this would give the proper mix of volume quality-running and conditioning to keep a high aerobic base, quicken his reflexes, keep him strong, and refine his fast-running abilities. One primary objective of his development was directed so that in the last hundred metres in Stuttgart, he would be so strong that no-one could go past him. Training became only part of this process. The other element centred around rest and recovery. Seb would need to be supremely fresh and hungry to race.

He managed to get the timing exactly right in Stuttgart, even though it was miserably cold leading up to the races. Two days before the heats, he ran a 200 in 21.8. That's fast. One of the black sprinters came up to him to give him some arm action advice, he was so impressed. Seb was delighted. In the final, he was as smooth as can be and never tied up. And when it came to his best ever 1,500 in Rieti, a week after Stuttgart, the strength that had given him the 800 victory was still there. What I saw were the physiological components of an exact training programme. What Peter had done was near perfect, because he had this sixth sense of the capabilities of his athlete. I'm convinced, from his physiology, that Seb could have run a brilliant 5,000 if he had trained for it. You need the mix to be correct for that, with more miles of endurance and backing off the repetitions. And Peter was an expert at devising correct training.

Coe is not the only one to have caught a cold at the wrong moment. It happened to Steve Ovett in 1986, but the other way round. He had

Road test while pre-season training in Bordeaux. The 800 repetitions, up to six in sequence, scrutinised by Peter in following car: part of the secret of success.

Coe supports Bob Geldof, in the 1986 appeal for African famine.

With Eamonn Coghlan, Pelé and Grete Weitz for a SportAid appeal.

"Do you ever try running, PM?" "But of course! I twice retained my title." Number 10 reception for sportsmen.

It's all Greek to me. With Sir Arthur Gold, chairman of the British
Olympic Association during a conference in Athens.

With The Princess Royal and Arthur Mapp, 1984 judo competitor,
launching Olympic appeal fund for 1988.

Stripped for action: training in Florida with Peter Wirz of
Switzerland, early '88, in vain preparation for Seoul Games.

Three pupils, same teacher. Coe, Wendy Sly and Peter Wirz
working to Peter Coe's schedules in Florida.

Last bend, foot down, nothing there. Coe, cold-ridden, winces in '88 Olympic trial.

Despair. A cold foils Coe's bid for third Olympic title, eliminated at trials in Birmingham.

Coe pips Cram in re-creation of Trinity Great Court run from
"Chariots of Fire', October '88. Did he beat the clock chimes?
They weren't sure.

Coe staggers after tripping on fallen Crabb (on ground) in
Commonwealth trial for '90, a falsely-acclaimed "confrontation"
with Ovett, second left.

Politician or athlete? Coe announces he is interrupting one career
to maintain another, September, 1989.

British swansong: Coe's last race, 800 in McVitie's meeting, Crystal Palace, September, '89, aged 33.

Arms aloft, Coe salutes a British crowd which has followed his feats during almost fourteen years of senior racing.

Silver salver in recognition of all those medals and records – only one, a share in 4 × 800 relay, at Crystal Palace.

The dream that dissolved. Coe in supreme form in Sydney two weeks before the Auckland Commonwealth Games.

Illness and anguish, again, as Coe fights a cold rather than competitors in his final competition, Auckland Commonwealth Games.

Reluctant acceptance as a sick Coe is scratched from Commonwealth 1,500 heats by John Jeffries, England's team manager.

Coming to terms with failure, a third championships frustrated by illness.

Previous page left A different kind of defeat. The chairman of London 2,000 reflects on capital's defeat by Manchester to bid as Olympic host city.

Previous page right Best of friends. Steve Ovett, former arch-rival, subsequently discovered much in common with Coe.

Sir Roger Bannister, hero of the past, congratulates the 1980 Olympic champion at the Coca-Cola meeting, Crystal Palace.

Greatest of all? Herb Elliott of Australia, never beaten over four laps, winning for Cambridge University at White City.

Britain supreme. Elliott, Commonwealth champion beats Cram, multiple ex-champion, in memorable finish, Sheffield, '90.

Below Grete Waitz of Norway and Sebastian Coe receive their *Runner's World* awards, a world-wide critics' choice as the best middle distance runners of the past twenty-five years.

Nicola Coe takes the water obstacle at Badminton Trials on the way to winning the coveted three-day event in 1990.

Heading for new horizons. Nicky and Seb taking the air in Falmouth Bay during election campaigning.

converted to 5,000 following the Olympic Games, and it possibly came more easily to him; his nature enjoyed the camaraderie of longer distances, of cross-country and road running. Ovett won the 5,000 in Edinburgh, but was then laid low by a cold before Stuttgart. "The transition took a few years," Ovett says. "To be honest, I didn't enjoy it as much as I'd *expected*. You can't run that many 5,000s in a year. I managed one shot at it, and it gave me the chance to win a gold medal at a third distance." Harry Wilson was especially disappointed at the illness that denied his man a chance in the European championships.

Steve was in fantastic shape [Wilson said]. I'd also trained Julian Goater, who had a personal best of 13:16. I *knew* what was needed to break thirteen minutes, and I thought Steve could do it. He beat Jack Buckner in Edinburgh, and it was Buckner who then won in Stuttgart, with a brilliant 13:10. But Steve had bad flu, and never recovered in time. There was a time when there was a break in my relationship with Steve, for a year or so I didn't see much of him, when Andy was arranging races. After that, we got back together again. He'd been with me since he was sixteen, but I've always believed athletes should be independent. By 1986, we were as close as ever, and I was convinced he could get near to Aouita's record.

Knowing there was no time to be lost in throwing off the effects of his influenza, Coe returned to London the afternoon that Cram was winning the 1,500 metres in Edinburgh, and set off by car with Steve Mitchell and Malcolm Williams for Macolin in Switzerland. The mountain air was clean, warm and soothing. His cold soon shifted. Steve took part in the track running, picking up every second or third repetition, to help provide momentum, while Malcolm assisted with work on weights in the gymnasium; hoodwinking a group of Italian athletes into purveying tales of Coe's super-human capacities by leaving, at the end of one session, weights of almost double the normal amount standing on the rest bar. Rodda of *The Guardian* came and wrote an article about "the last of the summer wine"; appropriate for the mood of Coe, who had not taken kindly to a series of articles by Pat Butcher in *The Times* with Cram that talked about the state of the art of middle-distance running, the demise of Coe and Ovett, and the fact that Cram was the new broom who was going to race (and beat) everybody. Coe took breaks from Macolin for a couple of 1,500 metres bench-marks, in Zurich and Berne, following Scott home in the first in reasonable time and then running a sharpish 3:35 in the second, from the front. He was coming to the boil again. The unfulfilled ambition for a championship 800 metres was looking more hopeful.

Even more so when, arriving in Stuttgart where it was persistently almost as cold and wet as Edinburgh, Coe ran some two hundred repetitions in under 22 that were sufficient evidence for some of the British sprinters, mightily impressed, to put money on Coe for the 800 final. They even began offering coaching advice on his arm action. Mike McFarlane was later said to have won more than £2,000. It was during training sessions prior to racing that Coe was involved in an escapade that could have led to his being sent home: one of the few irreverent moments in the athletic career of one whose image, so much of the time, had been that of the school swot. He hijacked a bus.

SC: A group of us, including Daley, Ade Mafe, John Isaacs, and some of the other sprinters, were picked up for training by a German driver who didn't know the way to the training track. After more than an hour winding around the suburbs of Stuttgart, he was completely lost, and pulled up at what was clearly the wrong place. The driver got out, leaving the keys in the ignition, and refused to co-operate any further. On an impulse, I jumped into the driver's seat and pulled away, leaving the driver standing there shouting and waving his arms. When we arrived at the training track where we were supposed to be, we were met by Frank Dick, looking several shades of white, and the local police. I just handed over the keys to the police and we heard nothing more.

Recalling the incident years later, Dick says: "I can't see any of the other runners doing that. He was lucky to get away with it. I think there was always a streak of devilment in him." It was a story that never made the back pages.

Part of the appeal of Jimmy Hedley, Cram's coach, is that as long as he is awake, he is talking. Enthusiasm runs out of him like perspiration, although with it comes a tendency to say what's on his mind, which often, in the nature of things, is subjective. In the count-down to Stuttgart, Hedley was predicting a "double-double" for his man. In an interview the weekend before the heats of the 800 metres, Hedley was saying:

Steve's bent on winning both, and he's in the best shape he's ever been. I know I'm biased, but I've truthfully believed for a couple of months now that Steve will win them both. He's getting faster and faster, and he's right on cue. I don't think he's worried about anyone. Steve may be doubling-up in a major championship for the first time, but I feel he's capable of it. I think Seb will wait until the dying seconds [in the 800] before taking him on, because he'll feel he's faster than Steve. But Steve won't allow him to get away with that. Steve will go from further out. I know Seb did that to Steve in LA, but he knew that Crammie wasn't fit. There's nobody else in either field who can do very much about the pair of them. I'm not saying Seb's over the top at twenty-nine, because although you don't tend to get faster at that age, Seb is holding on to what he's got.

SC: In Stuttgart, there were no tomorrows. This had to be it. If I didn't do it now, I would be remembered as a semi-complete athlete. But after racing in Berne, I felt very strong, I'd hardly broken sweat. This was going to be *my* year.

Peter, as they like to say in previews of football cup ties, was quietly confident.

PC: The year was geared to speed. Seb ran only a dozen races. In very windy conditions at Haringey, in July, he'd run a thousand in 2:14 in training, and that was why we thought the Commonwealth Games would be a cinch. His recovery from the cold was fairly quick, and when he came second to Scott three weeks later, I had no worries about the European Championships. Doubling-up for him was always a good idea. The 800 was the *focus* for Stuttgart. We didn't need to prove anything at 1,500, but we longed for the confirmation that we were right about preparation for shorter distances. The failure to win a championship had always irritated Seb, knowing that he was streets ahead of the next man, but without a gold medal to show for it.

The course that the final would take, the speed at which it would be run, was unpredictable. Cram had won in Edinburgh, going very fast. McKean, criticized by his coach for a lack of commitment, had later admitted that he had been running for second place. If the pace was now between 1:44 and 1:45, then McKean's kick might still come into effect. Coe considered that anything faster than 1:44.5 "would sort out McKean".

The red synthetic track glistened in the rain as the runners went to the line, the packed stadium of spectators huddled under umbrellas. Besides the three British runners there were Braun, the West German European indoor champion with an outdoor time of 1:44; Druppers, the World Championship bronze medallist; and Collard, a promising Frenchman. Going into the second bend, the order once the runners had shaken free from the lane break was Braun and Druppers in lane one, followed by Collard and the Russian Kalinkin in lane two. McKean and Ostrowski of Poland were fifth and sixth; Cram and Coe contentedly were biding their time at the back. The order remained the same around the bend, but going down the home straight for the first time, McKean moved past Kalinkin and Collard to take up third position. At the back, Coe was gently handing-off Cram as the two of them merged, then parted.

Braun went through the bell in 52, with Druppers half a stride down and McKean a further two yards back. Then came Collard and Kalinkin, followed by Ostrowski with Cram, and Coe running wide in lane two. Into the penultimate bend, Collard and Kalinkin collided, and while they were off balance Cram swiftly darted between the two of them, Coe running round the outside of the staggering Kalinkin. Half-way down the back straight, it was still Braun leading by half a stride from Druppers; then McKean, Ostrowski and Cram, who was moving wide in lane two; then Collard and Kalinkin together in lane one, with Coe poised . . . lying eighth! A mere six yards covered all eight runners.

Approaching the final bend, Coe accelerated suddenly to close in behind Cram in lane two. Simultaneously, McKean had surged to overtake Braun and Druppers; so that Collard, Braun and Druppers were now boxed behind the three British runners fanned out across two lanes. Into the bend, McKean held the inside, with Cram at his shoulder in lane two, and Coe tracking Cram along the line between lanes two and three. McKean, it seemed at this moment, would take some beating.

Ten yards into the final stright, Coe kicked. Cram was starting to knot, as he tried to respond, while McKean was maintaining his stride pattern yet losing ground. As they passed the victory rostrum half-way down the straight, Coe was level with McKean, Cram a yard back. In the last forty metres, with eyes hollowed, teeth gritted, Coe ground his way past McKean, who cast a pained glance sideways but could do nothing. By eleven-hundredths of a second, Coe was there in 1:44.50, with Cram beaten into third place and Druppers taking fourth.

During the medal ceremony, and the playing of the anthem for the British trio, Coe turned to comment to McKean. Cram looked despondent. "I'd picked up a niggling injury after Edinburgh, and went to Stuttgart *just* over the edge," Cram recollects. "Yet I was still very confident, thinking I had only to put my foot on the pedal and it would all happen. On the back straight I moved up level with Tom, with Seb just behind, and felt comfortable. I put my foot down . . . and so did Tom. I couldn't get past! That was the critical moment. Into the final straight, Seb suddenly appeared. I couldn't believe it. I'd been too blasé. I'd thought, after the performance in Edinburgh, that if I turned on the pressure, the other two would crumble. It didn't happen." Hedley reflects: "Steve left his effort too late, considering he had two sprinters with him. Steve always needed to do it the hard way, that's the way he's made."

SC: In European terms, there was no-one of frightening ability in the final. There'd been a chance in LA for a clean sweep in the 1,500, and now it could happen for the 800. I felt Cram and I were sure of medals, so McKean could make it three, if he did nothing silly. We hadn't yet come to his tactical blunders of '87 and '88. He'd come out of a 400 background, and this was the first time I'd run against him. Steve, I think, had raced him only once, in '85, when McKean had out-kicked him at Gateshead. McKean had replaced me in the European Cup in '85, and won the first of his four titles in that competition. McKean was especially tough to beat at any race between 1:45 and 1:47, but Steve had shown in Edinburgh that if you didn't want to be vulnerable to McKean in the last 120 metres, you mustn't let it drift slower than 1:44.

That day, I wasn't worried if it picked up to 1:43 pace: I didn't mind whether it was a slog or a kick, but I didn't want it to be 1:47. Looking at the video afterwards, it proved my hunch; that if I was out of sight in the first lap at the back, it might cause concern for the other two. Once I was sure the pace was under 1:45 – thanks to Braun over the first lap – I could continue to stay out of eye contact. As Braun had continued in the lead, Cram and McKean were following, but constantly looking round. In doing this, I'd probably drifted a fraction too far off the pace. By the end of the second back straight, I'd picked up on Cram. I'd calculated that if no-one else was leading Steve with 200 to go, it would have to be me. But McKean was there and already going for home, doing the job for me. I wasn't aware at this stage that Cram was not finding it easy. When I got to Cram's shoulder at the corner of the bend, with McKean still leading, I realized Steve had spurted yet still hadn't, or couldn't, catch McKean. I went past Cram coming off the bend, and had to dig deep for thirty or forty metres to get ahead of McKean by a stride.

Back in the tunnel after a lap of honour, I found McKean cross that he had not won, feeling he'd done enough to do so. Steve was there with a physiotherapist and ice-packs on his calf, part of his on-going problem. Peter was delighted after all these years, the dejection of Athens, though he'd been worried by my staying at the back as long as I had. He joked that I should have "dipped" at the finish. I'd said I would have a go at Steve at the medal interview, if I won, voicing my annoyance at his *Times* articles, but in the event discretion was better. The interview was lengthened by the necessity of having to translate McKean's Motherwell accent, for the benefit of the official German interpreter: "I thought I'd won till the little shit came past me."

Frank Dick was wondering how to handle a coach's responsibility towards three athletes who have come first, second and third. "It was difficult for me in the tunnel afterwards," Dick recollects. "Steve's head is down. Seb has done what he always wanted. McKean is wondering how he should have done it differently. How does the coach divide his loyalties? It's a fascinating part of the job. I said to Steve, 'The 1,500 is still to come, that's *yours*'."

That evening, Seb was having dinner with Daley Thompson, who was winding himself up for his awaited meeting with the home favourite, Jürgen Hingsen. Thompson and Coe had spent many hours together around the world since the day they made their international indoor debut together at Dortmund in 1977: and Daley had been youthfully envious of the "007" race number which Coe had been allocated. Coe had been told the previous year by Mike Corden, a Sheffield teacher who had competed in the decathlon at the Montreal Olympic Games, that a youngster who finished eleventh "would be the greatest decathlon competitor ever". Coe found Thompson's individuality, occasional eccentricity and passionate competitiveness one of the most pleasant aspects of being a part of British teams for twelve years.

SC: Keith Connor, the triple-jumper, was also in that team in Dortmund. It was the start of the new face of British athletics, of inner-city black dominance in our country, and a healthy broadening of our athletics team. Most of the competitions Daley utilized were club events, where he could compete as "training" for his decathlon events. What was impressive was that at international meetings he could hold his own in individual events, such as the long-jump and 100 metres. Until I talked to Daley, I didn't understand the decathlon viewpoint: that it really was one event spread over 48 hours. I remember his deep disappointment at being beaten at Prague in '78 after winning in Edmonton. Moscow I don't remember. I was too absorbed in my own problems, though I do recall Daley coming to my room the morning after the 800, asking how the weather was and my saying glumly, "It looks a bit silver to me." In LA, he confirmed my impression of his greatness when he threw a personal best in the discus to stay in contention with two events to go. On his last throw he sent the discus metres further than he'd thrown before. You don't witness this mental strength in many competitors. He tended to think middle-distance people were a bit casual about racing, but that was because he didn't have the opportunity to prove himself more than once a year or so. If there had been a decathlon every week, Daley would have competed. I've had one or two opportunities to watch him at close quarters. He has a Stalinist attitude: it wasn't enough to *beat* someone, you had to destroy them, destroy their system, their reasoning, their belief. It wasn't a physical battle in LA, it was emotional intimidation. On the second day of the decathlon, the same as my semi-final in the 1,500, Hingsen was sitting with a towel over his head in the sun, like a defeated boxer. I said to Jürgen, "He's an animal, isn't he?" Jürgen gave me a glazed nod. Half an hour later, Daley had won.

I was with him at training in Australia in the winter of '89–'90, when I was preparing for the Commonwealth Games. He's complicated, and sensitive; there's an inner driving force that's hard to explain. If he were to brush up on his social graces, which have been criticized, he would have to be more conventional, and that would knock a chunk off his talent. I've been in so many situations where he *is* friendly. He has an encyclopaedic knowledge of track and field, other events that he has no business to know about. You'll get more sense out of Daley talking about middle-distance running than you will out of some national middle-distance coaches. That's why he won't discuss his own event with anyone he doesn't consider understands it. I've got to know him better in recent years, he and Rachel were at our wedding. Although in reality the odds are stacked against him, or anybody at the age of 34, winning an Olympic medal in Barcelona, I've seen in him recently a lot of the old fire which has been rekindled. His pride, of course, won't let him step into the arena if he thinks he has no chance. The decathlon is unforgiving—you only have to get one event wrong to be out of it. Yet Daley could come through on experience and an even performance, never mind that some of his speed has declined. He'll have to be so focussed that he won't have time to design any funny T-shirts for the closing ceremony.

How would Coe react to the attainment of his 800 title when it came to running the 1,500 metres a few days later? In such form, he ought to have been in confident mood. Indeed he was. "He was in splendid spirits, jumping around his parents' room at their hotel, laughing with satisfaction in a particularly wicked way he has," Jane Williams remembers. "I don't think he was aware that Steve was only two rooms down the corridor. Seb had been a lot more nervous even than usual before the 800, though it was never really apparent if you didn't know him." The euphoria that understandably was flowing through him was to have its price in his challenge to Cram at the longer distance.

PC: I don't think he *cared*. When I said to Seb afterwards, "You could have buried him," he merely replied, "Maybe." I didn't suggest to him how he should run the race, only to stay out of trouble. I had been worried in the 800, because he nearly got it wrong, thinking that Cram was the danger rather than McKean. *They* expected him to push it out earlier, at 300 out, or even 400. In the 1,500 final, there was an element of over-confidence, though that's conjecture.

One of the surprises of the Stuttgart four-lap race was the failure of the two Irish runners, O'Mara and O'Sullivan, who came with a background of consistent indoor success in America. Coe believes this was their limitation.

SC: I wouldn't want to tackle either of them on a wooden 160-yard track in January, yet they seldom trouble a strong European field in the summer months. You can mostly discount athletes who commit themselves to heavy indoor competition from being involved in the spoils outdoors. The only ones to have done it are Delany, who took the Olympic title in 1956, and Coghlan, who won the 5,000 in the first World Championships after deliberately having a quieter winter.

For Cram, victory in the 1,500 was now paramount. Hitherto, his championship victories in 1982 and 1983 and this year in Edinburgh, had been in the absence of Coe; when they had met in Los Angeles, Coe had triumphed. Cram had only once failed to do what was asked of him in championships, and yet the second time he had come to confront Coe, profoundly confident here in Stuttgart, he had lost again. There were the sort of question marks being raised that hovered over Coe in Moscow.

I wasn't suddenly a bad runner, because of the 800 defeat [Cram reflects]. I needed to get back my confidence, by reassuring myself that I would now be running in *my* race, the distance in which I'd set the world record. Yet on the day it wasn't a good race, even though it went as I expected: I'd go somewhere between 300 and 400 out, Seb would challenge, and I'd have to run it out of him from the front. Maybe I was hungrier on the day. At the end, I had relief more than satisfaction. The elation came later. It was important to me to keep winning at 1,500 – the 800 would have been a bonus.

Brendan Foster reflects on the irony of the situation: "Because Coe and the Kenyans were not there in Edinburgh, it should have made it easier for Steve to achieve the double-double," Foster says. "So inevitably he felt down after Stuttgart, not having done what he wanted. Seb and Steve both began the season hoping for four gold medals. Steve won three, and felt he'd had a disappointing season; Seb won one, and was happy!"

In a slow final, Cram retained his title, winning his sixth championship gold medal, with a last lap of 50.9, and a last 800 in 1:49. His winning time was 3:41.09. Coe, seeming to be in the position to take his rival on the final lap, could not do so, failing to remember the principle he had recognized in LA and that had been repeatedly spelled out by Norman: that to beat Cram, you had to be *leading* him with 300 metres to go, not following him.

SC: I made errors. I was slightly knocked in the third lap, just at the point when Cram decided to put the pressure on, and I was four strides out of touch at the bell. I pulled two of these back, but you don't give a runner of Steve's class four strides with 400 to go, especially someone with his style. So I was never in the position to put him under pressure. Steve took his chance and closed the door, so at the finish we were all-square. It was a race I should never have lost. A week later I knew how foolish I'd been, especially when it was evident that, towards the end of the season, Steve was "running tired". It was the last title he was to win for a while: up to 1990, he never recaptured the same kind of form.

I'd felt after the semi-final that I was having difficulty maintaining focus, and conscious on the "spare" day before the final that I would have to work hard to retain a championship routine: the rigorous daily schedule of jogging, lunch, sleep, jogging, massage – all of which I did, as though it were a race day. I remember feeling under pressure in the warm-up area before the final, though not damagingly so. All that week we'd had to warm up indoors, which is unnatural, and I remember thinking again beforehand that he is at his best when leading at the bell. Out in front, Steve always grew in stature. If *you* could lead *him* you could prevent him gaining confidence.

The mood in the whole team that week was so good, the talent was there, and everyone was beginning to think we were as strong as any other country. Roger Black was brilliant in the 400; the old guard was still there, Christie was beginning to establish himself belatedly, Regis was emerging, and there were McKean and Buckner, and Hill in the javelin. This was the first time when the usual discrepancy between the Commonwealth Games and the European Championships was not going to be so marked, when Commonwealth champions weren't embarrassed in the first round of the European.

In the 5,000 metres final, Jack Buckner, having run poorly in Edinburgh, now ran a last 800 metres in 1:56.7 for a thrilling victory over Stefano Mei of Italy and Tim Hutchings of Britain, the latter having led after 4,000 metres. Ovett, unwell, dropped out before the 3,000 metre mark. Dave Bedford questions just how good Ovett was at 5,000. "He never convinced me that he was anything but an opportunist," Bedford says. "In Edinburgh, Hutchings and Buckner ran badly. At 5,000, you have to make it hurt, early. Had there been three Kenyans running in Edinburgh, Steve wouldn't have been able to run it the way he did. The odd thing is the way both Ovett and Coe failed to provide conclusive answers in a particular year. Ovett could have done so in Moscow and Coe in Stuttgart, could have ended the questions. Neither of them did."

A week later, running in Rieti, Coe recorded 3:29.77, to become with Sydney Maree the equal third fastest-ever behind Cram and Aouita, 0.31 seconds outside Aouita's record of 1985.

SC: I think I would have broken the record but for an incident during the third lap. I was following James Mays, the pacemaker, to about 1,100 metres, and then Chesire of Kenya took up the lead. At the bell, I started to move for a hard final 400, when Chesire also decided to make a run. After a dozen strides he suddenly slowed, and I went into the back of him. I must have lost at least half a second with that stumble. I won by about 40 metres, and but for the collision the record would have gone.

"Seb was so thrilled, and so annoyed," Jane Williams recalls. "I travelled down with some others on the bus to the track, because Seb had gone before, to get himself in the mood. The pattern was always the same on race days: I'd see him at meal time, and then not speak to him again until hours later. The pattern was unchanging, even in Rieti. After the race, he was off for a long warm-down. The discipline was unvarying."

Steve Mitchell is left with permanent speculation about his friend. "When you look back and consider that he ran under 3:30 just before his thirtieth birthday, you have to wonder what he might have done earlier in his career," Mitchell says. "There was some dire pacemaking at times in the early Eighties. Age was never a factor with Seb, yet an athlete is at his peak at about twenty-seven, so, logically, he should at some time have run much faster."

IX · Elliott

When considering Britain's four championship-winning middle-distance runners of the past decade, Andy Norman, who is no mean judge of character, once made a telling summary. "If I built a brick wall across the track fifty yards from the finishing line, I know how each one would react," Norman said. "One would wave his arms around and ask what the hell was going on, one would sit down and protest it wasn't fair, one would run clean through it, and the other would go off and hold a press conference." I leave it to the reader to decide to which athlete Norman was applying each description, but there can be no doubt in anyone's mind about who would be running through the brick wall; and probably not even noticing it was there.

SC: I recognize in Peter Elliott a streak of belligerence that is there in me, much more than there is in Ovett or Cram. So for that reason, among others, I have an admiration for him. What he has always had, and I respect, is a thirst for championship racing. You could never question Peter's desire for racing or his courage, especially in championships. Win or lose, you know he's going to give his absolute limit. It has to be said that Peter has admitted at the end of a season, if he's finished poorly in a particular event, "What do you expect, I've had forty races over 800 metres this year!" I think he recognized, by a certain point in his career, that he *was* racing too much. In terms of athletic purity, he, like Cram, did try to put too many races into the programme.

It's odd how my championship fortunes, more often than with the other two, have been interwoven with Peter's. He's the least naturally talented of the four of us, but for mental toughness, he's as tigerish as any of us and sometimes more so. You'd have to be blind-folded too, not to recognize that Peter's the son of the area in which he was brought up: gritty, realistic, unyielding south Yorkshire. My formative years were in Sheffield, nine or ten miles down the road from Rotherham, where Peter lived. At the height of the various controversies over our respective selection credentials, I read more about north v. *south* than I can recount. You look at Peter on the track, and you have confirmation that life is hard. There's a Lowry-like, dour element in his physical profile, that thread of melancholy from hard-pressed industrial England, whatever his state of fortune.

In Sheffield, and maybe south Yorkshire, there's a lack of self-belief that's not there in Newcastle. The Geordies are much more naturally confident. If you go to a pre-race reception in Gateshead, there's a bounce you don't always find in Yorkshire, a confidence about who they are, without having stated it in any way, a bit like Cockneys. In Yorkshire, they're more closed, and some of Peter's public utterances have had the same blend of self-defensiveness and aggression that we've seen at various times from Don Revie or Brian Clough. And in Rotherham, they even feel outsiders to Sheffield!

When I first went to Sheffield, which was when I really started in athletics, it was always assumed by others that I was a northerner. We'd come from the Midlands, and my father was working with a Sheffield cutlery firm. At twelve or thirteen, I joined Hallamshire Harriers, and I remember some people did feel, one or two coaches and others, that it wasn't as easy to get into the national team if you were up there in Yorkshire rather than down south. If this element did exist, I don't think it was deliberate or in any sense outrageous. Generally speaking, if you were good enough, you were selected. Someone like John Sherwood or Trevor Wright the marathon runner, would have no trouble. If you were that outstanding, you were in the team. Where there may have been a margin of doubt was at the fringe of selection – certainly something that could never have affected anyone like Peter Elliott. But if there were five or six athletes of similar standing, there might have been an instance when expense was taken into account on a last-minute inclusion. Peter might cite examples when cards were stacked against him, but I don't know that this was ever true. Perhaps my advantage was that my father, right from the start, had a national view of the sport, and when I was 14 or 15 he would enter me in races in the south, at Luton, say, or Barnet, and would drive me down. So I was never looked upon as a *regional* runner. That was a coincidental strength for me, based on my father's willingness.

I raced Peter on numerous occasions in Yorkshire, when he was sixteen and I was twenty, at Cleckheaton and elsewhere, with him giving me a hard lap then. Over the years, there's a tradition of milers in Yorkshire that's second to none: Ibbotson, Simpson, Whetton, Walter Wilkinson, myself, Elliott, though Peter for some years concentrated on two laps.

The first international rivalry between us came in 1984, at the Olympic trials, when he beat me at 1,500 metres and threatened my place. Until Auckland in 1990, I would never have considered that Peter Elliott was a serious threat if I was at the top of my form: I would never have sat down with my father for a race analysis to consider how we should handle him. By Auckland, though, I knew that I would have to run outstandingly well to have any chance of beating him, and in the event that chance never came. Peter's difficulty in any championship was often surviving the semi-final: the 800 metres in Helsinki and again in Rome, both World Championships. His style and tactics were suited to a final, to the stretching of mental limits. Once he was in the final, he did what he knew he had to do, which was break the field to the point where he could pick up one of the medals. A weakness in him is a limit to the range of tactics he can adopt. He can't *sit* in until the right time to react, so that in heats he's usually qualifying the hardest way. His strength is the mental commitment he brings to a final, together with hard, sustained speed. It's a tough way for a runner to try to win, because you risk letting yourself be the pacemaker for others. But Peter could pull two or three runners into an area, physiologically, where they didn't want to be. I remember sitting down with Kim McDonald after the semi-final in Rome, and saying that Peter would beat McKean for a medal in the same way that he got fourth place in 1983 behind Wülbeck, Cruz and Druppers, with Wülbeck standing off, and then scooping up people that Peter had killed off.

At some stage between 1986 and 1989–90, Peter significantly improved his sprinting ability, though it would be over-stating it to say he produced a real kick. He produced a change of pace that added a dimension to his racing. Probably on account of the way he felt about himself, you wouldn't say that he looked as though life was kind to him, and that was imposed by his style of running. He is a better running machine than Cram, biomechanically, in his foot plant. If Cram was biomechanically flawed, Peter made it look harder than it really was.

There is little doubt in most people's minds that, in 1990, Elliott should have taken over the mantle of Cram in 1982 and 1986, by winning both Commonwealth and European Championships at 1,500 metres. Unhappily, following his fine victory in Auckland, he was out of phase with his training schedule on account of the January timing of the Commonwealth Games. The summer period went awry; and at the European Championships in Split, Elliott was sent tumbling in the semi-final. His controversial re-instatement was a trauma he dearly wished had never happened: besides which, he was way out of touch in the final.

"For sheer guts, Peter has more than any, and has quite a lot of talent too," John Walker says. "But *no-one* has the same guts. When he ran 1:42 at Seville early in 1990 he should have gone for a mile or 1,500 metres that same week. Some people get a peak for two years, some for a month. Sometimes you don't know. I ran a personal best of 3:32.4 for the 1,500 metres, and world records for the mile and for 2,000 metres, all in the same fifteen days in 1975. You've got to go for it when you're *right*. I don't think we'll see 3:46 for the mile being beaten for some time, unless Peter pulls one out of the bag. The champions are not there at present, though Joe Falcon of America may go faster. Americans on the whole have it wrong, but I think Falcon may get it right. He's half-Mexican, he's hungry, and he knows what it's like to work hard."

One American who got it right, or so nearly so, was Scott. He, too, thinks Elliott may break into the all-time list of champions and record-breakers.

With intelligent planning, there's little that would hold Peter back [Scott says]. You have to admire his front-running, and up to now he's worked harder at the sport than almost anyone, even when he was holding down a job as a joiner at the steelworks; the kind of thing no other top runner has done. At one time Peter's attitude didn't seem that serious, when he was running hell-for-leather all over the place. Now, he's obsessed by the sport. In 1990, he flew straight from competition in Europe to New York for the Fifth Avenue Mile, at a time when Cram was saying, "Stuff it, I'm tired, and I don't want to train." Peter couldn't possibly miss *one* work-out if he could help it. To a degree, good or bad, I am not sure if Peter's calculated the difference between dedication and obsession. I first noticed him in Australia in '82–'83, when he won just about every race and I was asking "Who's this?" More than anyone else in Europe, Peter should be an *American*! He races too much and it's to his detriment. He's never yet been able to have that *one* race that sets him apart, in the way of Ovett, Coe or Cram, though he has the potential to be in that category. It's a pity he didn't jump into a mile or 1,500 race early in 1990. Life is timing: Peter's been there at the top, but not at the *right* moment.

Peter Coe, who tends to judge a runner as much initially in terms of design as in mental or physical potential, feels Elliott does not look right, stylistically. "He carries his arms too low. But then so did Peter Snell. Even when he's not under pressure, he doesn't really flow. Cram did, including under pressure. Peter's strength is his *strength*. Peter's had the same problem as Cram, of arriving in the shadow of Seb and Ovett; but some of his comments when trying to break clear of this shadow, about class and education, have really been a bit silly."

Ibbotson, one Yorkshire miler admiring another, sympathizes with Elliott's lust for racing, because that was the accusation so often levelled at him. In 1957, running at the AAA championships at the White City, the day after his first baby had been born, Ibbotson failed to qualify for the final of the mile, not having had time to warm up. Newspaper headlines labelled him a "chump", said that he was burned-out after too many races. A London taxi driver saucily asked him if he'd like tickets to watch the final the next day. Incensed, Ibbotson returned next day for the three miles championship, and proceeded to break the Commonwealth record. The next day the newspapers were calling him "champ". It is a thin line between success and failure.

Ibbotson drove himself as hard as any. "Success is as much determination and training as talent," Ibbotson says. "I never used to arrange anything for after training, because that takes your mind off the training when you're doing it, and you never know how you're going to feel: maybe knackered, maybe fine and doing some extra. I'd always try to meet beforehand at someone else's house: that way you're made to do the work, you can't put it off. With Peter, for a time I thought his forté would eventually be 5,000 metres. Talent-wise, you can't compare him with the other three. The ingredients of a great runner come from four or five factors, and Peter's strength is that he never gives in. He's worked it out, like Cram, and for him it's always got to be a wind-up process." Ian Hague, the Sheffield teacher, recalls Wilf Paish telling him when Elliott was a mere boy, "a strong lad without finesse" that eventually he would run under 1:44. It is perhaps a pity, given Paish's judgement, that the relationship between him and Elliott ran off the rails.

Peter would follow training schedules to a T [Paish recalls]. He started with me at the age of fifteen, and was good for anything from 800 to cross-country, an immensely hard worker. He came to the fore in '83, when he was fifth in the World Championships [*the kind of in-attention to detail – Elliott was fourth – that helped lead to the downfall of their partnership*] and in 1984 I thought it would be a good experience for him to try for the 1,500 in LA, as well as the 800 metres. I already had in mind that he could win the 1,500 in Seoul four years later. But when he switched training, to join Kim McDonald, his agent, in my opinion it was quite wrong to try to double, because I didn't believe you could do that with all the talented Kenyans there. When Coe and Ovett were doubling, it was at the time of boycotts, and was that much easier, even if Coe and Cram were still doing it in the European Championships in 1986. Peter needed to gain experience at 1,500 metres between '84 and '88, but if I'd had my way, I think he would have won the 1,500 in Seoul and *not* run in the 800. It didn't help him in Seoul that the British Board split the training camps, and that McDonald was with his middle-distance runners at one camp and I was with my throwers, Mick Hill and Tessa Sanderson, at the other. Because of my knowledge of injuries, I might have detected Peter's hip problem in time.

I agree that part of the difficulty may have been that championship athletes like him need exclusivity with their coach; and that I couldn't give this to Peter because I was working with a squad of athletes, maybe thirty at a time, and would be invited to go to Australia, South Africa or China. But that's my income for the rest of the year. A Sunday newspaper article appeared, claiming that I was annoyed that Peter didn't pay me, but I didn't *want* that. I never asked athletes for a penny, and I spend £12,000 a year on travelling. I get my income from my work in soccer, cricket and Rugby League, with Leeds United, Yorkshire and Halifax.

Peter was needing more of me personally, yet I'm positive that he agreed with what I was doing for him. I like to think my experience helped win him his gold and silver medals. I nursed him through the winter of '87–'88 with a foot injury, and he had a good physiotherapist in Rotherham. In Edinburgh in '86, it was disappointing: Peter ran to *win*, was pipped by Cram and McKean, and got the bronze, and missed selection for Stuttgart, when it was vital to have been there. At that time, with a personal best of 47.4 for 400, I could see he was unlikely to win the Olympic 800, even though he took the silver at the

World Championships in Rome the next year, when he was beaten by Konchellah, a good runner. I felt the schedule for Seoul was too demanding for two events, though I expected one of the classics in the 1,500, with Bilé, Aouita, Cram, Coe and Peter. In the event, he was the only one in it besides Cram, who was off colour. Peter's a man to win gold medals, I think, more than world records, he's so much better in a *series*.

That Paish's instinct was correct is confirmed by Brendan Foster. "In my estimation, for too long Peter was running the wrong event, a 1,500 runner competing at 800. When he stepped up to 1,500 in Seoul, I warned Cram that he was going to be a danger. It was exceptional that he should take the silver medal when having pain-killing injections. All the years of 800 running were good preparation. If I'd been his coach, I would have moved him up long before. He wasn't taking it that seriously, I suspect, in 1984; he'd hardly tried the event."

Elliott says that McDonald usefully and factually altered his training prior to the silver medal in Rome in 1987.

Training hadn't been going well with Wilf at that stage [Elliott recalls]. Kim had been representing me as my agent, and had been helpful. For '88, Wilf was still there at the track, doing the timing, but not coaching. They'd both been there with me in Rome in the warm-up area. Then I started to find I was getting inaccurate training times from Wilf, careless errors, and that's what decided me on making the change. Kim was an athlete himself, and he had some back-up from Alan Storey, another athlete. Kim is sure that my potential is *still* untapped. It's only with him that I've really shifted focus. I'm sorry about Wilf, but I needed more commitment, and he was becoming unreliable. There's no animosity: when someone asked my opinion, I recommended him for the MBE.

I wouldn't have considered both races for the World Championships in Tokyo in 1991, and won't for the Olympics in Barcelona in '92. I learned my lesson in Seoul, seven races was too demanding. A lot of people have said I race too much, but I *love* racing. It's something in me.

Ibbotson wonders just how much the campaign of denigration against Elliott in 1988 by the *Daily Mirror*, aimed at getting Coe to Seoul, served to give Elliott motivation towards his silver medal. "There's nothing finer for an athlete than needing to prove someone wrong. Cerutty used to goad Herb Elliott for this purpose, and the same thing happened with Seb in 1984."

Many middle-distance athletes would have been content to reach retirement with Elliott's silver medals from 1987 and 1988. In a British environment in which the public had been surfeited with success by home runners over a period of sixteen years, Elliott felt unfulfilled.

That was why his victory in Auckland, in a Commonwealth Games otherwise short on quality, was so welcomed by him, and by all those who appreciated what he had contributed to the sport.

SC: I had spoken to Peter on the infield when, though knowing I was ill, I was going through the motions of warming up for the 1,500 heats. He said he'd be very disappointed if I wasn't running, but that there was no point in stepping out there if not well. I was just starting to realize I'd gone two days past the end of my career without knowing it. Peter came of age in that final: he ran well, confidently. The moment he arrived in Auckland I realized he was not only supremely fit, but more confident than ever before. There's a particular look about people in this state, a condition we've all striven for: not an "I'm going to win" attitude, but that someone's going to have to hurt themselves to beat me. That's what Peter had in New Zealand. And when I look back at my training in Sydney, that's the way I'd felt too – that I couldn't lose, either.

It was the kind of 1,500 final I enjoy watching, a fully committed run by Peter. He took up the pace a lap out and ran the legs off the field. He should be proud, because he ran it the hard way, and this reaffirmed his degree of fitness. He had probably benefited from the year out after Seoul, coming back fitter and stronger.

The portent for further major medals was close at hand, at the start of the European summer season.

The 800 metres in Seville, when I ran 1:42.97, which has only been beaten by five men, came as a shock to *me* [Elliott says]. I didn't think I was that good. Seb's 800 record is the one I'd love to break, it's stood so long, and it's the hardest of all to challenge, I think (1:41.73). If I'd gone on to run that weekend in the 1,500, I think I could have broken Aouita's record, I *was* in such good shape. Two weeks later I had a calf injury – probably trained too hard when I would have been better racing. When I think back, I'd been sailing close to the wind, the amount of work I'd been doing. I think I can break the record for the mile or 1,500 but in 1991 I was concentrating on the World Championships, chasing *nothing*. If it happens that I break a record, that will be marvellous. But medals: they can't take that away from you, that's what *counts*.

Instead of records or medals in the summer of 1990, Elliott met only disillusionment. Second to Falcon in the Dream Mile in Oslo, he went to Belfast to race, and the calf-tear now moved up to the back of the knee. To compound his problems, when out for a walk with his dogs back home in Rotherham, he suddenly found he could hardly move; he discovered that it was not only Coe who could be struck down by a virus, and for a while he was confined to bed at his mother's house. Arriving in Split, Yugoslavia, for the European Championships with only seven weeks of track work behind him, Elliott was short of what he needed.

His main rival in Split was expected to be the East German, Jens-Peter Herold, sixth in the World Championships in 1987 and bronze medallist behind Elliott in Seoul. His coach was Bernd Diessner, the same man who had guided Beyer and Straub a decade earlier.

Herold is very different from the other two, a more elegant runner [Diessner says]. He has a pulsating rhythm, more spring in his style. Although he was from my city, Potsdam, I didn't start training him until he was sixteen, under the group system that we then had still operating in the GDR. At one stage, they tried to take him away from me, but he didn't want to move because he was very close to his family, and he was permitted to stay. He was a country boy, living side by side with the hen house, with animals wandering in and out of the kitchen door. Olaf Beyer had been his hero as a boy, and he'd been able to train together with him from about the age of eighteen. By the time of the championships in Split, he was the near-perfect age of twenty-five. I felt sure he'd win a medal, but that it would all hang on the last 200 metres. I knew Elliott was the stronger, more like Straub, but I felt it was anyone's race.

What happened was a nightmare for Elliott. Knocked innocently to the ground in his semi-final, he was reinstated for a place in the final, following hours of debate by the jury of appeal. The majority of athletes, coaches and critics were against the decision, never mind Elliott's innocence, or the fact that similar disasters have befallen great runners in the past, such as Ryun at the Olympic Games in 1972. The crestfallen Elliott, characteristically accepting misfortune and resigned to waiting another year for a chance at a championship, was reluctant to accept his reinstatement:

I'd watched the AAA trials at home, in which I wasn't required to run, and when Morrell handed off Halliday, I telephoned Kim to say jokingly, "Here's another controversy, and I'm *not* involved." The biggest controversy of all was waiting for me around the corner. After they'd reinstated me, I sat for an hour outside the hotel thinking about it the next day, before I went down to the track. People don't believe me, when I have said in interviews, that if I had led into the final straight, as I did in the Commonwealth Games, I would have pulled off the track. If I had won the final, I knew people would say I didn't deserve it. The whole thing was wretched. I was booed on the warm-up track by Spaniards, there were nasty glances in the dressing-room, and when we walked out for the race. It was the longest walk I've ever had to the starting line. I never *asked* to be put back in the race. I accepted that I was *out*. I thought after Seoul, and the problems there, that nothing could ever bother me, yet this was worse. I was the big, bad villain. I knew I should not have run, but the Board's officials had done so much for me, well-meaningly, that I just had to fulfil the decision taken by the appeal committee.

It was sad for Herold too, that his victory, in a race which Elliott inevitably ran without commitment, should have been denied its proper acclaim. For Elliott there was one consolation. Returning to Sheffield, he closed the season with a memorable race in front of his own people, defeating Cram in a swaying tussle in which Elliott got home for his fastest ever time of 3:32.69. He had been left with something on which to build for the next two years.

SC: The difficulty for Peter and for his coach McDonald had been the fact of producing 3:33 pace in January/February, and then knowing that they had to produce that, or faster, in September in Split. That's the art of coaching, of peaking and retaining form. For anyone, what Peter faced was going to be a tall order.

Peter *was* pushed over in Split, and that was from the idiocy of having sixteen athletes on the track at the same time. In that situation, no-one's doing more than is strictly necessary to qualify, everyone's trying to keep their ground on the track. With Peter's speed and form, he didn't need to be there in the ruck – if I'm to be critical – he could have been running wide, keeping clear of the inevitability of a nervy race. With his new sprinting ability, he didn't need to be sitting in the middle of the field. It's a very tough place to be, always jostled, knocked off your stride, looking down avoiding other feet and legs instead of thinking about race tactics.

I didn't really think Peter should have been reinstated, because that opens the door to so many things: someone not in a position to win the race dives in order to get the nod. I'm concerned that track-and-field is not geared for that kind of assessment, in the way horse-racing is; there you have overhead cameras, clearer rules about taking someone else's line or space, and disqualification happens even without *touching*. If you're going to reinstate, you've got to have cameras above the track. We don't know if the East German was himself pushed. If two or more had fallen, would they all have been reinstated? The argument was lost years ago, in the mid-seventies for example, when I was banged into lane five by Wülbeck in the Europa Cup. There was plenty of it around, including at times from Steve Ovett!

Fulfilment for Elliott was again denied in 1991, when injury forced him out of the World Championships in Tokyo. Would Barcelona and the Olympic Games be his final fling?

X · Swan-song

SC: When I heard the news, driving along the M25, that I had been left out of the Olympic team for Seoul, I knew instantly that I would carry on: a determination to finish top of the rankings domestically in 1989, in both events. I may have said, publicly, that I was carrying on "only because I enjoy athletics". That wasn't so. Previously, when I'd had injuries, illness and major disappointments, I'd always felt I would come back, that there would be other great days. Now, when such circumstances were combined with criticism, it generated inside me a lethal mixture.

For 1989, I wanted not only to finish top domestically but also as high as possible internationally, with a string of good races that I could be proud of. It wasn't for the British Board to tell me my career was *over* because they hadn't selected me, because there were better athletes around. By that rationale, the logical conclusion, whether I agreed with their decision or not, had to be that my representative international career *was* over. That was the reason for my comments at the Grand Prix in Berlin, in 1988, that I "wouldn't be wearing a British vest again". I was obliged to believe that this was the British Board's opinion. It would not have rested happily with me had I just petered out after Birmingham, with a couple of end-of-season races. I didn't care *what* the Board's opinion was: I wanted race-judgement for my own satisfaction: *and* in a sport that is always improving, even though I was thirty-two. At this point, I had decided that I would finish at the end of the summer of '89, with no serious thought of continuing until the Commonwealth Games. The Amateur Athletic Association, which selects the England Commonwealth team, and the British Board are much the same thing; so should I expect favours for the Commonwealth Games, when they would again be selecting from the English runners, as for the Olympic Games? There was no point in gearing a season to a selection process that had changed in no feature at all, and indeed was no proper process for selecting a team. This was again proved: in 1988, I was the one who suffered, and in 1989 it was Cram, when both he and Elliott were good enough to win the title in Auckland.

Various newspapers in '88 said I was "turning my back on Britain". I didn't respond. I raced for my club, Haringey, in the European Club Championship, at the beginning of the '89 season in Belgrade. I *did* reject running in minor indoor international events for Britain, because it was the wrong time of season and they clashed with my plans with Haringey. If they'd come to me honestly, and said, "We're maintaining our policy of last year and giving experience to younger people," you could have understood. Instead, I suspected, it was the old game of "He's still an attraction, he'll put bums on seats." Then there was a nonsense mid-season. Suddenly I'm invited to run in the European Cup final at Gateshead. Not in the 800 – that's pencilled in for

McKean. For the 1,500, Cram was selected but couldn't make it, Elliott was still injured, Crabb was invited but had stomach problems. So the choice is now between me and Morrell. I make no bones about it, I was not disposed towards the selectors, and said "No". I'd also been asked to stand by as a *reserve* for both 800 and 1,500, when I'd planned races in Italy, for which I was criticized by some of our senior athletes. It must have been a serious embarrassment for the Board to have to consider me because so many others were unfit or unavailable. John Regis, I think, said I shouldn't be selected for the World Cup after refusing to run in the European Cup; but the aim of my season was fast times in the Grand Prix meetings at the end of the year . . . under 1:44, and some good 1,500s. Although the Board had said *everyone* was eligible for the World Cup, it wasn't likely I'd get the nod, so I went looking for what I wanted.

When Coe was training one Sunday morning, towards the end of June at Haringey's Riverside Stadium in North London, John Hovell mischievously reminded him not to forget to submit his entry forms for the AAA Championships in Birmingham in mid-August. These were again to incorporate the selection trials, this time for the Commonwealth Games; and again on the first-two-past-the-post principle, never mind that they would be taking place *five* months in advance of the championships in which athletes wished to compete. The next day, Coe telephoned the Board, and happened to speak to Charles Taylor, who had been the British official in charge when Coe ran in the European junior championships in 1975. Taylor assured him that he would submit forms on his behalf, and on asking whether Coe wished to be entered for the 800 as well as the 1,500, was told to put him down for both. The seed had been sown for some bizarre subsequent events.

Coe's eventual decision, to prefer the 1,500, was at the time no more than a matter of personal expediency. It was taken ten days beforehand, sitting in a coffee shop by the seafront in Viareggio, where he had just run 1:46. He and his father considered that he had reached the level he needed over two laps, and should now look for something comparatively severe over four. Throwing the AAA into confusion was not a calculated objective; though this was already happening on account of Coe's 1:45.97 in Rovereto. Elliott was injured and out for the season; Cram was fluctuating; Ikem Billy and Tony Morrell had finished behind Coe in Rovereto. Now, running legitimately for his own interests, Coe would coincidentally become a candidate for Commonwealth selection at *both* distances if he finished in the first two in Birmingham. When Coe realized that, if he claimed a 1,500 qualifying place in Birmingham, then Elliott and Cram would be left disputing the discretionary third place for Auckland, a mischievous cunning began to creep into his race-plan.

If the Board could be made to look foolish two years running, maybe it would be obliged to change its policy. An equivalent dilemma was likely to be facing the Board on the decision for the 5,000 metres, with neither Hutchings nor Buckner likely to be fit and the two therefore disputing a single discretionary selection. There was no pressure on Coe as he headed for Birmingham.

His concerns were outside athletics. He was busy seeking selection elsewhere: as Parliamentary candidate for Falmouth and Camborne, in Cornwall. He would not, as had Christopher Chataway in similar circumstances twenty years before, be riding the back of a concurrent career in television. Coe's move in that direction had come to a halt. Towards the end of 1988, he had been approached by the BBC as a potential presenter for Breakfast Television, where they were intending to sharpen the programme and increase the news element. Coe was cautious: he had no wish to rise at 4.30 in the morning for a half-minute slot reading the close of play scores from the previous evening in the West Indies, or giving the highlights of last night's match at Highbury. If they wanted him in a sporting capacity, he was not interested. The BBC assured him this was not so, and invited him to discuss details. Coe was intent on establishing three points: that he was not interested in a sports role; that he was planning a political career with one of the major parties, and hoped soon to be adopted, which could cause difficulty with the BBC if, say, he was required to interview the opposition spokesman on the NHS; and that he wanted assurance that, if he was to be an anchor-man, he would be given time for proper training in the technology of studio work. The BBC seemingly accepted his conditions, though Coe was disconcerted to find a story relating to this appearing in the *Sun* newspaper. Also, the launch date was continually postponed. A planned series of five-minute film slots, by way of introduction, never began. Simultaneously, Coe was having to consider the offer from Colin Moynihan, the Sports Minister, of the chairmanship of the Sports Council. Although there was the suggestion that he could take a two-year period of office as chairman, he was worried about becoming pigeon-holed. He had enjoyed his period as vice-chairman, and being involved in a drugs report and the Council's "Olympic Review", but he had no ambition in the sports field. The BBC venture came to a standstill when it became clear that, after all, it *was* intended to utilize him on sport. That would be even more of a pigeon-hole than the Sports Council. By December of 1989, he had been selected as Conservative candidate for Falmouth, and his route had become resolved.

Whatever the Board might decide about discretionary Commonwealth places as a result of the trials at the AAA Championships, it was inevitable that this Birmingham meeting would also be a major influence on their selection for the World Cup, to take place in Barcelona a month later. For Coe to be selected for that would be exceptional even by his standards. He would then be two weeks off his thirty-third birthday. Still to be racing beyond thirty, in a middle-distance event dependent on kick finish, is rare. Kip Keino was thirty-two when he took the 1,500 silver medal behind Vasala of Finland, in the Munich Olympic Games in 1972, and won the steeplechase ahead of Ben Jipcho. Miruts Yifter was thirty-five when he did the long-distance double, 5,000 and 10,000, in the World Cup in 1979, and repeated it in the Moscow Olympics a year later, while Sydney Wood-erson was thirty-two when he won the European Championships 5,000 in Oslo in 1946. Here was Coe using Birmingham primarily as a warm-up for a confrontation the following week with Bilé, the world champion, and Aouita in Zurich. A coincidental oddity of the event in Birmingham was that, for the first time in seventeen years, Coe and Ovett would be standing on the same starting line in Britain. Their clash would send fewer reverberations through the sport than it would have done eight or nine years before; yet in spite of its irrelevance in current racing terms, Independent Television was playing the card for all that it was worth.

SC: I drove across to the meeting from Loughborough with Steve Mitchell, the same as the year before. This time I won my heat comfortably, with a strong finishing kick. I'd already had a minor dust-up with the Board the previous Monday. Following the European Cup final at Gateshead, when there'd been some inflammatory comments about my not appearing – I'd been in Viareggio – I'd telephoned Mike Farrell, the secretary, to clarify the position. The tabloids had made meat and drink of comments about me by Board officials, and this was the last thing I wanted in my final year. It was during this 'phone call that I made clear that I would be running the 1,500 and not the 800 in Birmingham. Peter had talked early in the week to Andy Norman about stand tickets for the final, saying, "I suppose they're like gold dust." Norman had said the reverse was the case, that for every two you bought, you were given one free. That began to provide an explanation for me why ITV had been going overboard all week about my alleged "showdown" with Ovett. The *Mirror*, among many, had joined the hype, with the headline "It's On!". Yet I'd had an odd feeling earlier in the summer, when a couple of journalists, Randall Northam and Vic Robbie, had asked me, for no particular reason, whether I would agree to run against Ovett. There was no indication when. Had someone been prompting them? I'd merely said, yes, if it happens.

Things were a little odd on the day of the heats. Warming up with Mitchell, we'd seen Steve Ovett standing in a group with Harry Wilson and Rachel. Although Steve and I were at very different stages in our respective careers, it was evident, in spite of what Norman had said to Peter, that the hype was working, because there was a fair-sized crowd. On principle, I'd been refusing requests for interviews during the week to discuss the "showdown". Now Ovett came up to me and said, "I must talk to you after the race." I joked a bit, and Steve said, "I'm serious." In case I missed him, I gave him the telephone number at Mitchell's. Harry and Rachel continued to look bothered, and I asked what the problem was. Steve said, "There's some very dodgy business going on." I laughed, and made a remark I would later regret: "Steve, you know me, if there's any dodgy business, count me in!" My comment is there in the text of the official inquiry which was later to take place, and will mock me to my grave. David Pickup, the director of the Sports Council, who was to conduct the inquiry, said, "Can I confirm a few of your comments at the time?" I couldn't help but laugh.

After the heats, I noticed Ovett talking in the car park with Les Jones, the British team manager. I walked over, and Les moved away. Again I asked Steve what was the problem. "I want to clear up things that have been bothering me," Steve said. "Are you being paid to run in these championships?" I didn't realize subventions were being paid to run at championships, yet, why would someone like Buckner be there, when he was less than fit but assured of selection as European champion? Anyway, Steve said, "Well, I've been offered money, and I'm angry, we're both being used to sell tickets." I said I was happy to be there for my *own* interests. Steve said he was being paid a substantial sum. He was most agitated. He clearly didn't want me to find out later that he was being offered £20,000, and said he had a good mind to drive home to Scotland that night. I said he ought to be careful in his considerations, because if he pulled out, it would only be remembered as another Ovett–Coe race that didn't take place, and he'd be hammered by the press. Yet things were falling into place. If he'd been offered that kind of money, it tied in with what I was offered the year before to run in the McVitties meeting (£25,000). I don't know if Andy Norman was involved in this offer to Steve, though I do know he's a great judge of athletic horse flesh, of what anyone will do. I didn't think much more about the situation that evening, but the following morning I had a call from Colin Hart of the *Sun*, from the athletes' hotel in Birmingham, saying he was with Ovett, who wanted to speak to me. I was becoming a bit tired of the issue, what with this and reading Cliff Temple in the *Sunday Times*, writing, "Don't be sure they'll both be there, one of them may still catch a virus or fall down a lift-shaft." I spoke to Steve, didn't discuss money, but repeated my warning about pulling out. At midday, I had *another* call from Steve, on the car phone, saying he wasn't in the mood to run. I told him he'd better watch out, because there were probably people already in a traffic jam on the M1 trying to get to the race. Besides, I *was* worried about adding to the Coe–Ovett mythology. I told him if he withdrew, it was on his own account; that even if there was a two-tier (payment) system, I wanted to be in the race for my own needs. I didn't speak to him again until just before we ran, though when Peter arrived at the stadium, independently, he was approached by Jim Rosenthal of ITV, saying, "I suppose you want to talk to Ovett about all this business." Peter, in all ignorance, said yes, he wanted to give Steve a bottle of wine he'd brought from Freddie Schaefer, the promoter of the Koblenz meeting. What Peter didn't know was that, all morning, ITV had been attempting to persuade Steve that he *must* run. Many interests were interwoven that day.

It was a cold and windy evening for the final. Those looking for a Commonwealth nomination, apart from Ovett and Coe, included Horsfield, Crabb and Morrell, plus Steve Halliday and Chris McGeorge. It was a typical selection race: slow, edgy, with elbows all over the place and no-one willing to make the pace. Down the third back straight, Coe was lying second and Crabb third, with Ovett seventh. Coming into the home straight approaching the bell, Crabb made a move to go to the front, was caught from behind on the heel by Morrell, and went down. Morrell, who was running wide in lane two, was able to move by on the outside, but Coe had to leap over the fallen Crabb, moving sideways and jarring a hamstring as he landed. By the time he recovered his balance and had started running again, he was twenty yards adrift of the leaders.

SC: Crabb ridiculously cut in immediately in front of Morrell, and when I landed badly on the outside of my foot, leaping in the air to avoid stepping on Crabb, Ovett ran into the back of me, and I nearly fell again. I realized the best chance I had was to keep cool, not to try to eat up the 20-metre gap in 100 metres, but to erase it with level running, one metre for every twenty. Down the back straight I passed three or four people, and now had the leaders, Morrell and Horsfield, within range. I eased for a dozen paces, and then went past the others with 80 metres to go, managing to hold on to the finish. It was one of those occasions I've been most aware of a crowd, who thought it was splendidly spectacular. I had a sore leg, but coasted a gentle lap of honour, unaware of what was happening to Steve (Ovett, fourth down the final back straight, had finished tenth). When I came to a standstill, Rosenthal was there with a microphone and camera. What I didn't know was that Ovett had already been interviewed, and had broken down in tears, giving his side of the story. I was busy trying to explain the last 500 metres, and all Rosenthal was asking about was Steve and money.

In a performance that brought back, for spectators and television viewers, all the former enchantment of Coe's magical running in his prime, he had finished four yards ahead of Morrell. Theirs by right were the places in the Commonwealth team; the World Cup team would be announced the following Thursday, though it was said that the 1,500 metres place for that would be left open for a fortnight, pending possible return to fitness by Elliott and Cram. Andy Norman denied that he had spoken with Ovett, or that subventions had been offered for these championships. It was alleged that ITV had threatened to drop Ovett from their commentary team if he did not run, and the Board promised that there would be an inquiry. When that eventually took place, under the chairmanship of Pickup, predictably nothing was proved one way or the other about what had been a disreputable affair. From Birmingham, Coe went to Zurich where, his leg still sore, he ran carefully, on three-quarter throttle, to come second in the 1,500 metres; he then ran the world's third fastest 800 metres of the year, 1:43.38, in Berne, which together with 3:34 in Zurich told him that he could win the World Cup, *if* selected.

The Zurich race – defeating among others Rono, the Olympic champion, Di Napoli and Falcon, improving young runners from Italy and America, and Scott, Cheruiyot and O'Sullivan, fifth, seventh and eighth respectively in the '88 Olympics – when not going flat out, was Coe's fastest time since his best ever in Rieti in 1986. The Berne time was his fourth fastest ever, and by one and a half seconds was the best English time of the year. So much for the young cubs and the old lion.

It was inevitable that the Board would have to swallow antagonisms of the previous year, having been proved demonstrably wrong, and select Coe for the World Cup. Tony Ward, the Board's press officer, who during the controversy of 1988 had behaved more like a cheerleader at an American football match than an objective provider of facts and information, was decent enough to admit to Coe that the old lion still had breath, and this was accepted with good grace. The decision in '88, after all, had been by Ward's employers. Coe now headed for the sunshine of the Costa Brava and a meeting with the world champion, Bilé, who had avoided him in Zurich by switching at the last minute to a 1,000 metres race. Besides Bilé, there would be Herold, the Olympic bronze medallist. Coe was also riding comfortably on an option to run both distances in the Commonweath Games. He had been named by the AAA in England's team, not only for the 1,500, for which he had qualified, but for the discretionary place at 800, following his performance in Berne; and had been given until 19 September, a week after the World Cup, to make his decision. Cram and Elliott still did not know whether, in the Commonwealth Games, they would be running at either distance or neither.

SC: The first time I was aware of Bilé was in '87 in Rome, working with the BBC, when I used to enjoy sitting with Stan Greenberg, the statistician who is their back-up man, looking through video tapes at the end of the evening. At the time you're commentating, you tend to concentrate on the first three. In Bilé's semi-final in Rome he'd sat at the back, fifth or sixth on the last lap, over-hauling by up to thirty metres over the last 200. Watching the re-run, I'd been convinced there could be only one possible winner, and that's what I'd said in my preview the next day. I'd raced him in '88, and knew you couldn't mess about with him: I'd tried to break him in Lausanne, and failed. Now I would be giving away ten years, so the very latest I could leave it would be 300 yards out. If there was a format where he looked vulnerable, it was when put under pressure over the last 200 from *in front*. Nobody had yet really given him a race: he missed Seoul with injury, and I'd seen him beaten only once, in Cologne this year, by Kip Cheruiyot of Kenya. There was a bubbling feeling in the British team, following the Europa Cup victory in Gateshead, a mood that maybe we could turn over the Americans. I avoided all encouragement offered by the media to discuss being back in the team.

The two favourites would begin as predicted. After 300 metres, Coe, representing Britain, lay third, in touch with the pace, behind Oliveira (Americas), Nakayama (Asia), with Bilé (Africa) bringing up the rear. With Herold (GDR) tucked in behind Coe, it remained much the same as they went through the 800 mark in a leisurely 1:58.68; as they moved down the home straight towards the bell the order had rearranged, with Coe, Bilé and Herold poised behind Nakayama. Into the back straight for the last time, Coe made his move.

SC: I remember feeling very strong, and perhaps with hindsight I should have gone earlier. I kicked hard at 300, right on the 1,500 start line. I was aware Bilé responded instantly. I wasn't flat out down the back straight, and thought I would wind it up at 200, really dig in round the last bend. I was still in the lead on the crown of the bend, and felt I had another gear to go. At about 120 metres out, Bilé comes alongside me, we're shoulder to shoulder, and as we come off the bend, he's crowding me, he's narrowing into lane one. The next thing I know, he's shot right across my path, into my stride. I had to put out both hands to push him off on his shoulder, but more to keep my own balance. Bilé's correct when he says I pushed him, but for me the damage was done. My stride was checked: I'd lost one and a half strides, and that was about how it stayed to the line, though Herold closed in on both of us. Then the politics started.

Bilé's time was 3:35.56, Coe's 0.23 seconds slower. Irrespective of the foul, it had been an exhilarating race and an astonishing performance by a runner of thirty-three. In order to bring himself to a single exclusive peak for the season, just as he had intended to do for Seoul – and had done unerringly so often in the past – Coe had voluntarily forfeited more than £50,000 in half a dozen available race fees over the previous two months. He had done so not because he was racing for his country, against all expectations, but because for Peter and him the search for perfection had always been the priority. Whether he was

running for Britain or for himself, he ran with the intention of getting
it right. It was an ironic final twist of history that the British Board
management, which had treated him so shabbily in excluding him from
Seoul, should now be obliged to lodge a protest against Bilé, the
representative of the African team: and was so slow in doing so, that
there was little chance that the IAAF's jury of appeal would withdraw
Bilé's gold medal and nine points for Africa, even with a disqualification that would have been justified. There was little or no chance with
the three-man appeal committee containing an African, though he
could have been out-voted by an American and a Finn.

The appeals procedure needs reviewing. A steward's inquiry in
horse-racing, for instance, having viewed the video, would have reversed the order of first and second places, thereby denying Africa only
one point instead of nine. Coe, whose career had contained enough
controversy to have made him retire long ago, was wholly against a
protest, but in such circumstances the responsibility lies not with the
athlete. Coe argued strongly with his father against an appeal, having
no taste for victory in the committee room, such as Chris Brasher
achieved when he won his steeplechase gold medal in the 1956
Olympic Games.

SC: Peter was steaming. I'd not seen him as angry for a long time, he was
spitting. Frank Dick was angry, too, *and* Ward. Les Jones seemed embarrassed to be involved, and was trying to say it was "the athlete's decision". I
pointed out the futility of a protest, the politics of the situation, that it was not
an individual but a team event, that there would never be an overturn of the
African victory.

Bilé gave a poor performance at the medallists' interview, pretending
that he didn't understand what the fuss was about, that Coe had fouled
him more than he had fouled Coe, maintaining an offended naïvety
wholly out of place in someone conditioned over several years by the
American way of life. Bilé had twice been US college champion since
1985, for George Mason, and in a sycophantic interview with *Track
and Field News* he maintained the pretence of innocence. "There was
no doubt who was responsible," Peter recalls. "All around me, at the
moment of the incident, there were gasps of 'Oh!' from people sixty
metres or more from where it happened but with a clear view of how
Bilé cut across for the inside of the lane. The give-away is that before
there had been any protest, Bilé was trying to apologize to me. I don't
forget that Bilé was disqualified in his Olympic semi-final in Los
Angeles." The give-away from the appeal committee was that they
returned to the British the fee that has to be deposited with each appeal
and is forfeited if the appeal fails.

Five days later, Coe made his domestic swan-song in the McVitties International at Crystal Palace. Although such international figure-heads as Aouita, Herold, Barrios, Buckner, Greg Foster, Backley, the new javelin world record holder, Christie, Regis, and Wachtel were on display, the final appearance of the most celebrated runner in British history undoubtedly did much to attract the 17,000 crowd. Coe duly rewarded them, with an easy win over Billy and Morrell in 1:45.70. His run was distinguished by the fact that Konchellah, the Kenyan world champion, was willing to make the pace for him. The cloud over the evening was an anonymous performance by the fading Ovett, a distant tenth behind Aouita in the mile. It was sad to witness the decline in Coe's great contemporary, upon whom increasing age had not smiled so benignly. Coe would be the first to agree that his career could never have shone with the same intensity had it not been set against the equivalent talents of this other unique runner, whose appeal had been so strong and so different.

SC: When I ran a lap of honour, it seemed that it lasted twenty minutes. My appearances have been relatively infrequent at Crystal Palace, though athletics isn't just about London audiences or invitation events. Between 1984 and 1990, I think I probably turned out more for my club than most people running at my level, and for twenty years I ran every year in the county championships. This was the end of my racing after sixteen seasons as a senior. In the ups and down, there had been some very low moments, but now I was glad I was leaving a sport that had never been in a healthier state. I had been able to do almost all of what I'd set out to do, all those years ago. I would like to have had an Olympic gold at 800 metres, but I think I got it right more times than I got it wrong.

On the morning of the race at Crystal Palace, at a portentous personal press conference given in central London, it had not been clear whether Coe was appearing as athlete or politician. Journalists of both cultures were in attendance at the Connaught Rooms, where he announced that he was accepting the invitation to run both distances in the Commonwealth Games in January. For three years, he said, he had been a politician fitting in the occasional track race. In the past twelve months, he had made speeches at forty political gatherings, and could not reasonably hope any more to do both activities, he asserted, without one suffering; though for the next three months his political ambitions would be put on hold. He would be running for England in Auckland, he said, because the call to compete in his country's vest remained irresistible, and because twice previously in this event his health had let him down. He neatly embraced both schools of journal-ism – some of the political scribes beginning to move to the bar during discussion of lap times – by presenting his views on South Africa and the Commonwealth. Expressions such as "I believe that the Commonwealth remains an important and influential bonding of nations" were the very stuff of constituency meetings. Coe the public figure, as opposed to Coe the athlete, had drawn his audience: and it did not go away empty-handed.

SC: When I ran in Barcelona, I didn't know whether to go to Auckland or not. Arthur Gold (Sir Arthur Gold, chairman of BOA) had been pushing me. There were advantages and disadvantages. I was racing well, and the situation was free of administrative pressure. I'd tumbled into the Commonwealth team almost inadvertently. To go didn't mean another whole season of maintaining form, but holding on for a few months. Against that, I was into the selection process for Falmouth. The final meeting should have been on the day of the race in Barcelona, and I'd been able to arrange a postponement. In the end, I went because it was a competition from which I had never brought back a medal. I wanted '89 to be the end, and this way it could be. I'd achieved this year what I wanted, I'd salvaged some personal esteem, proving that at thirty-three I was still among a small refined group. Internationally, I'd just finished second in the world, and come top of the rankings in Britain at 800 and 1,500. The risk was to go to Auckland and perform *badly*. The decision to go gave rise to quite a lot of thought: where to go from September, with performances of 1:43 and 3:34, and not break down, not lose speed-work, maintain endurance work. In the end I took a couple of weeks' holiday, and treated November to January as a mini-season, with October having the same kind of training I would normally do in March–April.

I went to Melbourne early in December to acclimatize, and in order to have one or two preliminary races. Daley was down there with me, and I had five weeks of marvellous preparation. Melbourne was beautiful, with lovely runs and cycle paths in its parklands and down by the Yarrow river. The people were so hospitable and I would have voted for Melbourne for the Centenary Olympic Games of 1996. My decision had meant that England had to choose between Cram and Elliott for the discretionary place at 1,500 metres. Billy and Yates had the other two places at 800. It was clear that Elliott was coming back strongly after injury, and sometimes it can help to have had a break. He'll enjoy looking back on his career and seeing a Commonwealth title. Cram had had an in-and-out season. It was tough to choose between the two of them, and I guess the selectors got it right. In Auckland, my father and I rented a bungalow on the edge of town. I did a lot of 400 repetitions, all under 50, with short intervals. I was as fit as I could possibly be; so much so, that Peter was having to ease me off.

Fortune, however, was not to smile upon him. It is odd that out of the seven championships in which Coe competed, four should have had

abnormally cold weather; and that for two of them he should have
been struck down with flu. His first European Championships, in
Prague, were wretchedly cold, but he remained fit, as he did in Stuttgart in 1986; in Edinburgh and Auckland he was laid low. Auckland
was especially perverse. The sun shone almost all the time, yet there
was always a fierce wind blowing, and certainly I found, as a
European, that one had only to step into the shadow of a building to
be shivering if wearing no more than a sports shirt. In the press box,
we were mostly dressed in anoraks. The schedule for the middle-
distance races consisted of heats and semi-finals of the 800 on consecutive days, then a two-day rest, followed by the final, and heats and
final of the 1,500 on successive days.

As Coe and John Walker stood side by side for the 800 semi-finals,
it had been strange to recall that eleven years earlier these two
illustrious runners had lined up for the Golden Mile in Oslo: Walker,
the world record holder, Coe the suddenly emerging star. And half an
hour later Walker had been saying that "around the final bend I could
only watch from behind, knowing he was going to take my record."
Too many years had now accumulated for Walker, aged thirty-eight,
but there was no public premonition of problems for Coe. He
appeared, from the trackside, to have a comfortable fourth place in
mid-race behind Kiprotich and Tirop of Kenya, and Whittle of Scotland. The appearance was illusory. As Whittle, Coe and Ikem Billy,
the AAA champion, followed the two Kenyans into the bend, Billy
suddenly surged ahead of Coe, who failed to respond and came into
the finishing straight fifth. In what was the sterner of two semi-finals,
Billy had timed his effort well, and though down the straight Coe
passed him fifteen metres out, Billy qualified with the fastest fifth
position: 1:47.80, to Coe's 1:47.67, and Kiprotich's winning 1:46.92.

There was general alarm in the press box at Coe's lack of zest, at that
phlegmatic look about his stride which had been so easily distinguish-
able from the flow that characterized his stride when all was well.
Journalists hurried down to the warm-up track to find out what might
be amiss, only to be assured by runner and coach that this had been
nothing more than a matter of preserving energy for the final. Unhappily, their explanation was a blind. Peter said that the plan had been to
qualify with the least possible effort, to run wide, and on no account to
slog it out to the finish. His son agreed that this had been the intention,
and said he felt comfortable and untroubled, yet admitted to his slow
reaction on the final bend. In the second semi-final, McKean, momentarily boxed on the back straight, comfortably kicked clear in the
finishing straight to win by a chest in 1:46.83, ahead of Kibet of
Kenya. Coe had beaten Kiprotich and Kibet in Berne, with the third
fastest time of the year; and Peter Coe, in a last, despairing pretence as

ring-master, said to me over dinner in the Village that evening: "It is going to be furious for 600 yards and then eyeballs out round the last bend."

The anguish for Peter, privately aware that the runner he had nursed, guided, driven and inspired for twenty-two years, was about to collapse in harness on his last appearance, was too great a pain for him to admit the truth to me. When his son had put his foot down in the home straight, little had happened, and Peter's prediction for the final was no more than bravado. Two days later, Coe was to finish a dispirited sixth, a shadow of his normal self, in a moderate race won by Tirop; memorable only for the clashing on the track, and the face-to-face confrontation afterwards, between McKean and Billy. It was McKean's second disaster in a championship final, for the same had happened to him in Rome in 1987. Only quick action by Coe, stepping between his England colleague and the Scot, prevented them coming to blows. Billy had finished fifth and McKean seventh, with Matthew Yates of England surprisingly taking the bronze medal. Twenty-four hours later, protesting against the advice to do so from the England team doctors, Coe would withdraw from the heats of the 1,500 metres. On a windy warm-up track in New Zealand, the flame of one of the most illustrious careers in the history of the sport had been finally extinguished.

SC: I'd felt signs of cold over the weekend before the heats of the 800, though I'd not wholly come clean with Peter. Not feeling so good, I'd been to Ken Kingsbury, the doctor. He knew immediately what was up and had been to tell Peter privately I was ill. I'd been trying to kid myself I was suffering from dehydration, because the symptoms for this can sometimes ape a fever. That whole weekend I was *drinking* for England, in the belief that I might cure myself. By Thursday, however, the day of the 800 final, I was feeling no better, and had hardly slept. My resting pulse-rate was 47 instead of 38, so I knew something was wrong. Tactically, I ran a reasonable final, but was swallowed up by the field when I reached for the kick that wasn't there. I remember thinking it was vaguely humorous, knowing how badly I was running, that I should be in armed combat with Tom McKean for *sixth* place. I walked off the track at the finish, knowing, as ever, that you cannot run through illness. As Dave Moorcroft was busy saying on BBC television, as an international athlete "you're either world class or nothing at all." McKean was shell-shocked: though in fairness to him, it's very difficult to come out of a European season and adapt to winter. In the changing-room, he and Billy were about to have a punch-up, McKean accusing Billy of robbing him of a medal. I got between the two of them and said to Tom, "Shut up, and go and win the European championship" . . . which is what Tom did. The team manager had stood there doing nothing.

I'd said to the press that it was "just one of those days". I didn't want to make excuses. I had a fearful headache, and went to the doctor again, took some aspirins, and saw him again the next day. He advised me not to run. I chatted to Peter, who was dead against it. He was right: in that state there was no guarantee I'd even get through the heat, any more than in '88 in the Olympic trial. I decided to wait, to warm up before the heat and see how I felt. Frank Dick pleaded with me not to run. There was *another* instance of how our sport is administered: the chief coach of the British Board was not even accredited, and was only able to get into the stadium with an accreditation from the Falkland Islands!

I was still undecided, but finally John Jeffrey, the team manager, said, "I've seen enough, you're withdrawn, I'm making this decision as team manager." And that's how my athletic career finished. I was very disappointed, and things were made no easier by the tangibles: Matthew Yates flowing past for the 800 bronze, O'Donoghue of New Zealand taking a bronze in the 1,500, when I could remember a training session in Melbourne of 300 metre repetitions in which I'd been trying to give *him* encouragement. Those are the things you recall. On the day of the 1,500 final, I decided to sit in the stadium and watch with Peter, David Martin and Wendy Sly. It was so different . . . suddenly to be cut off, and be a spectator. The next day I flew home.

Peter, while on the one hand distressed beyond measure at the manner of the exit his son was forced to endure, remained characteristically objective.

PC: If you can't take that kind of disappointment, how could you ever work in politics! [Peter says, with that pinched, squinting look he has when grasping something prickly]. It *was* a wretched frustration – all the time and effort – but what else could you have done? Apart from the pelvic displacement he had in 1980–81, all the setbacks that have pulled him down seriously have been infections rather than physical. It happened twice in eighteen months in 1988–90. It's only metaphorically a matter of life and death to those at the highest level of competition, where a difference of half a per cent means the difference between being first or at the back of the field. In any other walk of life, you're OK. Otherwise the hospitals would be swamped. There are permanent risks for unique performers at a superlative level of fitness. Nowadays Seb is still running, maybe preparing for a social effort in the London Marathon, but with none of the hard stuff, and he's never felt better, though he couldn't now do a series of 300s in the low 30s. It's clear that the lowest point of the super-athlete, in resistance to illness, is at moments of peak fitness. A paper in the *Lancet* has described how the cells of a fit athlete are more permeable. Seb had a peak of brilliance that ran from '79 to '84, or, if you include his 3:29 in Rieti, from '79 to '86. Ken Kingsbury and I knew in Auckland that he had a bug, but I didn't say anything to you after the 800 semi-final because I knew he was determined to run. To have said something would have been the ultimate disloyalty.

As the years went by, we found that longer recovery periods were needed after hard training sessions: probably an indication that his tolerance to physical stress was decreasing. After the 800 gold medal in Stuttgart, I would have been happy to call it a day. It was *he* who wished to keep going. After the non-selection in '88, Seb got the needle, he wanted to prove things once more, and it was his inclusion in the World Cup that led to going to Auckland. I felt he only had to stand up to get a couple of medals. After Bilé's foul, he wanted to finish on a good note. He had *always* had to come back.

SC: It gets no easier, looking back on Auckland, the last exit being a seat in the stand. Yet I'd been lucky. I'd never had surgery, never trained through injury or illness to a point of threatening my career. Yet I was always vulnerable at a peak. My problems did get more coverage because they were so damaging to publicly perceived prospects. It's a bit like flying accidents: when you get a cold at a quiet time, you think good, that's eliminated another chance of being side-swiped in the middle of the summer. The vulnerability of sports competitors is renowned. In the World Cup soccer in Mexico, it's the players who go down with sickness, not the octogenarian FA councillors! Yet for so much of the time, it did go well for me. The good times I had are not within many people's frame of reference. Sport in general, but especially measurable sport, is so exposed to minute fluctuations of physical condition. And we're nowhere near to knowing the relationship between illness and physical stress. I would make a plea to physiologists to pay more attention, for interest's sake, to this problem, though in global terms it is admittedly a narrow field for study.

The decline in performance by sport's supreme achievers must always be a process more difficult for them to accommodate than for an adoring public. The public merely moves on to the newest phenomenon, while yesterday's star must adjust his or her life to different dimensions. Only golfers may continue to believe their sun will never set. The achievers' self-perception can be so difficult to adjust when achievement is no longer there. For Coe there is the compensation that he is moving into fresh and even more challenging fields in what many call, as he well knows, the *real* life.

"The vanity element did still matter to him, to the end," Angela Coe says. "He enjoyed being recognized, for the confirmation that he could still do it. It's a kind of gratitude. He continued even after '86, because he knew he was still a winner, even though there were longer gaps to accommodate other aspects of his life. In one way, the sporting challenge became greater: there were people of twenty-four trying to beat him, and not doing so. From sport beyond himself, he became switched off. If someone said, 'Did you see about Aouita?', he often hadn't heard or noticed."

As Derek Ibbotson says: "His span was extraordinary. To be there in Auckland at the age of thirty-three was exceptional."

XI · Neglect

The attitude of British governments towards sport is a conundrum. The British, having invented much of modern competitive sport, have persistently regarded it throughout the twentieth century as something essentially unimportant. Millions of the population would spend hours and hours, to the point of tedium, talking about sport, yet no politician could be persuaded to regard it seriously. Sport, never mind that it occupies more television time than any other human activity – except, perhaps, violence – is regarded by politicians as a topic for the pub, the club, the men's washroom, possibly the train going to work, and dinner, if the ladies can be persuaded to talk about something else. The governments of the United States and Britain have been alone, in the developed world, in ignoring the value to a nation of staging an Olympic Games, refusing to invest public funds in assisting the creation of those facilities that might persuade the International Olympic Committee to grant one of their cities the honour of staging the Games. The recent election of Los Angeles and Atlanta as host cities was wholly due to the energy and efforts of private individuals backed by corporate business.

The role of Minister for Sport in Britain is a continuing controversy. A succession of ministers – Eldon Griffiths, Hector Munro, Neil Macfarlane, Richard Tracey, Colin Moynihan and Robert Atkins – have conducted high-profile campaigns while in office . . . and achieved little. There is no major legacy for sport left by any of them to which we can point with gratitude. There is the impression that the post is little more than a stepping-stone to a knighthood, and a quiet seat on the back-benches. Whoever hears much these days of Sir Eldon, Sir Hector or Sir Neil – flags that flew strongly from the top of the tent, and were then pulled down and quietly put away when the show left town. What had they all been doing?

SC: A succession of ministers have been involved in a misconception. They have all tended to say that they cannot be *expected* to do more, because only one-fifth of their time in office can be directed at sport, on account of other responsibilities as junior ministers within the Department of the Environment – which is what the job was until John Major moved it to the Department of Education. Any permanent civil servant in sport will tell you that ministers spend the majority of their time engaged in sporting business, as Parliamentary Under-Secretary of State, but suggest that they do not, simply because there is little respect or consideration given to sport by the senior department Minister. This is what Macfarlane discovered as junior minister. The Minister is often an enthusiast, and enjoys the position; but there is *no* job description and he has no budget, even if three-quarters of his time is occupied with sporting matters. The government budget for sport is wholly distributed by the Sports Council, together with whatever the Department of the Environment, under the old Rates Support Grant, designated to regions for Sport-and-Leisure. The Minister can develop certain initiatives, but can enshrine nothing in legislation. Just look at the trouble Colin Moynihan had trying to obtain a ban on anabolic steroids in civil law. All that happened was that the Home Office made it an offence to pass steroids to minors, whereas Moynihan had wanted *any* possession to be an offence. Civil servants will advise a sports minister never to get into a head-on situation within sport. Colin Moynihan did, with the identity-card scheme, but he was running with a ball that had been passed to him. What finished Macfarlane was trying to explain on television how five hundred yobs had smashed up Luxembourg at an England football match, or attempting to deal with the aftermath of Heysel. Dick Tracey lasted a year.

Inheriting the sports ministry can be a lead weight for anyone, no matter how much the Minister may try to stress that what he is *really* involved with is waterways, parks and national monuments, his "other" responsibilities. There is the often-quoted story of one civil servant saying to another, upon his return from working in sport: "Glad to see you've got a proper job at last!" Against such a political background, I did not feel it made sense for me to accept the offer, at a time when I was vice-chairman of the Sports Council, of taking over the chairmanship from John Smith, who was also then the chairman of Liverpool Football Club. And, it has to be asked, what really is the difference between the Minister for Sport and the chairman of the Sports Council.

British sports administration is very much a product of Victorian institutional attitudes, and it's difficult to dissociate much of its attitude from other aspects of nineteenth-century labour and union organization. There's a strange logic about the way the three umbrella bodies of British sport have come together: the British Olympic Association, governing Olympic sport; the Central Council of Physical Recreation, which is the forum of governing bodies; and the Sports Council, the executive arm of government. If they haven't come together sufficiently, or effectively enough, it's because of the quality of the people running them. All three bodies would still be necessary under an amalgamated "British Sports Confederation", but would they work any better? Who would fund them, and would there be discipline? Individual, divisional chairmen would still be competing with each other. Although the Rossi Report recommended the abolition of the CCPR – the original owners of the National Sports Training Centres before these were handed over to the Sports Council, at the creation of its Royal Charter in 1972 – I believe the CCPR *does* have a place. Under the leadership of Peter Lawson, the general secretary, it has campaigned for fair play, for the retention of public sports grounds, for more swimming pools. The Sports Council has no scope for such campaigns, though it would claim it does have a public relations function.

There is a limit to what it can do. What can the Sports Council do if it thinks it is under-funded by central government, with its annual grant in 1991 approaching nearly £50 million? Very little. I remember the Sports Council being on a standstill budget, and deciding with the chairman that we should campaign. I was filmed at inner-city sports facilities that would suffer from under-funding, but we couldn't really *let loose*.

Does the BOA satisfactorily meet its obligations? You used to get the impression that they were content with a moderately quiet life tucked away at Wandsworth, though they have now expanded their operation. If the BOA were given more exposure and status, it could exert a great deal of influence. Charles Palmer, when chairman, substantially improved BOA's finances – as even his many critics would agree. The BOA cannot continue to find powerful leadership from a general-secretary when paying less than £30,000; and I find it hard to understand why John Boulter, a former British Olympic athlete earning £75,000 as corporate head of Adidas in France, applied for the post before then withdrawing. The short answer to most problems in British sports administration is that publicly we under-value the importance of the work. The responsibility within government has been lessened to the rank of junior minister; and no departmental Secretary of State with, say, a housing budget of £2.7 billion, is going to risk his job going out on a limb regarding some quango with a sports budget of £45 million. Atkins' re-shaping of the Sports Council in December 1991 was less than radical.

Britain, having provided inspiration with its organized games for Baron Pierre de Coubertin to recreate the Olympic Games in 1986, has twice staged the Games: in 1908 and 1948, London both times coming to the rescue of the IOC in the absence of other willing host cities. People within British sport would like the Games to return to Britain, and with good reason: though the logic of this ambition has hitherto been lost upon the government. The Olympic Games in Barcelona in 1992 are expected to bring a commercial benefit to the city, in tourism and development, to the tune of £500 million. The Games' budget of £650 million has cost the taxpayer nothing and will provide permanent sports facilities for the population. The boost to Catalan morale in the north-east of the country is inestimable, let alone to the whole of Spain. In 1988, the Seoul Olympic Games made a profit of £250 million, and transformed South Korea's political and trade relations, particularly with communist countries. In 1984, the Los Angeles Games made a similar profit. The cities expected to be bidding, in 1993, for the vote from the IOC to host the Games of 2000 include Beijing, Berlin, Milan, Sydney, Brasilia and possibly Istanbul, with Johannesburg a likely candidate in the event of sudden further liberalization within South Africa. And Manchester.

SC: Birmingham and Manchester tried and failed for the Games of 1992 and 1996 respectively. I think Birmingham were blown into touch by a combination of inadequate personnel and too many town councillors out for a ride. Both cities had features that were flawed. Birmingham's, technically, was quite a good bid, but it was weak on presentation. I believe Birmingham had more to offer than Manchester, though some IOC members thought more of Manchester, which had the advantage of being less politically orientated. Bob Scott, the leader of Manchester's bid, was impressive, though some IOC members wondered how much substance there was behind him. If Manchester had polled fifteen votes or better – they had eleven in the first round, and dropped to five in the second, which means that with two British votes they retained the confidence of only three others – then I would not have considered that Manchester should be challenged as Britain's bid for 2000. Having experienced Birmingham's bid, however, there was nothing to suggest to me that Manchester would do any better a second time, though they left a better taste than Birmingham, and knew how to handle themselves better when they lost.

I was commentating on the vote by the IOC for 1996, made in Tokyo in 1990, for Sky Television, and was asked what I thought. Manchester attacked me for daring to say that I thought London would have more chance. Yet Manchester's chance of finding another 43 votes had to be questioned. If I'm critical of *both* Britain's recent bids, it is that neither asked sport for its opinion. There were key members of the BOA who were disillusioned. The most unifying factor, in getting rival London bids together as a single contender in January 1991, was Bob Scott saying on radio that we were a bunch of amateurs. London 2000 made a decision not to get drawn into public personal dispute. Obviously, the IOC is unlikely to have had any city as different as London in mind when drawing up bidding regulations, London being without a strategic authority since the abolition of the Greater London Council.

On the Board of London 2000 we had John Lelliott, chairman of a large construction company, and vice-chairman of the London Council for Sport and Recreation, but unfortunately the City of London was unwilling to be a counter-signatory for any contract with the IOC. The major consideration was the siting of venues, and we needed something that would satisfy the BOA. We thought we had it. We discussed the acknowledged transport problems with an expert, David Bayliss, a prominent figure with London Transport, who was consultant for Barcelona. We believed beforehand that we had behind us a consensus of individual national sports federations on the question of venue sites; though of course Bob Scott was right in saying that there must be approval in every instance by the international sports federations, because they are the people during a Games who administer the sports day by day and have to resolve logistic problems. My own role in the London bid was always clear: I wanted to help get it launched, while recognizing that I would never have the time to devote the seven-days-a-week application for two years or more that is necessary for any candidate city hoping to win. The postbag we had from Londoners, expressing approval, was impressive, with hundreds of letters offering spontaneous support.

What happened on the day of decision – we lost heavily by 28 votes to 5 – was not entirely a surprise. We were competing against a city that had been in the ring for four years. Manchester had more time to give flesh to their bid. There's no point in second-guessing. What the BOA told us, in effect, was that in 1993, when the IOC will be making their decision, Manchester is an easier concept to sell than London. Obviously I have to disagree, but I openly accept that Manchester is now the British bid, and we all have to support it wholeheartedly.

As a journalist who has been closely associated with Olympic and IOC affairs for many years, I had to share the scepticism of Chris Brasher regarding the prospects of a London bid. Brasher believes London is too big and too congested; that one cannot contemplate an Olympic village and facilities in re-developed east London docklands, for example, when it can take over an hour and a half by road from London Airport. Like Brasher, I believe that for the benefit of British sport the conception of the Manchester bid, incorporating much of the north-west, will provide the most valuable legacy for British sport into the twenty-first century. For the people of Britain, a Manchester Games would be seen to embrace the whole country, and would have an immeasurable public relations value that would not be achieved by London, which would absorb the Games as merely another large entertainment event that created inconvenience for the local inhabitants. Against this, I partially accept the foreign perception, especially within the IOC, of London as being the historic and romantic heart of England, and being therefore much more electable. Yet, encouragingly, by the end of 1991, John Major was showing a substantial, formal interest in Manchester's bid for 2000, inviting serious application by the city for financial subsidy.

It is not an unfair description of British administration of individual sports to say that predominantly it is honest, well-intentioned, inefficient and out-of-date. Some of it is not as good as that. The main disability, in the second half of the twentieth century, has been an unwillingness to adopt a more professional approach during an era of ever-increasing commercialization. Elected officers, mostly coming from within the ranks of sport – which is no bad thing – have been reluctant to appoint professionals who might usurp their authority and status. A conspicuous instance of this was in athletics, when in 1961 Geoff Dyson, the chief coach of the Amateur Athletic Association, resigned to take up a post in Canada because he could no longer endure the frustrations of being over-ruled, even on technical matters, by the honorary officials of the AAA. Dyson was outstanding in his field, but the administration of the sport was a cosy little corner operated with proprietary self-interest; and it was sad that one of those who did little to protect the position of Dyson was none other than the former Olympic 100 metres gold medallist, Harold Abrahams, the honorary treasurer, and then chairman: himself a runner dependent for his fame, 37 years previously, partially on the advice of a coach.

Coaches, upon whose function and intelligence the future of the sport is dependent, were then of lowly status. And still are. Harry Wilson recalls that he was excluded from the official party for the Olympic Games in Montreal, in 1976, following the accusation, absurd though it now seems, that he had exhibited prejudice towards the *athletes*, in attempting to obtain improved accommodation – instead of five to a room – during the European Championships in Rome in 1974. He was said to be *disruptive*. The situation continues to this day, with low-paid administrators and coaches in a sport with an annual income approaching eight figures. Coaches remain second-class citizens, their budget for training athletes a reflection of this. The selectors, the professional coaches, as we have seen, are not allowed to select. The chief national coach is not provided with a ticket to attend one of the four major international championships. In almost any other commercial administration, the council running British athletics would not survive six months. Belatedly, there has been a re-organization of the twenty different bodies that administer the different branches of athletics in Britain into one "British Athletics Federation", from the autumn of 1991. The limitation of such a scheme is that the same personnel are running it as before. The one outstanding recent secretary of the British Board, David Shaw, found himself unable to tolerate the antiquated regime, and soon departed.

SC: The British Board could be both criticized and defended. Between the Sixties and the Eighties, people were being asked to do a different job. By 1984, ITV had come to the table with £11.5 million over three years, which together with guaranteed sponsorship meant an income of more than £20 million. The financial implications were vast. Yet management is not just a financial venture: it demands skills too, for ascertaining and establishing necessary targets and insuring they are met. You could soon discover flaws in governing bodies, for instance, by asking what was their strategy, where would they be in ten years' time, what was their intended balance between grass-roots and elite sport? As Denis Howell, the Labour minister for Sport, who gave more status to the post than almost any other, used to say, British sports administration is all about Buggins's Turn.

The criticism of the British Athletics Board was that for too long it was promoting from within its own ranks. In its flawed structure, it was quite unable to provide the management skills needed at the top. Without that, you are selling your competitors down the road, not providing a coherent support system. Yet without the competitors, they don't have a sport. Management is a skill common to any activity. If you can manage a division of Heinz, you can run a governing body: though that is not to say a governing body can ignore the essential feel for sport, can depend on well qualified people who are no more than technocrats. One of the difficulties that has militated against successful management appointments is the multi-fractured *structure* of the sport. The problem has not been discussed since the Byers' Report in the Sixties and came to a head with a poor British performance at the Olympic Games in 1976, when Brendan Foster was the only medallist, with a bronze for the 10,000 metres. But what can you expect with twenty separate organizations, some of which are regional committees? Those in charge of athletics were reluctant to bring in someone capable of running the show. Malcolm Jones, who now has the job, is walking into a sea of vested interests and structural mayhem.

Coaches are vocation people, they don't want money from athletes. The problem across the board in the UK, the reason we've fallen behind in coaching standards, is that there is not enough time, money and planning devoted to national coaching development. Too many of the best coaches work *outside* the governing body. There is the misguided idea that Steve Ovett, Daley Thompson and I are some quirk of nature, rather than long-term products of sensitive, sustained, knowledgeable coaching. In defence of some governing bodies, and this you learn quickly when sitting on the grants committee of the Sports Council, many of them are operated from someone's front room in a private house in Balsall Heath or Oxford. They don't have the *time* to raise their level of operation, and they are under-funded. It's correct for the government to question whether the Sports Council is getting value for money as a distributor of a public fund; but if the grant is covering nothing more than subsistence level, those administrators are hardly likely to be thinking in terms of a ten-year plan.

It is particularly regrettable that Association Football, the most important of all the British sports – with the largest following, the highest television coverage and the biggest sponsorships – should be among the worst administered. It should be conceded that the Football Association is consistently well-intentioned, whatever its inadequacies – reluctant in the past to impose behaviour discipline on the field in the national team, a shameful commercial exploitation among school children of endorsed national playing kit – but the wanton power-lust together with incompetence exhibited for 45 years by the Football League is hard to credit. That these two bodies should spend so much time in dispute has been a public disgrace; they too have suffered from resentment of the employed professional, resisting at every turn, out of willfulness or ignorance, the kind of management, financial and structural, that would have enabled them to do so much good for the community upon which they ultimately depend. The creation of the new Premier league, splitting away from the derelict Football League, may provide a partial solution.

SC: Football is the worst case. The disaster at Hillsborough, in the FA Cup semi-final of 1989 between Liverpool and Nottingham Forest, was caused on the day, by police error as much as anything. Yet I have sympathy for the police, under the kind of pressures put on them. The fault that afternoon was with the FA and the Football League, for their lack of co-ordination over the years. The most charitable thing you could say is that they have communication problems, being three hundred miles apart; but when they do speak to each other, they are often gratuitously rude. Something is seriously wrong when, as at Hillsborough, the FA, who do not have day-to-day jurisdiction over the League, take charge of a match that, outside Wembley, is the largest, most emotional and sensitive of the year. No governing body properly organized would have allowed the police traffic-planners to have operated the system they did that day. Where was the governing body, or the League, when the decision was made? There were many contributory factors, but there was a basic failure of central football administration.

The Bradford City fire disaster, and the Heysel catastrophe during the European Cup final between Liverpool and Juventus, both occurred during my first year on the Sports Council, in 1985. Justice Popplewell was appointed by the government to hold an inquiry, and it was the first that would combine the institution of law through the parliamentary legal process. The government realized that these incidents were damaging, nationally and internationally, and that the government's electoral reputation could be affected by such issues. Over-simplified, Liverpool Football Club had travelled abroad and thirty-eight people died. Football was given a platform to initiate responsible change that it had never had before. Yet out of ninety-two letters sent by Popplewell inviting comments, he received replies from barely a third of the clubs, including only *five* from the First Division. In 1984–85, the DoE conducted a study of football violence, and one of their recommendations was that high-risk matches, specifically those involving teams chasing promotion and playing at seaside towns on a Bank Holiday, should be rescheduled. After Leeds fans ran riot during the promotion match in Bournemouth on Easter Monday 1990, the reaction of the Football League was, pathetically, that "it is easy to be wise with hindsight". The only aspect of football that has remained constant during a decade of human tragedy is that predominantly the same people are still running the game.

XII · Greatest?

In 1948, Roger Bannister, a nineteen-year-old undergraduate at Oxford University, preferred not to run in the Olympic Games in London, which he could have done. Instead, he decided to wait until he was more mature, and to compete in Helsinki in 1952. His preparations for the 1,500 metres that year were calculated on two races: heats and final. When he arrived in Finland, it was to discover there was an additional semi-final. Though running his fastest time yet, a new U.K. record of 3:46.0, he was able to finish only a tired fourth behind Barthel of Luxembourg, McMillen of USA and Lueg of Germany. This disappointment, for a sporting figure who had generated acclaim in Britain for his thrilling sprint-finishes over the last lap when coming from behind, determined him more than ever to triumph in the European Championships in 1954; and in what were then still known as the British Empire Games, the same year, where Bannister's rival would be the renowned John Landy of Australia. Jungwirth of Czechoslovakia would provide the challenge in the European final in Berne.

I knew that I had to develop a capacity to run the mile in four minutes, or less, if I was to have a chance of beating Landy in Vancouver [Sir Roger, who is now the Master of Pembroke College at Oxford, recalls]. I was disappointed at missing a medal in Helsinki. I would compare the rivalry between Coe and Ovett in 1980 with the way my mind was concentrated by the prospect of racing against Landy. As a medical student, I was only able to train for half an hour a day, five days a week; and for three races in Helsinki that clearly had not been enough. I had to become more earnest, and started to extend my training, together with Chris Brasher and Chris Chataway. It was a matter of adjusting the schedule between May, when I broke the four-minute mile, and the Empire Games in August. I was proved right in my estimation of Landy, because six weeks after I had broken the record, he beat my time in Turku in Finland.

On a wet and windy Thursday in May, I and some friends at Peterhouse, in Cambridge, looked out of the window, saw that the clouds were racing low across the sky, and said to each other, "No, he'll never do it today." We had been planning to hire a car, which in those days you could do for a fiver for the day, and to drive across to Oxford for this eagerly-awaited meeting between Oxford University and the AAA. We didn't go. A record attempt by Bannister had been heavily publicized. For more than a decade the world's best four-lap runners had been pounding the face of the four-minute barrier; the mile distance was as popular in Scandinavia and other parts of metric Europe as was the 1,500 metres. In 1945, Gunder Hägg had set the record at 4:01.3, which is a little under ten yards short of the magic time. The gap of 1.3 seconds had stood unbeaten for nine years; though, in 1953, Bannister and Landy had both recorded times of 4:02.0, with Landy running 4:02.4 and 4:02.6 in the early months of 1954, during the Australian summer. Wes Santee of America had run 4:02.4. Hägg's record was under fire. When Bannister went to the starting line that May day, on the cinder-track at Iffley Road in Oxford, he had not raced for six months, devoting his running exclusively to the training schedules set by his Austrian coach, Franz Stampfl. There had been pessimism about the chances at lunchtime in Oxford; but shortly before the race began, the rain stopped and the wind fell.

Brasher went to the front of the six-man field, and after 200 yards was ignoring Bannister's request at his shoulder to make it faster. Brasher kept his head, ran the first 440 yards in 57.4, and stayed in the lead for almost two and a half laps, passing the half-mile in 1:58: perfect judgement of even time, allowing for the inevitable slower third lap and the compensation of Bannister's finishing kick.

At the bell, Chataway, who had picked up the lead, went through in 3:0.4, with Bannister a couple of feet behind. A last lap of 59.4 was needed. With 230 yards to go, Bannister kicked past Chataway; and was on his own. "I felt at that moment that it was my chance to do one thing supremely well," Bannister would write later, in his account of the race. His long stride picked up time lost on the third lap, and, sustaining his kick, he flung himself at the tape – as there still was in those days – and collapsed in the arms of supporters. He had achieved the goal that would make him famous for life, whatever he might subsequently do in the fields of physiology and neurology, or as chairman of the Sports Council. "I felt that the moment of a lifetime had come . . . the world seemed to stand still or did not exist . . . the tape meant finality: extinction perhaps!" So Bannister later wrote when describing his historic run of 3 minutes, 59.4 seconds.

The record, you could say, was a by-product of my preparation for the race against Landy [Sir Roger said recently, sitting in his study at Pembroke]. In the AAA Championships that year, though winning with a slowish time of 4:7.6, I'd put in a last lap of 53 seconds, as a frightener. Landy had said that his chance would be best if he was leading, and I wanted to compel him to expend his energies too early. I thought he would try and make it fast, because he had said it would disappoint everyone if it was a cat-and-mouse race.

It was a classic. Landy, as predicted, quickly took the lead in

Vancouver, attempting to run the lungs out of the eight-man field. At one stage, he had built a ten-yard lead, but Bannister doggedly held on. In the last lap, Bannister began to close. Some seventy yards from the finish, a tiring Landy looked over his shoulder on the inside of the bend, only for Bannister to go surging past on the outside, to win in 3:58.8: faster than his time at Oxford, but 0.8 seconds slower than Landy's new record set in June.

Having qualified as a doctor that summer, Bannister was retiring from the sport, and knew that his 1,500 metres in Berne would be his last race. Contentedly taking up a position at the back of the field, he let Dohrow of Germany lead Jungwirth through the first lap; and at 800 metres, in 2:00.2, Bannister was fifth, then third at the bell just behind Jungwirth. With 200 metres to go, Bannister leapt past Jungwirth, and held his lead to the line, ahead of Nielsen of Denmark. His winning time of 3:43.8 was more than a second faster than Barthel's Olympic record: and only two and a half seconds slower than Sebastian Coe's time in winning the AAA Championships thirty-five years later. The legend of Bannister would rest alongside the famous deeds of the young man to be born two years and one month later.

The story of the first four-minute mile is fascinating [Brasher recollects]. Roger was concluding his medical studies in London, and the three of us used to meet for training at the Duke of York barracks in Chelsea, where we would do 10 x 440, with two-minute jogging intervals. We managed to bring it down from an average of 68 to 60. For the four-minute mile, Roger was going to have to get *below* 60. We worked at it week after week, and it still wouldn't come. At Easter in '54, Franz, who was also my coach, told us to go off and relax, to find some girls. I was going climbing in Scotland, and Roger said he'd like to come. John Mawe, a doctor from Bethnal Green, whom I was going with, had an Aston Martin, a two-seater. The journey took ten hours, with Roger or me lying in the luggage space at the back. At one stage during the climbing, standing shivering in pouring water on the mountainside, I thought Roger was going to pass out. We were drenched, drove back another ten hours . . . and went out and averaged 59-something. The intensity had been relieved, it had done the trick. I don't think this factor is sufficiently realized in modern athletics. Yet a coach must be hard, as Stampfl was. A coach like Peter Coe has to understand the experience of driving you to a point at which you think you'll die. Mihaly Igloi, coach to the great Hungarians such as Iharos and Rozsavolgyi, had it. Stampfl had it. He'd been torpedoed during the war, while being taken as an Austrian internee to Canada on a merchant vessel, and was swimming for eight hours in the Atlantic before he was rescued. Peter Coe was twice a prisoner of war, escaping from the Germans and being recaptured by the Spanish across the border from France. You achieve nothing in sport without some pain, and athletes of the class of Coe and Ovett nowadays press themselves so hard in training that they are teetering on a border-line between extreme fitness and every virus that's there in the air. They're like a genius writer on the borders of insanity.

What Brasher did not know, when telling the story of Stampfl – and nor at the time did I – was that Peter had also been blown out of the water in a merchant ship by shell-fire from the battle cruiser *Gneisenau*, and been picked up by the Germans from one of the few lifeboats successfully launched.

So what are the measurements of greatness? Is it mind, or muscle, or planning, the availability of an exceptional coach, the sheer love of running as attributed to Ovett by Walker? I think it is an amalgam of all these, together with that imponderable of which Coe has spoken: the quirk of nature, the hazardous combination of genes between man and woman. Ultimately, the quality of the runner who has these various talents will depend upon his or her ability to marshal them. It is one thing to say that Cram or Elliott have run too frequently because of the availability of financial reward, but their tendency is no different from that of Derek Ibbotson, thirty-five years before. Might Ibbotson have run faster than his single world record of 3:57.2, when he took the record from Landy in London in July 1957? He ran more than seventy races in 1957. Did he reduce himself by running here and there for fifty quid in the pocket?

Maybe so [Ibbotson says], but I *enjoyed* running, the sheer exuberance of racing was what I loved. What let *me* down was a spell in 1957–58 when I was ill, my system off the rails, a huge carbuncle on my back, maybe from stress with my work as an electrical engineer salesman. I missed a whole winter's work that is vital, missed out on the European Championships team, ran the three miles in the Commonwealth Games in Cardiff, and was sixth. I did think of living in Finland. Six races there would have paid me a *year's* salary. When I ran hard, I could make it hard for anyone, thinking, "If I'm feeling the pinch, what will *they* be feeling?"

When I ran the world record, Jungwirth took the third lap, but there was a hesitation, and he didn't pick it up straight away. He ran 62, which wasn't quite fast enough. I've always thought that if he'd run 59, as I'd hoped, maybe I could have run 3:54, which was the time Herb (Elliott) ran the next year in Dublin. Herb retired after the Olympic Games in Rome because he basically didn't like running, he found the training too hard. Bannister was the same, he didn't enjoy the *business* of running. It was something Bannister did, I felt, because he was *good* rather than because it was fun. But then, he also had his medical studies to occupy him. If you ask me who was best of all, I'd have to say Herb Elliott: never beaten. He retired untapped at twenty-two, and we'll never know. But I'd place Coe second, because he's done everything, gold medals *and* records, and maybe Ovett next, just ahead of Snell.

"Of all the people of recent times, Coe had a magnetic, charismatic quality about him" Herb Elliott says. "As soon as he walked onto the track, he created an aura that has epitomised the last few years. He was outstandingly the star of recent times. For me he was the most exciting, the most likely to pull it out for the big result on the big day. I wouldn't attempt to rank him, because I wouldn't nowadays have an idea about record times, and don't even remember my own."

One of the difficulties of attempting to compare different generations is that circumstances vary, and the cycle of some great runners does not coincide with an Olympic Games. Sydney Wooderson won the Commonwealth and European Championships, and broke the world 800 metres record at Motspur Park in South London, in 1938, with 1:48.4, but was injured at the time of the 1936 Olympic Games in Berlin. When Jim Ryun, then current world record holder for both 1,500 metres and the mile, ran in the Olympic Games of 1968, he was at the perfect age of twenty-five. Yet the altitude factor proved to be too much of a geographic aberration for his personal physiology, and he could only take a silver medal in the 1,500 behind the altitude-adjusted Keino of Kenya. In 1972, Ryun was tripped in his heat: an experience that he was to find infinitely more deranging than did Peter Elliott in his fall in 1990. In the Worldmark Films documentary *The Supermilers*, released on the thirtieth anniversary of Bannister's record and recounting the subsequent progression of the record, Ryun said:

Munich was a terribly difficult situation for me, not so much because of the fall. A day later they would show the videos, that I was indeed fouled. The hard part would come about twenty-four hours later, when the International Olympic Committee Jury of Appeal, having looked at those films, would simply say: "That's too controversial, we don't want to do anything; come back in four years and try again." Now I am paraphrasing that a little bit, but in essence that is what they said, and I was angry at that time, because I simply couldn't justify the sacrifice that it would require.

It was at that point in my life that I turned to God, and I said, Lord, I need some help, I need some kind of way to resolve this. And eventually the Lord would show me that I had to forgive those men, which was the most difficult thing I could ever do. It took me months before I could sit down and say OK, I forgive them for what I thought was a very poor decision. And because I was able to do that I can now go back to running and say it is fun again. But right after the Munich Olympics, I didn't want anything to do with running for a long time.

I could play the ranking game for a long time [Brasher says] and these are the results of my own deliberations and also those of the Fox and Grapes Debating Society – the Fox and Grapes being the pub on Wimbledon Common where members of Thames Hare and Hounds, the oldest running club in the world, meet on a Saturday evening. Out of six votes present (including John Bryant, formerly with *The Times*, now the *European*) there were three votes for Coe and three votes for Elliott as the number one. The clear number three was Snell, because all six people ranked him somewhere, three in third place and one in fourth. After that, the situation was highly confusing, with Walker getting a 3 and a 4; Keino getting a 2, 5, and 4; Cram getting a 2 and a 5; Bannister getting a 2 and Said Aouita getting no votes in any position whatsoever.

You have to differentiate between those who ran from the late 1970's onwards and those who ran earlier than that. The difference is that the former were able to earn a living, provide for their dependents and for their old age, and so went on running for much longer. Whereas the latter had to retire in order to earn a living. Those who had to retire in order to earn a living include Bannister, Ryun, Snell and certainly includes Elliott, who went to Cambridge on a Shell scholarship and had to provide for a wife and children. I also believe that the ultimate test is the Olympic Games and the World Championship, but one has to take into account that Ryun was disadvantaged in 1968 because of altitude and that Walker's opposition was decimated in 1976 because the Africans were not there. Then there were the 1980 and 1984 boycotts. When you take these points into consideration then my ranking is clear:

1: Elliott. He was the most competitive runner I have ever known, marginally more competitive than Kuts. These two stand head and shoulders above anyone else because Elliott was never beaten over 1500 metres or the mile and Kuts, outside his own country, was only ever beaten by two people – Pirie and Chataway – who had to break the world record in order to do so.

2: Coe. Second because of his two Olympic Gold Medals and because of his six world records (I leave out odd distances like 1000 metres) but principally because of the way he picked himself up from the floor in 1980 after his defeat in the 800 metres.

3: Snell. Third because of this three Olympic Golds, and a suspicion that he might have come even higher if he had not been such a lazy athlete.

You can juggle with the order of those three but there is no doubt in my mind that they are the three medallists in this ranking competition. The next three places are nearly impossible to put in any order – they finish in a bunch and would include seven athletes in no particular order: alphabetically, they would be Bannister, Bayi, Cram, Keino, Ovett, Ryun and Walker. One must remember that Bayi might have won an olympic Gold in 1976 if he had been allowed to complete.

There was a perfectionism about Ryun that was an echo of the Bannister of the past and of the Coe yet to come. Harry Wilson, a shade dismissively, says that neither Bannister nor Ibbotson could be included in any estimation of the all-time greatest, on the grounds that when they were initially failing to break four minutes, this was merely because they were not *fit* enough. The anecdote of Brasher's to a degree substantiates this; though no one can do more than be a champion of his own time.

If you look at the old films [Wilson says], when runners were finishing a mile in those days, they were collapsing. Now, they stroll off the track after running 3:50. Bannister ran under four minutes once he was fit enough. Nowadays, he could do it twice a week. I think best performances have to be related to the major Games. When you consider that Herb Elliott was twenty-two when he won in Rome, and that a miler doesn't mature until twenty-five, he was *awesome*. When I talked to Herb once, he said, "I've seen some of them training nowadays: if you'd seen me training with Cerutty, you'd have been *frightened*." On the day, no one beat him. Nor do I think anyone would have ever beaten Juantorena at 800, but he'd gone before the Grand Prix began. After Herb Elliott, it would be difficult to judge between the rest of them.

John Walker, who set the mile record at 3:49.4 in 1975 in Gothenburg, takes an opposite, and extreme, view:

I would never rank Herb as the greatest, not someone who retires at twenty-two when he's only just beginning [Walker says]. I once asked him why he did that, and he said, "I couldn't take the pressure of *winning*." Would Snell have beaten him? Tactically, I think Snell would have won. He was five years ahead of his time when he ran 1:44.3 on *grass* in Christchurch in 1962, taking almost one and a half seconds off the time of Moens. Snell admits his oxygen uptake was nowhere as good as runners today.

The British public came back to athletics, following the Fifties, because of Coe and Ovett. We were years ahead in New Zealand in the Seventies, but now we've gone backwards: now we have to *pay* TV to come to meetings, and are lucky to get a crowd of more than a thousand. I don't think I'd rank Ovett too high, it was Andy (Norman) who gave him his confidence. Andy's man-management was so helpful to your British runners: the same for Cram, then Elliott, even for Coe at times. But Seb made his own destiny. Different runners all contribute at different times and everyone should be grateful. Ovett should have won the 1,500 in Moscow, but didn't believe in himself. Coe was so positive, he knew what he wanted and went after it. He did the impossible with two Olympic victories, and I'd have to rank him top because of that. Cram was awesome when he broke the mile record in '85, I felt for Coe that evening, coming third, the same as had happened to me in '79. And Cram at his peak beat Aouita.

Andy Norman's tribute to Walker is that the New Zealander was the man who did most for contemporary athletics by setting standards of speed, competitiveness and sportsmanship.

We tend now to forget what he did [Norman says], but he was the first of the new era. To an extent, British track and field was built on the efforts of John Walker. The best? Put me on the line, and I have to say Coe. Then Ovett, then Cram, out of the British runners. Peter Elliott's got to win something first, and he's not yet won an "open" or set a record. The Commonwealth? Who gives a damn south of Dover or east of Sydney? At his peak, Coe was ruthless, an absolute professional. There was nothing I could have done for him, had I been more involved. You couldn't have made him better. He was so focused. I set up the pacing for him twice for the 1,000 metres record in Oslo, and the second time Mike Solomon, who had made the running for him, went to congratulate Seb and shake his hand, and Seb didn't recognize him.

Mel Watman, consultant editor of *Athletics Today*, was fascinated with Coe's search for excellence. "What impressed me was his desire to see how fast man can run at those distances," Watman says. "I think Ovett was essentially a *championship* racer." Watman is one of those to rank Herb Elliott first, then Coe, ahead of Snell. "Seb was almost freakish" Ron Clarke, the multiple long-distance record-holder, reflects. "He was so good, phenomenal, that no one can repeat what he did. There will be a general decline in running because of the distraction for youngsters of television and videos, reducing the exercise and involvement in the sport they used to have: the old formula of 'give me the boy of eleven, and I'll show you the man'. Coe has been accused of being aloof, but at club level, out of sight, he did a lot of work with young runners."

Andreas Brugger, the Zurich promoter, places Coe ahead of Herb Elliott, Snell third, Aouita fourth, Cram and Ovett joint fifth. "We are missing athletes of this quality right now," Brugger says. "My view about Herb Elliott is that competition was not as severe at his time, compared with the last ten years, once he had raised his training to the level he did. What Coe did in winning in Los Angeles for the second time was exceptional. In the records he set here, there were fine runners who just couldn't stay with him through 1,200 metres. He seemed to be able to get *anything* out of his body if he wanted to. For me, it was a highlight when he finally won his 800 metres in Stuttgart."

Steve Scott, for fourteen years in the front line along with Coe, and a believer in the fundamental importance of championships as against records, is worried about declining standards because of over-racing. "We've seen it already, in the Olympic Games in Seoul, with Rono winning," Scott says. "There was the potential there for a great final,

204 · Born to Run

with Cram, Peter Elliott, Cruz, Bilé, Aouita, Herold, myself. All of those racers had problems due to over-racing – and then along comes Peter Rono, who hasn't over-raced, who's single-minded, and had the class on the day. If my training goes well, I may continue following the World Championships of '91, though I'll be thirty-five. I'd like to go on to the Olympics in '92. When I don't have the motive any more, I'll quit. My problem in Barcelona will be finding the strength to endure *three* races, though age is not necessarily a factor, it's more mental and emotional. There's nothing at present I'd rather be doing. If I was offered $70,000 a year, but not to run, I'd turn it down." Scott, like Walker, has mixed feelings about Herb Elliott: perhaps it is a psychological and subconscious disapproval by the older runners of the kid who quit. You have to consider the durability of a great athlete's performance, as Scott says: he ranks Coe ahead of Aouita, Walker and Snell.

The case for Coe as the best of all time – the view to which I am inclined on the basis of his combination of medals and records, and the depth of character demanded in both Olympic victories – is partly scientific. Peter Coe regards the 1,000 metres record, relatively unfashionable though it may be, as the extreme expression of his son's running attributes. "It's probably the cream of them all, and explains why he was equally good at 800 and 1,500," Peter says. "The fourth 200 of his second 1,000 record, 2:12.18, was run in 26.2, which gave him an interim 800 time of 1:44.56, faster than the main 800 event of that day. The relevant percentages of the contribution of aerobic and anaerobic running gave him the ability to sustain very high speeds."

Dave Martin extends the explanation.

When we first began testing Seb, which was during his aerobic-emphasis endurance build-up in 1985, I was impressed with his far-better-than-average running economy, i.e. at any given sub-maximum running pace, Seb consumes remarkably less oxygen than other athletes. This may provide a physiological basis for what many have described as his "poetry in motion", implying a smoothness of gait. During such aerobic endurance phases, athletes typically have little *an*aerobic fitness (for sprinting) and thus measurements such as maximum end-of-treadmill-test lactic acid are typically not very high. This is because those muscle cells specialized for lactic acid production (the fast-twitch cells) are not well-developed during this period of training: they are stimulated by speed-orientated training. It was interesting that Seb's maximum post-test lactic acid measurement was really quite high: which suggests that either he had not lost much of his *an*aerobic fitness from the previous season, *or* that he was able to recruit the use of these fast-twitch cells in maximum-effort-exercise better than most athletes who had a comparable lay-off. Subsequent testing enabled us to help Peter refine Seb's training plans (1) to help increase his maximum oxygen intake, thereby minimizing lactic acid production until the highest of work-loads were reached; (2) to help raise his anaerobic threshold, thereby keeping metabolic acids from accumulating until only very intense work-loads were reached; and (3) to help develop the ability to produce and endure the highest possible anaerobic work-loads with maximum-effort work, as in end-of-race sprints.

It is this refinement and attention to physiological and anatomical detail, by a scientist whose research work and laboratories are available for examination by any serious student of the art, that should be sufficient to persuade any doubter that Coe's exceptional performance owed nothing to drugs. Coe has been tested countless times, and to those who say "Well, so was Johnson", Coe would reply that throughout his career anyone was free to test him randomly, any day of the year. Also, he says, just look at the size and shape of his frame.

SC: My stand on drugs hasn't altered since the time I recommended a life ban during the IOC Congress of 1981 in Baden-Baden. The use of drugs is the *total* antithesis of fair competition, in which the judgement should be by ability and hard work. It's like climbing over the stadium wall to watch without paying. The majority of other people recommending life bans has not altered. What has hardened those seeking a life ban is governing-body ambivalence. An argument in which I agree with Charlie Francis, Johnson's coach, whom I otherwise don't defend – and most athletes at the top level agree with me – is that if we're going to force drugs out of the sport, we have to have a system by governing bodies that the athletes agree is workable. While some countries continue to turn a blind eye, no one feels the principle is sincere. We know there have been Americans who failed tests, with the governing body equivocating. It was Ron Pickering's argument that you cannot expect athletes to toe the line until governing bodies give the lead: not while you see governing bodies mutely wishing the problem would go away.

When, jointly with Colin Moynihan, I chaired a drugs inquiry, random testing was taken away from governing bodies and put in the hands of Chelsea College testing laboratory, to avoid inconsistency and manipulation. Now, if you are eligible for international competition, your name will come up randomly on the computer. In 1989, one of the officials at the Sports Council helped me set up the system: you *know* that it will be put into action. The Sports Council ring up and say, "There'll be someone knocking on your door at two o'clock this afternoon." Someone from the Boxing Federation came to take a sample from me, just like that. Athletes are being asked, impromptu, to give samples at a motorway service area. It's a good system, and better than most countries. I was disappointed that the Home Office didn't go far enough on steroid-possession being an offence. I'm beginning to suspect, moreover, that the IOC, on whose medical commission I sit, is worried about the cost of testing and its supervision. I'm hearing more and more an argument for making a distinction between drugs dangerous to health and those that are "merely" performance-enhancing. I think that's capitulation.

When I asked coaches, athletes and professional colleagues for their views on who was the greatest over four laps, none was more fastidious in his selection than Stan Greenberg, the statistician. He thought about it for a week, before sending me a lengthy letter. There were some athletes and coaches, such as Bannister, who were disinclined to give a view: only because they felt the criteria between one generation and another were too variable, or they wished not to offend friends and associates who might disagree with what they believed was the truthfulness of their view. Greenberg wrote:

If we consider between the Wars, then few can compare with Nurmi, the Finn, who in 1923 ran 4:10.4, and was known to be *aiming* eventually for four minutes. He ran a faster last lap in the 1924 Olympic Games 1,500 metres than Elliott and Ryun when setting *their* world records. If we consider the early post-war years, there was so much less to beat than there is now. There are, too, so many random factors: Ryun ran 3:33.1 from the front, and Bayi 3:32.2 from the front, but they never won major championships. Bannister failed in the Olympics, but beat everybody who was anybody in Berne in '54. Regarding injuries, these have been more prevalent throughout the Seventies and Eighties, as training becomes more severe. Coe, in my opinion, takes top place – for his two Olympic titles, primarily; while Cram must take second, with his championships, European (2), world (1) and Commonwealth (2), plus two wins in the European Cup. Cram is also the only one to make three Olympic 1,500 finals, placing eighth, second and fourth. Keino gets the edge over Herb Elliott, with his two Commonwealth golds to add to his Olympic gold and silver. Snell never ran as many 1,500/mile races as Elliott, and so goes after him, but his Olympic and Commonwealth titles give him the edge over Ovett, whose championship record at 800 is surprisingly better than at 1,500. Ovett only took a bronze out of three Olympic Games at 1,500, to which must be added a European title, two wins in the World Cup, and fourth place in the World Championships. Roberto Quercetani, esteemed statistician from Florence, wrote to me: "Coe's weight in Olympic gold medals and world records appears to be *nonpareil*. Elliott was head and shoulders above his contemporaries as few have ever been — before or after. So was Snell, to a slightly lesser degree. Ovett and Cram had impressive careers in the midst of a 'hot' age." [see Appendix D.] Of the thousands of letters and tributes that Coe has received since he burst on to the global stage with his three records in 1979, two in particular are worthy of notice. On 18 July 1979, he received the following from Roger Bannister:

May I join your many admirers in sending my heartiest congratulations to you on your absolutely magnificent two world records (800 and mile). I think this undoubtedly ranks as the greatest middle-distance feat for many years, and the apparent ease with which you accomplished it betokens more world records to come. It is particularly heartwarming to see the world record for this traditionally British distance back in this country, when national pride is not at a very high point and everyone may feel rather more inspired to try harder. Many years ago, my wife and I had some ties made for the then rather few sub-4-minute milers in the world. We ran out of ties a long time ago, but I kept one for a special occasion, and this occasion has now arrived! Please accept it as a small token of my admiration of your performance and with my best wishes for many further triumphs – not least Moscow 1980, though I would not wish to burden you with tiresome expectations. With kind regards, yours sincerely, Roger Bannister

In February 1982, Coe gave a lecture at Ezra Stiles College in America. Heinrich von Staden, the master, made the following introduction:

I didn't know exactly what Frank Ryan had in mind when he asked a scholar of ancient Greek culture to introduce a contemporary English runner, but it is easy enough to find connections between ancient Greece and modern English athletics. It was, after all, the ancient Greeks who first seem to have shown us how and why to bestow honour upon those who could run the fastest, throw the farthest, and jump the highest or farthest. It also was the Greeks who found deep significance in such individual achievements and who tried to sort out the controversial relation betwen the individual meaning of athletic achievement and its civil import – its value for the *polis*. And it was, of course, the Greeks who organized the first Olympic Games in 776BC.

But once one moves beyond classical antiquity and the dark ages of athletics that ensued, England clearly emerges as the cradle of modern track and field. It was the English who, in the twelfth century, revived the practice of running, jumping, and throwing "for the sport of the thing"; it was Mr Coe's compatriots who in 1834 first set down rules and minimum standards for major track contests (the standard for the mile was five minutes); it was the English who in the 1860s organized the first inter-collegiate track and field event on record; it was in England that the first international track and field event on record took place in 1894 (Yale v. Oxford, in London); and in 1954 it was Mr Coe's countryman Roger Bannister who astounded the world by running the mile in 3:59.4, the first such effort under four minutes.

And then, on 28 August of last year in Brussels, our honoured guest, Seb Coe, continued this fine tradition and accomplished the remarkable feat of breaking the world record in the mile for the second time within nine days. In the span of a mere century the record had dropped from 4:32.6 to an astounding 3:47.33. This is, however, not Mr Coe's only claim to fame; he currently holds three other world records: 800 metres, 1,000 metres, and 800 metres indoors. Queen Elizabeth II gave recognition to the significance of these accomplishments last Tuesday by making Mr Coe a Member of the British Empire.

With his four world records, however, Mr Coe transcends whatever national meaning athletics might have; he has also become a citizen of the world, a kinsman whom all members of the human race can honour as one of their own, trans-national heroes. There is something else Mr Coe possesses, other than his records – something on which the press does not dwell at length but which should mean more to all of us. I'm referring to his degree in History and Economics, to his commitment to education, to his deep desire to continue both his formal and his informal education.

Finally, what struck me most in my conversations with Seb Coe the last two days are what I've come to appreciate as his greatest strengths, perhaps his greatest accomplishments, to wit: his sound perspective on the relation of running to his education and to other dimensions of his life; his exemplary patience; his modesty; the civic courage with which he has spoken out against drug use by athletes and their coaches, and against the prescription of drugs by team physicians; and the profound decency that shines through every conversation with him.

Better than most accomplished runners or other athletes I have known or read about, Mr Coe is equipped for life – for a life with or without running. I can think of no better example that the Yale scholar-athlete – or any scholar-athlete – might strive to emulate than our Kiphuth Fellow, Seb Coe.

Sebastian Coe was one of the contemporary sporting heroes of the end of the twentieth century: smooth of manner, ruthless in intent, competitively supreme, financially well rewarded, yet his instincts were old-fashioned. Although for almost twenty-two years he went in search of athletic perfection with his father, and was motivated by curiosity to discover what were the possible limits of his capabilities, he was motivated, too, by sporting patriotism. At the time he announced, in the autumn of 1989, his intention to have one last stab at the Commonwealth Games, an area of previous failure, he said:

For me as a young club athlete in Sheffield twenty years ago, it was people like Dorothy Hyman, Sheila and John Sherwood, Trevor Wright, the athletes who made it to the Olympic Games and came back home with medals, who were the ones you revered. They were our heroes, and I've always found the call to wear my country's vest irresistible. For me, championships in athletics are what matter. Nothing motivates me like preparing for a Games. Perhaps I'm one of a dying breed.

It must be hoped that his sentiment will prevail into the next century:

that athletics will not turn a corner to follow down the same direction as tennis, in which financial self-promotion has become not just the first but perhaps the only motivation. When I went to talk with Jimmy Hedley, sitting in his little office beside the running-track in Jarrow, where he has conducted a lifetime's vocation, he said whimsically: "I've got all Steve's medals, and I look at them from time to time. I'd swap that silver for a gold. There's something about the Olympics, isn't there? It's different."

Appendix A

A complete list of the track races in which Sebastian Coe has competed since 1973

Abbreviations

pb	personal best	sf	semi final	UK	United Kingdom record
h	heat	cr	championship record	WR	World record
f	final	CR	Commonwealth record	OR	Olympic record

Date	Event	Track	Distance	Place	Time
1973 (age 16)					
17 Mar	AAA Indoor Youths Champs	Cosford	800 m	4th	2:02.6
1 May	B. Milers' Club	Stretford	800 m	3rd	1:56.6
5 May	Longwood Youth	Huddersfield	1,500 m	1st	4:07.4
13 May	B. Milers' Club	Crystal Palace	800 m	2nd	1:56.0(pb)
18 May	West District Schools	Sheffield	800 m	1st	2:01.1
18 May	West District Schools	Sheffield	1,500 m	1st	4:15.4
23 May	Sheffield Selection	Sheffield	3,000 m	1st	8:43.7
3 Jun	Northern League	Sheffield	1,500 m	3rd	4:07.5
9 Jun	Yorks Schools Championships	York	3,000 m	1st	8:49.0
16 Jun	N. Counties Youths	Sheffield	1,500 m	1st	3:59.5(pb)
7 Jul	English Schools	Bebington	3,000 m	1st	8:40.2(pb)
17 Jul	S. Yorks League	Doncaster	800 m	1st	1:59.7
21 Jul	City Championships	Sheffield	800 m	1st	1:57.0
21 Jul	City Championships	Sheffield	1,500 m	1st	4:07.4
4 Aug	AAA Youth Championships	Aldersley	1,500 m	1st	3:55.0(pb)
14 Aug	Stretford League	Manchester	3,000 m	6th	8:34.6(pb)
9 Sep	Hallam Harriers Championships	Sheffield	400 m		–51.8(pb)
15 Sep	Rotherham Festival	Rotherham	1,500 m	1st	3:58.0
1974 (age 17)					
10 Apr	Training run	Rotherham	800 m		1:55.1(pb)
Apr–Nov	Injured with stress fractures				
1975 (age 18)					
21 Mar	Indoor Under 20 Championships	Cosford	1,500 m(h)	2nd	4:08.0
22 Mar	Indoor Under 20 Championships	Cosford	1,500 m(f)	1st	3:54.4(pb)
13 Apr	Pye Cup	Cleckheaton	1,500 m	1st	3:49.7(pb)
30 Apr	B. Milers' Club	Rawtenstall	1,500 m	1st	3:54.0
31 May	Yorks Senior Championships	Cleckheaton	1,500 m	1st	3:51.3
8 Jun	Pye Cup	Cleckheaton	800 m	1st	1:53.8(pb)
8 Jun	Pye Cup	Cleckheaton	4 x 400 m	–	50.5
21 Jun	N. Counties Under 20	Gateshead	1,500 m	1st	3:50.8
25 Jun	Northern League	Sheffield	300 m	2nd	36.2(pb)
28 Jun	N. Counties Under 20	Blackburn	3,000 m	1st	8:14.8(pb)
26 Jul	AAA Junior Championships	Kirkby	1,500 m(h)	1st	3:52.0

Date	Event	Track	Distance	Place	Time
27 Jul	AAA Junior Championships	Kirkby	1,500 m(f).	1st	3.47.1(pb)
10 Aug	GB v France/Spain	Warley	1,500 m	1st	3.50.8
22 Aug	European Junior Championships	Athens	1,500 m(h)	4th	3.48.8(pb)
24 Aug	European Junior Championships	Athens	1,500 m(f)	3rd	3.45.2(pb)

1976 (age 19)

Date	Event	Track	Distance	Place	Time
24 Jan	AAA Indoor Championships	Cosford	1,500 m	5th	3.51.0
6 Mar	Loughborough Match	Crystal Palace	4 x 800 m	–	1:52.0(pb)
20 Mar	Loughborough Match	Cosford	600 relay/leg	–	80.4
28 Mar	B. Milers' Club	Stretford	1,500 m	1st	3:47.4
14 Apr	H. Wilson Mile	Crystal Palace	1 mile	1st	4:07.6(pb)
1 May	B. Milers' Club	Stretford	1 mile	1st	4:05.7(pb)
12 May	Loughborough Match	Loughborough	800 m	1st	1:53.0
16 May	Yorkshire Championships	Cleckheaton	1,500 m	1st	3:43.3(pb)
19 May	Loughborough v Borough Rd	Isleworth	800 m	1st	1:53.0
31 May	Inter-Counties Championships	Crystal Palace	1 mile	2nd	4:02.4(pb)
11 Jun	Olympic Selection	Crystal Palace	1,500 m	7th	3:43.2(pb)
17 Jun	Loughborough v AAA	Loughborough	800 m	1st	1:50.7(pb)
24 Jul	Heckington Sports	Heckington	1 mile	1st	4:09.1
1 Aug	Open Meeting	Nottingham	1,000 m	1st	2:30.0
8 Aug	B. Milers' Club	Stretford	800 m	1st	1:47.7(pb)
13 Aug	AAA Championships	Crystal Palace	1,500 m(h)	3rd	3:45.05
14 Aug	AAA Championships	Crystal Palace	1,500 m(f)	4th	3:42.67(pb)
21 Aug	Rediffusion Games	Gateshead	1 mile	3rd	4:01.7(pb)
30 Aug	Emsley Carr Mile	Crystal Palace	1 mile	7th	3:58.35(pb)
14 Sep	Bell's Games	Gateshead	1 mile	2nd	4:01.5
20 Nov	Indoor Meeting	Cosford	600 m	1st	79.7

1977 (age 20)

Date	Event	Track	Distance	Place	Time
29 Jan	AAA Indoor Championships	Cosford	800 m	1st	1:49.1
19 Feb	GB v W. Germany	Dortmund	800 m	1st	1:47.6(CR)
26 Feb	GB v France	Cosford	800 m	1st	1:47.5(CR)
12 Mar	European Indoor Ch'ships	San Sebastian	800 m(h)	1st	1:50.5
13 Mar	European Indoor Ch'ships	San Sebastian	800 m(sf)	1st	1:48.2
14 Mar	European Indoor Ch'ships	San Sebastian	800 m(f)	1st	1:46.54(CR)
3 Jul	Dewhurst Games	Spalding	800 m	1st	1:51.7
23 Jul	AAA Championships	Crystal Palace	800 m	2nd	1:46.83
30 Jul	Philips Games	Gateshead	800 m	2nd	1:47.4
14 Aug	Europa Cup	Helsinki	800 m	4th	1:47.61
16 Aug	Ivo Van Damme	Brussels	800 m	3rd	1:46.31(pb)
24 Aug	Club Meeting	Rotherham	400 m	1st	49.1
28 Aug	GB v W. Germany	Crystal Palace	800 m	1st	1:47.78
29 Aug	Emsley Carr Mile	Crystal Palace	1 mile	1st	3:57.67(pb)
7 Sep	Courage Games	St Ives	800 m	1st	1:48.1
9 Sep	Coca-Cola	Crystal Palace	800 m	2nd	1:44.95(UK)

1978 (age 21)

Date	Event	Track	Distance	Place	Time
26 Apr	Loughborough Match	Crystal Palace	400 m	1st	48.0(pb)
10 May	Loughborough Match	Isleworth	400 m	1st	47.7(pb)
14 May	Yorkshire Championships	Cleckheaton	800 m	1st	1:45.6(CR)
1 Jun	Loughborough v AAA	Loughborough	800 m	1st	1:50.0
9 Jul	Philips Games	Gateshead	800 m	1st	1:46.83
15 Jul	UK Championships	Meadowbank	800 m	1st	1:47.14

Date	Event	Track	Distance	Place	Time
10 Aug	International Invitation	Viareggio	800 m	1st	1:45.7
18 Aug	Ivo Van Damme	Brussels	800 m	1st	1:44.25(UK)
29 Aug	European Championships	Prague	800 m(h)	1st	1:46.81
30 Aug	European Championships	Prague	800 m(sf)	1st	1:47.44
31 Aug	European Championships	Prague	800 m(f)	3rd	1:44.76
15 Sep	Coca-Cola	Crystal Palace	800 m	1st	1:43.97(UK)
17 Sep	McEwans Games	Gateshead	1 mile	1st	4:02.17

1979 (age 22)

Date	Event	Track	Distance	Place	Time
27 Jan	AAA Indoor Championships	Cosford	3,000 m	1st	7:59.8(pb)
25 Apr	Loughborough Match	Crystal Palace	400 m	2nd	48.3
9 May	Loughborough Match	Loughborough	800 m	1st	1:51.0
20 May	Yorkshire Championships	Cleckheaton	800 m	1st	1:50.5
21 May	Yorkshire Championships	Cleckheaton	400 m	1st	47.6(pb)
23 May	Loughborough Match	Loughborough	400 m	1st	47.4(pb)
23 May	Loughborough Match	Loughborough	800 m	1st	1:54.8
31 May	Loughborough v AAA	Loughborough	800 m	1st	1:47.9
16 Jun	N. Counties Championships	Stretford	800 m	1st	1:46.3
30 Jun	Europa Cup Semi Final	Malmo	800 m	1st	1:46.63
3 Jul	Bislet Games	Oslo	800 m	1st	1:42.33(WR)
7 Jul	International Meeting	Meisingset	800 m	1st	1:54.8
13 Jul	AAA Championships	Crystal Palace	400m(h)	1st	46.95(pb)
14 Jul	AAA Championships	Crystal Palace	400 m(f)	2nd	46.87(pb)
17 Jul	Golden Mile	Oslo	1 mile	1st	3:48.95(WR)
29 Jul	Dewhurst Games	Spalding	600 m	1st	76.5
5 Aug	Europa Cup Final	Turin	800 m	1st	1:47.28
5 Aug	Europa Cup Final	Twin	4x400m	6th	45.5
8 Aug	International Invitation	Viareggio	800m	1st	1:45.4
15 Aug	Weltklasse	Zurich	1,500 m	1st	3:32.03(WR)

1980 (age 23)

Date	Event	Track	Distance	Place	Time
23 Apr	Loughborough Match	Crystal Palace	3,000 m	1st	7:57.4(pb)
7 May	Loughborough Match	Isleworth	1,500 m	1st	3:45.1
11 May	Yorkshire Championships	Cudworth	5,000 m	1st	14:06.2(pb)
21 May	Philips Meeting	Crystal Palace	800 m	1st	1:47.48
25 May	Inter-Counties Championships	Birmingham	800 m(h)	1st	1:48.93
26 May	Inter-Counties Championships	Birmingham	800 m(f)	1st	1:45.41
1 Jun	International Invitation	Turin	800 m	1st	1:45.74
5 Jun	Loughborough v AAA	Loughborough	800 m	1st	1:45.0
7 Jun	N. Counties	Champs Hull	800 m	1st	1:44.7
15 Jun	UK Championships	Crystal Palace	400 m	8th	47.10
1 Jul	Bislet Games	Oslo	1,000 m	1st	2:13.40(WR)
24 Jul	Olympic Games	Moscow	800 m(h)	1st	1:48.44
25 Jul	Olympic Games	Moscow	800 m(sf)	1st	1:46.61
26 Jul	Olympic Games	Moscow	800 m(f)	2nd	1:45.85
30 Jul	Olympic Games	Moscow	1,500 m(h)	2nd	3:40.05
31 Jul	Olympic Games	Moscow	1,500 m(sf)	1st	3:39.34
1 Aug	Olympic Games	Moscow	1,500 m(f)	1st	3:38.40
8 Aug	Coca-Cola	Crystal Palace	800 m	1st	1:45.81
13 Aug	Weltklasse	Zurich	1,500 m	1st	3:32.19
14 Aug	International Invitation	Viareggio	800 m	2nd	1:45.07

Date	Event	Track	Distance	Place	Time
1981 (age 24)					
24 Jan	AAA Indoor Championships	Cosford	3,000 m	1st	7:55.2(pb)
11 Feb	GB v GDR (Indoor)	Cosford	800 m	1st	1:46.0(WR)
3 May	UAU Championships	Crystal Palace	400 m	1st	46.9
13 May	Loughborough Match	Borough Road	400 m	1st	47.4
17 May	Yorkshire Championships	Cleckheaton	800 m	1st	1:46.5
3 Jun	England v USA/Eth/Bel	Crystal Palace	800 m	1st	1:44.06
3 Jun	England v USA/Eth/Bel	Crystal Palace	4 x 400	–	45.7
7 Jun	GB v USSR	Gateshead	4 x 400	–	46.5
10 Jun	International Invitation	Florence	800 m	1st	1:41.73(WR)
5 Jul	Europa Cup Semi	Helsinki	800 m	1st	1:47.57
7 Jul	International Invitation	Stockholm	1,500 m	1st	3:31.95(pb)
11 Jul	Bislet Games	Oslo	1,000 m	1st	2:12.18(WR)
17 Jul	GB v USSR	Gateshead	800 m	1st	1:47.47
19 Jul	Dairygate	Leicester	1,000 m	1st	2:17.6
31 Jul	Talbot Games	Crystal Palace	800 m	1st	1:46.72
5 Aug	International Invitation	Viareggio	800 m	1st	1:47.12
7 Aug	AAA Championships	Crystal Palace	800 m(h)	1st	1:45.84
8 Aug	AAA Championships	Crystal Palace	800 m(f)	1st	1:45.41
15 Aug	Europa Cup Final	Zagreb	800 m	1st	1:47.03
19 Aug	Weltklasse	Zurich	1 mile	1st	3:48.53(WR)
28 Aug	Golden Mile	Brussels	1 mile	1st	3:47.33(WR)
4 Sep	World Cup	Rome	800 m	1st	1:46.16
1982 (age 25)					
16 May	Yorkshire Championships	Cudworth	1,500 m	1st	3:39.1
5 Jun	International Invitation	Bordeaux	2,000 m	1st	4:58.85(pb)
4 Aug	Time Trial	Nottingham	800 m	1st	1:46.5
17 Aug	International Invitation	Zurich	800 m	1st	1:44.48
20 Aug	Talbot Games	Crystal Palace	800 m	1st	1:45.85
22 Aug	International Invitation	Cologne	800 m	1st	1:45.10
30 Aug	BAAB/Heinz Games	Crystal Palace	4 x 800 m	1st	(7:03.89)(WR)
			4th leg	1st	1:44.01
6 Sep	European Championships	Athens	800 m(h)	1st	1:48.66
7 Sep	European Championships	Athens	800 m(sf)	1st	1:47.98
8 Sep	European Championships	Athens	800 m(f)	2nd	1:46.68
1983 (age 26)					
12 Feb	GB v France (Indoor)	Cosford	1,500 m	1st	3:42.06
12 Mar	England v USA (Indoor)	Cosford	800 m	1st	1:44.91(WR)
19 Mar	GB v Norway (Indoor)	Oslo	1,000 m	1st	2:18.58(WR)
16 May	Yorkshire Championships	Cleckheaton	1,500 m	1st	3:45.8
5 June	GB v USSR	Birmingham	1 mile	1st	4:03.37
12 Jun	Loughborough v AAA	Loughborough	800 m	1st	1:44.99
24 Jun	Permit Meeting	Paris	1,500 m	2nd	3:35.17
28 Jun	Permit Meeting	Oslo	800 m	1st	1:43.80
15 Jul	Talbot Games	Crystal Palace	1,500 m	2nd	3:36.03
23 Jul	AAA Championships	Crystal Palace	1 mile	2nd	3:52.93
31 Jul	Gateshead Games	Gateshead	800 m	4th	1:45.31
1984 (age 27)					
12 May	GRE League	Wolverhampton	4 x 400 m	–	–
			2nd leg	–	46.8

Date	Event	Track	Distance	Place	Time
19 May	Middx Championships	Enfield	800 m	1st	1:45.2
2 Jun	S. Counties Championships	Crystal Palace	1,500 m	1st	3:43.11
24 Jun	AAA Championships	Crystal Palace	1,500 m	2nd	3:39.79
28 Jun	Permit Meeting	Oslo	800 m	1st	1:43.84
4 Jul	Beverly Baxter Meeting	Haringey	1 mile	1st	3:54.6
3 Aug	Olympic Games	Los Angeles	800 m(h)	1st	1:45.71
4 Aug	Olympic Games	Los Angeles	800 m(h)	3rd	1:46.75
5 Aug	Olympic Games	Los Angeles	800 m(sf)	1st	1:45.51
6 Aug	Olympic Games	Los Angeles	800 m(f)	2nd	1:43.64
9 Aug	Olympic Games	Los Angeles	1,500 m(h)	2nd	3:45.30
10 Aug	Olympic Games	Los Angeles	1,500 m(sf)	3rd	3:35.81
11 Aug	Olympic Games	Los Angeles	1,500 m(f)	1st	3:32.53(OR)
19 Aug	GRE League	Haringey	1,500 m	1st	3:45.20
22 Aug	Weltklasse	Zurich	1,500 m	1st	3:32.39

1985 (age 28)

Date	Event	Track	Distance	Place	Time
11 May	GRE League	Birmingham	800 m	1st	1:49.37
18 May	Middlesex Championships	Enfield	800 m	1st	1:44.0
8 Jun	Euro/Club Championships	Haringey	800 m	1st	1:48.37
9 Jun	Euro/Club Championships	Haringey	1,500 m	1st	3:47
16 Jun	Moorcroft Mile	Coventry	1 mile	1st	3:54.5
21 Jun	England v USA	Birmingham	800 m	1st	1:46.23
19 Jul	Peugeot Talbot	Crystal Palace	800 m	1st	1:44.34
27 Jul	Bislet Games	Oslo	1 mile	3rd	3:49.22
2 Aug	IAC/Coca-Cola	Crystal Palace	1 mile	2nd	3:56.89
21 Aug	Weltklasse	Zurich	1,500 m	2nd	3:32.13
25 Aug	Grand Prix	Cologne	800 m	2nd	1:43.07

1986 (age 29)

Date	Event	Track	Distance	Place	Time
25 Jan	AAA Indoor Championships	Cosford	3,000 m	3rd	7:55.58
8 Feb	GB v Hungary (Indoor)	Cosford	1,500 m	1st	3:45.65
8 Mar	England v USA (Indoor)	Cosford	3,000 m	1st	7:54.32(pd)
10 May	GRE League	Birmingham	1,500 m	1st	3:45.27
17 May	Middlesex Championships	Enfield	800 m	1st	1:47.9
4 Jun	Invitation	Madrid	800 m	1st	1:45.66
27 Jun	Invitation	Hengelo	1,500 m	1st	3:34.32
1 Jul	Grand Prix	Stockholm	800 m	2nd	1:44.17
11 Jul	Peugeot Talbot	Crystal Palace	800 m	1st	1:44.10
16 Jul	Beverly Baxter	Haringey	1,000 m	1st	2:14.90
28 Jul	Commonwealth Games	Edinburgh	800 m(h)	1st	1:53.13
28 Jul	Commonwealth Games	Edinburgh	800 m(sf)	3rd	1:48.07
13 Aug	Weltklasse	Zurich	1,500 m	2nd	3:35.22
20 Aug	Invitation	Berne	1,500 m	1st	3:35.09
26 Aug	European Championships	Stuttgart	800 m(h)	1st	1:47.64
27 Aug	European Championships	Stuttgart	800 m(sf)	3rd	1:47.10
28 Aug	European Championships	Stuttgart	800 m(f)	1st	1:44.50
29 Aug	European Championships	Stuttgart	1500 m(h)	2nd	3:39.03
31 Aug	European Championship	Stuttgart	1500 m(f)	2nd	3:41.67
7 Sep	Grand Prix	Rieti	1,500 m	1st	3:29.77(pb)
12 Sep	McVitties	Crystal Palace	800 m	1st	1:44.28

1987 (age 30)

Date	Event	Track	Distance	Place	Time
13 Mar	England v USA (Indoor)	Cosford	3,000 m	1st	7:54.33

Date	Event	Track	Distance	Place	Time
9 May	GRE League	Portsmouth	800 m	1st	1:46.18
9 May	GRE League	Portsmouth	4 x 400 m	–	46.8

1988 (age 31)

Date	Event	Track	Distance	Place	Time
13 Feb	Meadowlands Meeting (Indoor)	New Jersey	3,000 m	dnf	–
12 Mar	England v USA	Cosford	3,000 m	2nd	8:05.80
14 May	Middlesex Championships	Enfield	800 m	1st	1:48.8
19 Jun	GB v USSR/France	Portsmouth	800 m	1st	1:48.63
24 Jun	Grand Prix	Lausanne	800 m	2nd	1:45.50
8 Jul	Peugeot Talbot	Crystal Palace	800 m	1st	1:46.13
31 Jul	Invitation	Rapperswil	1,500 m	1st	3:37.74
8 Aug	AAA Championships (trial)	Birmingham	1,500 m(h)	5th	3:45.01
26 Aug	Grand Prix	Berlin	800 m	2nd	1:47.87
28 Aug	Grand Prix	Koblenz	800 m	2nd	1:43.93
31 Aug	Invitation	Rieti	1,500 m	3rd	3:35.72

1989 (age 32)

Date	Event	Track	Distance	Place	Time
20 May	Middlesex Championships	Enfield	800 m	1st	1:47.2
3 Jun	Euro/Club Championships	Belgrade	1,500 m	1st	3:51.89
24 Jun	Euro/Club Championships	Belgrade	800 m	1st	1:46.60
24 June	Invitation	Birmingham	800 m	1st	1:46.83
21 Jul	Invitation	Rovereto	800 m	1st	1:45.97
2 Aug	Invitation	Viareggio	800 m	1st	1:46.04
13 Aug	AAA Championships (trial)	Birmingham	1,500 m	1st	3:41.38
16 Aug	Weltklasse	Zurich	1,500 m	2nd	3:34.05
20 Aug	Grand Prix	Cologne	800 m	4th	1:45.13
29 Aug	Invitation	Berne	800 m	1st	1:43.38
9 Sep	World Cup	Barcelona	1,500 m	2nd	3:35.79
15 Sep	McVities	Crystal Palace	800 m	1st	1:45.70

1990 (age 33)

Date	Event	Track	Distance	Place	Time
4 Jan	Invitation	Hobart	1,000 m	1st	2:21.0
14 Jan	Invitation	Sydney	800 m	1st	1:47.66
29 Jan	Commonwealth Games	Auckland	800 m(h)	2nd	1:49.83
29 Jan	Commonwealth Games	Auckland	800 m(sf)	4th	1:47.67
1 Feb	Commonwealth Games	Auckland	800 m(f)	6th	1:47.24

Appendix B

Evolution of World Records

800 metres

Time	Runner	Nation	Date	Place
1:51.9	Ted Meredith	USA	8.7.1912	Stockholm
1:51.6	Otto Peltzer	Germany	3.7.1926	London
1:50.6	Sera Martin	France	14.7.1928	Paris
1:49.8	Tom Hampson	GB	2.8.1932	Los Angeles
1:49.8	Ben Eastman	USA	16.6.1934	Princeton
1:49.7	Glenn Cunningham	USA	20.8.1936	Stockholm
1:49.6	Elroy Robinson	USA	11.7.1937	New York
1:48.4	Sydney Wooderson	GB	20.8.1938	Motspur Park
1:46.6	Rudolf Harbig	Germany	15.7.1939	Milan
1:45.7	Roger Moens	Belgium	3.8.1955	Oslo
1:44.3	Peter Snell	New Zealand	3.2.1962	Christchurch
1:44.3	Ralph Doubell	Australia	15.10.1968	Mexico City
1:44.3	Dave Wottle	USA	1.7.1972	Eugene
1:43.7	Marcello Fiasconaro	Italy	27.6.1973	Milan
1:43.50	Alberto Juantorena	Cuba	25.7.1976	Montreal
1:43.44	Alberto Juantorena	Cuba	21.8.1977	Sofia
1:42.33	Sebastian Coe	GB	5.7.1979	Oslo
1:41.73	Sebastian Coe	GB	10.6.1981	Florence

1,000 metres

Time	Runner	Nation	Date	Place
2:32.3	Georg Mickler	Germany	22.6.1913	Hanover
2:29.1	Anatole Bolin	Sweden	22.9.1918	Stockholm
2:28.6	Sven Lundgren	Sweden	27.9.1922	Stockholm
2:26.8	Sera Martin	France	30.9.1926	Paris
2:25.8	Otto Peltzer	Germany	18.9.1927	Paris
2:23.6	Jules Ladoumègue	France	19.10.1930	Paris
2:21.5	Rudolf Harbig	Germany	24.5.1941	Dresden
2:21.4	Rune Gustafsson	Sweden	4.9.1946	Boras
2:21.4	Marcel Hansenne	France	27.8.1948	Gothenburg
2:21.3	Olle Aberg	Sweden	10.8.1952	Copenhagen
2:21.2	Stanislav Jungwirth	Czechoslovakia	27.10.1952	Stará Boleslav
2:20.8	Mal Whitfield	USA	16.8.1953	Eskilstuna
2:20.4	Audun Boysen	Norway	17.9.1953	Oslo
2:19.5	Audun Boysen	Norway	18.8.1954	Gävle
2:19.0	Audun Boysen	Norway	30.8.1955	Gothenburg
2:19.0	István Rózsavölgyi	Hungary	21.9.1955	Tata
2:18.1	Dan Waern	Sweden	19.9.1958	Turku
2:17.8	Dan Waern	Sweden	21.8.1959	Karlstad
2:16.7	Siegfried Valentin	GDR	19.7.1960	Potsdam
2:16.6	Peter Snell	New Zealand	12.11.1964	Auckland

Time	Runner	Nation	Date	Place
2:16.2	Jürgen May	GDR	20.7.1965	Erfurt
2:16.2	Franz-Josef Kemper	Germany	21.9.1966	Hanover
2:16.0	Daniel Malan	South Africa	24.6.1973	Munich
2:13.9	Rick Wohlhuter	USA	30.7.1974	Oslo
2:13.40	Sebastian Coe	GB	1.7.1980	Oslo
2:12.18	Sebastian Coe	GB	11.7.1981	Oslo

1,500 metres

Time	Runner	Nation	Date	Place
3:55.8	Abel Kiviat	USA	8.6.1912	Cambridge, Mass
3:54.7	John Zander	Sweden	5.8.1917	Stockholm
3:52.6	Paavo Nurmi	Finland	19.6.1924	Helsinki
3:51.0	Otto Peltzer	Germany	11.9.1926	Berlin
3:49.2	Jules Ladoumègue	France	5.10.1930	Paris
3:49.2	Luigi Beccali	Italy	9.9.1933	Turin
3:49.0	Luigi Beccali	Italy	17.9.1933	Milan
3:48.8	Bill Bonthron	USA	30.6.1934	Milwaukee
3:47.8	Jack Lovelock	New Zealand	6.8.1936	Berlin
3:47.6	Gunder Hägg	Sweden	10.8.1941	Stockholm
3:45.8	Gunder Hägg	Sweden	17.7.1942	Stockholm
3:45.0	Arne Andersson	Sweden	17.8.1943	Gothenburg
3:43.0	Gunder Hägg	Sweden	7.7.1944	Gothenburg
3:43.0	Lennart Strand	Sweden	15.7.1947	Malmö
3:43.0	Werner Lueg	Germany	29.6.1952	Berlin
3:42.8	Wes Santee	USA	4.6.1954	Compton
3:41.8	John Landy	Australia	21.6.1954	Turku
3:40.8	Sándor Iharos	Hungary	28.7.1955	Helsinki
3:40.8	László Tábori	Hungary	6.9.1955	Oslo
3:40.8	Gunnar Nielsen	Denmark	6.9.1955	Oslo
3:40.6	István Rózsavölgyi	Hungary	3.8.1956	Tata
3:40.2	Olavi Salsola	Finland	11.7.1957	Turku
3:40.2	Olavi Salonen	Finland	11.7.1957	Turku
3:38.1	Stanislav Jungwirth	Czechoslovakia	12.7.1957	Stará Boleslav
3:36.0	Herb Elliott	Australia	28.8.1958	Gothenburg
3:35.6	Herb Elliott	Australia	6.9.1960	Rome
3:33.1	Jim Ryun	USA	8.7.1967	Los Angeles
3:32.16	Filbert Bayi	Tanzania	2.2.1974	Christchurch
3:32.03	Sebastian Coe	GB	15.8.1979	Oslo
3:31.36	Steve Ovett	GB	27.8.1980	Koblenz
3:31.24	Sydney Maree	USA	28.8.1983	Cologne
3:30.77	Steve Ovett	GB	4.9.1983	Rieti
3:29.67	Steve Cram	GB	16.7.1985	Nice
3:29.46	Saïd Aouita	Morocco	23.8.1985	Berlin

1 mile

Time	Runner	Nation	Date	Place
4:14.4	John Paul Jones	USA	31.5.1913	Cambridge, Mass
4:12.6	Norman Taber	USA	16.7.1915	Cambridge, Mass
4:10.4	Paavo Nurmi	Finland	23.8.1923	Stockholm

Time	Runner	Nation	Date	Place
4:09.2	Jules Ladoumègue	France	4.10.1931	Paris
4:07.6	Jack Lovelock	New Zealand	15.7.1933	Princeton
4:06.8	Glenn Cunningham	USA	16.6.1934	Princeton
4:06.4	Sydney Wooderson	GB	28.8.1937	London
4:06.2	Gunder Hägg	Sweden	1.7.1942	Gothenburg
4:06.2	Arne Andersson	Sweden	10.7.1942	Stockholm
4:04.6	Gunder Hägg	Sweden	4.9.1942	Stockholm
4:02.6	Arne Andersson	Sweden	1.7.1943	Gothenburg
4:01.6	Arne Andersson	Sweden	18.7.1944	Malmö
4:01.3	Gunder Hägg	Sweden	17.7.1945	Malmö
3:59.4	Roger Bannister	GB	6.5.1954	Oxford
3:57.9	John Landy	Australia	21.6.1954	Turku
3:57.2	Derek Ibbotson	GB	19.7.1957	London
3:54.5	Herb Elliott	Australia	6.8.1958	Dublin
3:54.4	Peter Snell	New Zealand	27.1.1962	Wanganui
3:54.1	Peter Snell	New Zealand	17.11.1964	Auckland
3:53.6	Michel Jazy	France	9.6.1965	Rennes
3:51.3	Jim Ryun	USA	17.7.1966	Berkeley
3:51.1	Jim Ryun	USA	23.6.1967	Bakersfield
3:51.0	Filbert Bayi	Tanzania	17.5.1975	Kingston
3:49.4	John Walker	New Zealand	12.8.1975	Gothenburg
3:48.95	Sebastian Coe	GB	17.7.1979	Oslo
3:48.8	Steve Ovett	GB	1.7.1980	Oslo
3:48.53	Sebastian Coe	GB	19.8.1981	Zurich
3:48.4	Steve Ovett	GB	26.8.1981	Koblenz
3:47.33	Sebastian Coe	GB	28.8.1981	Brussels
3:46.32	Steve Cram	GB	27.7.1985	Oslo

Appendix C

Olympic Games Medallists 1896–1988

Abbreviations (in addition to those given in Appendix A)
tna   time not available

800 metres

	Gold	Silver	Bronze
1896	Edwin H. Flack (AUS) 2:11.0	Nándor Dáni (HUN) 2:11.8	Demitrios Golemis (GRE) 2:28.0
1900	Alfred E. Tysoe (GBR) 2:01.2	John F. Cregan (USA) 2:03.0	David C. Hall (USA) tna
1904	James D. Lightbody (USA) 1:56.0 OR	Howard V. Valentine (USA) 1:56.3	Emil W. Breitkreutz (USA) 1:56.4
1906	Paul H. Pilgrim (USA) 2:01.5	James D. Lightbody (USA) 2:01.6	Wyndham Halswelle (GBR) 2:03.0
1908	Melvin W. Sheppard (USA) 1:52.8 OR	Emilio Lunghi (ITA) 1:54.2	Hanns Braun (GER) 1:55.2
1912	Ted Meredith (USA) 1:51.9 OR	Melvin W. Sheppard (USA) 1:52.0	Ira N. Davenport (USA) 1:52.0
1920	Albert G. Hill (GBR) 1:53.4	Earl W. Eby (USA) 1:53.6	Bevil G. d'U. Rudd (SAF) 1:54.0
1924	Douglas G. A. Lowe (GBR) 1:52.4	Paul Martin (SUI) 1:52.6	Schuyler C. Enck (USA) 1:53.0
1928	Douglas G. A. Lowe (GBR) 1:51.8 OR	Erik Byléhn (SWE) 1:52.8	Hermann Engelhardt (GER) 1:53.2
1932	Thomas Hampson (GBR) 1:49.7 OR	Alexander Wilson (CAN) 1:49.9	Philip A. Edwards (CAN) 1:51.5
1936	John Y. Woodruff (USA) 1:52.9	Mario Lanzi (ITA) 1:53.3	Philip A. Edwards (CAN) 1:53.6
1948	Malvin G. Whitfield (USA) 1:49.2 OR	Arthur S. Wint (JAM) 1:49.5	Marcel Hansenne (FRA) 1:49.8
1952	Malvin G. Whitfield (USA) 1:49.2 OR	Arthur S. Wint (JAM) 1:49.4	Heinz Ulzheimer (GER) 1:49.7
1956	Thomas W. Courtney (USA) 1:47.7 OR	Derek J. N. Johnson (GBR) 1:47.8	Audun Boysen (NOR) 1:48.1
1960	Peter G. Snell (NZL) 1:46.3 OR	Roger Moens (BEL) 1:46.5	George E. Kerr (BWI) 1:47.1
1964	Peter G. Snell (NZL) 1:45.1 OR	William Crothers (CAN) 1:45.6	Wilson Kiprugut (KEN) 1:45.9
1968	Ralph D. Doubell (AUS) 1:44.40 OR	Wilson Kiprugut (KEN) 1:44.57	Thomas F. Farrell (USA) 1:45.46
1972	David J. Wottle (USA) 1:45.86	Yevgeniy Arzhanov (URS) 1:45.89	Michael Boit (KEN) 1:46.01
1976	Alberto Juantorena (CUB) 1:43.50 OR	Ivo Van Damme (BEL) 1:43.86	Richard Wohlhuter (USA) 1:44.12
1980	Steve Ovett (GBR) 1:45.40	Sebastian Coe (GBR) 1:45.85	Nikolai Kirov (URS) 1:45.94

Gold	Silver	Bronze
1984 Joaquim Cruz	Sebastian Coe	Earl Jones
(BRA) 1:43.00 OR	(GBR)1:43.64	(USA) 1:43.83
1988 Paul Ereng	Joaquim Cruz	Saïd Aouita
(KEN) 1:43.45	(BRA) 1:43.90	(MOR) 1:44.06

The performances listed below were Olympic Records set additionally in the preliminaries

2:10.0	1:59.0	1:47.1	1:46.1	1:46.1
Flack	Hall	Kerr	Kerr	Kiprugut
1896	1900	1960	1964	1964

1,500 metres

Gold	Silver	Bronze
1896 Edwin H. Flack	Arthur Blake	Albin Lermusiaux
(AUS) 4:33.2 OR	(USA) 4:34.0	(FRA) 4:36.0
1900 Charles Bennett	Henri Deloge	John Bray
(GBR) 4:06.2 OR	(FRA) 4:06.6	(USA) 4:07.2
1904 James D. Lightbody	W. Frank Verner	Lacey E. Hearn
(USA) 4:05.4 OR	(USA) 4:06.8	(USA) tna
1906 James D. Lightbody	John McGough	Kristian Hellström
(USA) 4:12.0	(GBR/IRL) 4:12.6	(SWE) 4:13.4
1908 Melvin W. Sheppard	Harold A. Wilson	Norman F. Hallows[1]
(USA) 4:03.4 OR	(GBR) 4:03.6	(GBR) 4:04.0
1912 Arnold N. S. Jackson[2]	Abel R. Kiviat	Norman S. Taber
(GBR) 3:56.8 OR	(USA) 3:56.9	(USA) 3:56.9
1920 Albert G. Hill	Philip J. Baker[2]	M. Lawrence Shields
(GBR) 4:01.8	(GBR) 4:02.4	(USA) 4:03.1
1924 Paavo J. Nurmi	Willy Schärer	Henry B. Stallard
(FIN) 3:53.6 OR	(SUI) 3:55.0	(GBR) 3:55.6
1928 Harri E. Larva	Jules Ladoumègue	Eino Purje
(FIN) 3:53.2 OR	(FRA) 3:53.8	(FIN) 3:56.4
1932 Luigi Beccali	John F. Cornes	Philip A. Edwards
(ITA) 3:51.2 OR	(GBR) 3:52.6	(CAN) 3:52.8
1936 John E. Lovelock	Glenn Cunningham	Luigi Beccali
(NZL) 3:47.8 OR	(USA) 3:48.4	(ITA) 3:49.2
1948 Henry Eriksson	Lennart Strand	Willem F. Slijkhuis
(SWE) 3:49.8	(SWE) 3:50.4	(HOL) 3:50.4
1952 Josef Barthel	Robert E. McMillen	Werner Lueg
(LUX) 3:45.1 OR	(USA) 3:45.2	(GER) 3:45.4
1956 Ron Delany	Klaus Richtzenhain	John M. Landy
(IRL) 3:41.2 OR	(GER) 3:42.0	(AUS) 3:42.0
1960 Herbert J. Elliott	Michel Jazy	István Rózsavölgyi
(AUS) 3:35.6 OR	(FRA) 3:38.4	(HUN) 3:39.2
1964 Peter G. Snell	Josef Odlozil	John Davies
(NZL) 3:38.1	(TCH) 3:39.6	(NZL) 3:39.6
1968 H. Kipchoge Keino	James R. Ryun	Bodo Tümmler
(KEN) 3:34.91 OR	(USA) 3:37.89	(GER) 3:39.08
1972 Pekka Vasala	H. Kipchoge Keino	Rodney Dixon
(FIN) 3:36.33	(KEN) 3:36.81	(NZL) 3:37.46
1976 John Walker	Ivo Van Damme	Paul Heinz Wellmann
(NZL) 3:39.17	(BEL) 3:39.27	(GER) 3:39.3

	Gold	Silver	Bronze
1980	Sebastian Coe (GBR) 3:38.4	Jurgen Straub (GDR) 3:38.8	Steve Ovett (GBR) 3:38.99
1984	Sebastian Coe (GBR) 3:32.53 OR	Steve Cram (GBR) 3:33.40	Jose Abascal (ESP) 3:34.30
1988	Peter Rono (KEN) 3:35.96	Peter Elliott (GBR) 3:36.15	Jens-Peter Herold (GDR) 3:36.21

[1] The Olympic record has only been set in those winning performances marked OR with the exception of Hallows, who achieved 4:03.4 in the 1908 preliminaries
[2] A. N. S. Jackson (1912) changed name to A. N. S. Strode-Jackson and P. J. Baker (1920) changed name to P. J. Noel-Baker

Appendix D

An arbitrary ranking list of runners over 1,500 metres or a mile since 1945:

	1	2	3	4	5	6
Dave Bedford	H. Elliott	Coe	Snell	Aouita	{ Ovett / Ryun	–
Chris Brasher	H. Elliott	Coe	Snell	Bannister	Keino	Bayi/Cran
John Bryant[1]	H. Elliott	Bannister	Coe	Walker	Cram	Snell
Andreas Brugger	Coe	{ Aouita / H. Elliott / Snell	–	–	{ Cram / Ovett	–
Ron Clarke	H. Elliot	Snell	Coe	{ Ryun / Ovett	–	{ Aouita / Walker
Stan Greenberg	Coe	Cram	Keino	H. Elliott	Snell	Ovett
Derek Ibbotson	H. Elliott	Coe	Ovett	Snell	Cram	{ Walker / Ryun
Derek Johnson	H. Elliott	Coe	Snell	Keino	Ovett	Aouita
Arthur Lydiard	Snell	{ Coe / Aouita		{ Keino / Ovett / Cram		{ H. Elliott / Ryun
Peter Matthews	H. Elliott	Coe	Cram	Ovett	Ryun	Keino
Gianni Merlo[2]	Coe	Snell	Aouita	Ovett	H. Elliott	Ryun
David Miller	Coe	Snell	H. Elliott	Ovett	Cram	{ Keino / Ryun
Wilf Paish	Coe	Ovett	H. Elliott	Keimo	Snell	Cram
Runners' World	Coe	Aouita	Keino	Walker		
Robert Paviente[3]	{ H. Elliott	–	Ryun	Snell	Aouita	Cram
Roberto Quercetani[4]	{ Coe / Coe	Elliott	Snell	Cram	Ovett	Aouita
Matti Salmenkyla[5]	H. Elliott	Bannister	Snell	Coe	Cram	Aouita
Steve Scott	Coe	Aouita	Walker	Snell	{ Cram / Ovett	Keino
Rudi Thiel[6]	Coe	Aouita	Snell	Cram	H. Elliott	Ovett
John Walker	Coe	–	–	–	–	–
Mel Watman	H. Elliott	Coe	Snell	Keino	Cram	{ Ovett / Walker
Harry Wilson	H. Elliott	–	–	–	–	–

Footnote: 1. Former Thames Valley Harriers Captain.

2. Italian author/journalist
3. Editor, *l'Equipe* (France)
4. Statistician/author
5. Finnish member, IOC press commission
6. Berlin promoter

Appendix E

Biographical details of leading 4-lap runners

Saïd Aouita
Morocco. Born 2 November 1959, Kenitra
Personal bests: 800 metres 1min 43.86 sec; 1,000 metres 2:15.16; 1,500 metres 3:29.46; mile 3:46.76
World records: 1,500 metres 3:29.46 (1985); 2,000 metres 4:50.81 (1987); 3,000 metres 7:29.45 (1989); 5,000 metres 13:00.40 (1985), 12:58.39 (1987); two miles: world outdoor best 8:13.45 (1987)
Championships: 1984 Olympic Games: 5,000 metres. 1987 world championships: 5,000 metres

Roger Bannister
Great Britain. Born 23 March 1929, Harrow
Personal bests:1,500 metres 3:43.8; mile 3:59.4
World Records: mile 3:59.4 (1954)
Championships: 1954 British Empire(Commonwealth) Games: mile. 1954 European Championships: 1500 metres.

Sebastian Coe
Great Britain. Born 29 September 1956, London
Personal bests: 800 metres 1min 41.73sec; 1,000 metres 2:12.18; 1,500 metres 3:29.77; mile 3:47.33
World records: 800 metres 1:42.33 (1979), 1:41.73 (1981); 1,000 metres 2:13.40 (1980), 2:12.18 (1981); 1,500 metres 3:32.03 (1979); mile 3:48.95 (1979), 3:48.53 (1981), 3:47.33 (1981)
Championships: 1980 Olympic Games: 1,500 metres. 1984 Olympic Games: 1,500 metres. 1986 European championships: 800 metres

Herb Elliott
Australia. Born 25 February 1938, Subiaco, near Perth
Personal bests: 880 yards 1min 47.3sec; 1,000 metres 2:19.1; 1,500 metres 3:35.6; mile 3:54.5
World records: 1,500 metres 3:36.0 (1958), 3:35.6 (1960); mile 3:54.5 (1958)
Championships: 1958 Commonwealth Games: 880 yards, mile. 1960 Olympic Games: 1,500 metres (in world record and by 20 metres)
Never lost at 1,500 metres or mile.

Steve Ovett
Great Britain. Born 9 October 1955, Brighton
Personal bests: 800 metres 1min 44.09sec; 1,000 metres 2:15.91; 1,500 metres 3:30.77; mile 3:48.40
World records: 1,500 metres 3:32.1 (1980), 3:31.36 (1980), 3:30.77 (1983); mile 3:48.8 (1980), 3:48.40 (1981); two miles: world outdoor best of 8:13.50 (1978)
Championships: 1978 European championships: 1,500 metres. 1980 Olympic Games: 800 metres. 1986 Commonwealth Games: 5,000 metres

John Walker
New Zealand. Born 12 January 1952, Papakura
Personal bests: 800 metres 1min 44.94sec; 1,500 metres 3:32.4; mile 3:49.08
World records: mile 3:49.4 (1975); 2,000 metres 4:51.4 (1976)
Championships: 1976 Olympic Games: 1,500 metres

Filbert Bayi
Tanzania. Born 23 June 1953, Karatu
Personal bests: 800 metres 1min 45.3sec; 1,500 metres 3:32.16; mile 3:51.0.
World records: 1,500 metres 3:32.16 (1974); mile 3:51.0 (1975); 2,000 metres steeplechase: world best 5:20.3 in 1980 Olympic 3,000 metres steeplechase final
Championships: 1974 Commonwealth Games: 1,500 metres

Steve Cram
Great Britain. Born 14 October 1960, Gateshead
Personal bests: 800 metres 1min 42.88 sec; 1,000 metres 2:12.88; 1,500 metres 3:29.67; mile 3:46.32
World records: 1,500 metres 3:29.67 (1985); mile 3:46.32 (1985); 2,000 metres 4:51.39 (1985)
Championships: 1982 European championships: 1,500 metres. 1982 Commonwealth Games: 1,500 metres. 1983 world championships: 1,500 metres. 1986 Commonwealth Games: 800 metres, 1,500 metres. 1986 European championships: 1,500 metres

Kipchoge Keino
Kenya. Born 1 January 1940, Kipsamo
Personal bests: 800 metres 1min 46.4sec; 1,500 metres 3:34.91; mile 3:53.1
World records: 3,000 metres 7:39.5 (1965); 5,000 metres 13:24.2 (1965)
Championships: 1966 Commonwealth Games: mile, three miles. 1968 Olympic Games: 1,500 metres. 1970 Commonwealth Games: 1,500 metres. 1972 Olympic Games: 3,000 metres steeplechase

Jim Ryun
United States. Born 29 April 1947, Wichita, Kansas
Personal bests: 880 yards 1min 44.9sec; 1,500 metres 3:33.1; mile 3:51.1.
World records: 880 yards 1:44.9 (1966); 1,500 metres 3:33.1 (1967); mile 3:51.3 (1966), 3:51.1 (1967)
Championships: None

Peter Snell
New Zealand. Born 17 December 1938, Opunake
Personal bests: 800 metres 1min 44.3sec; 880 yards 1:45.1; 1,000 metres 2:16.6; 1,500 metres 3:37.6; mile 3:54.1
World records: 800 metres 1:44.3 (1962); 880 yards 1:45.1 (1962, though ran an unofficial 1:44.9 relay leg in 1960, when the world record stood at 1:46.8); 1,000 metres 2:16.6 (1964); mile 3:54.4 (1962), 3:54.1 (1964)
Championships: 1960 Olympic Games: 800 metres. 1962 Commonwealth Games: 880 yards, mile. 1964 Olympic Games: 800 metres, 1,500 metres
Unbeaten in leading championships.

Bibliography

Norman Barrett and Mel Watman: *Profile, Steve Cram*, Virgin, 1984

Sebastian Coe and David Miller: *Running Free*, Sidgwick and Jackson, 1981

David Miller: *Coming Back*, Sidgwick and Jackson, 1984

Steve Ovett (with John Rodda): Ovett, An Autobiography, Collins/Willow, 1984

Roger Tames: *The Making of an Athlete*, W.H. Allen, 1984

Simon Turnbull: *Portrait of an Athlete*, W.H. Allen, 1982

Tony Ward: *The Golden Decade*, Queen Anne Press, 1991

Mel Watman: *The Coe and Ovett File*, Athletics Weekly, 1982

Harry Wilson: *Running Dialogue*, Stanley Paul, 1982

Index

Picture Acknowledgements

The author and publisher are grateful to the following for permission to reproduce photographs:
Michel Andre; Ashna; The Associated Press Ltd; Barn Owl Associates; Hugh Hastings; The Hulton-Deutsch Collection; Jack Kay/*Daily Express*; Eileen O'Connor/UNICEF; Popperfoto; The Press Association Ltd; *Runner's World*; Mark Shearman; Solo Syndication & Literary Agency Ltd; Sporting Pictures (UK) Ltd; Ian Stewart/*The Times*; UPI/Bettmann.